ROAD
RACE

ROAD
RACE

Chris Jones

David McKay Company, Inc.
New York

First American Edition, 1977

Library of Congress Catalog Card Number: 76–43547
ISBN: 0–679–50710–8

10 9 8 7 6 5 4 3 2 1

Printed in Great Britain

ACKNOWLEDGEMENTS

ADAC–Gau Niedersachsen—Alfa Romeo—Vicente Alvarez—Anglo-Argentine Society—Jean Angus—Arcon—Argentine Embassy, London—AC Argentino—Associated Press—*Automotor und Sport*—*Autosprint*—BP—Oreste Berta—BMW—British Leyland—British Museum—*Buenos Aires Herald*—Burmah–Castrol—AC Catalonia—AC Catanzaro—ASA de Cévennes—Chrysler—AC Colombia—Hugh Conway—Daimler-Benz—Mike Doodson—Automobile Association of East Africa—Chris Economaki—AC Ecuador—Vic Elford—Esso—Fiat—Emerson Fittipaldi—Ford—GM—José and Mary Garcia-Martinez—Mauricio Rozo Gomez—Hackney Public Library—Ronald Hansen—Hispanic-American Society—Veronica Hitchcock—Indianapolis Motor Speedway—Jaguar—F. A. Jones—Elizabeth Junek—Kensington Public Library—Karl Kling—Kozana—Lancia—AC Libya—Umberto Maglioli—Matra—Maserati—Mobil—Philip Morris—Stirling Moss—National Motor Museum, Beaulieu—Nissan—ASAC du Nord—Victor and Elena Pelli—AC Peru—Peugeot—Porsche—Publifoto—RAC—Renault—Doug Richardson—William R. Roff—Royal Auto Union, Liège—Shell—Don Smith—Automobile Association of South Africa—Alex Starkey—Colette-Ann Stasse—Steyr-Daimler-Puch—Hans Stuck—RAC Sweden—AC Ulster—ASAC Vauclusien—*Virage Auto*—Volkswagen—Westminster Public Library—AC 'Targa Florio', Ypres.

CONTENTS

ILLUSTRATIONS

Miglia, 1932 (*Alfa Romeo*)

36. Umberto Borzacchini, *Mille Miglia*, 1932 (*Alfa Romeo*)
37. Minoia/Balestrero, *Mille Miglia*, 1932 (*Alfa Romeo*)
38. Antonio Brivio, *Targa Florio*, 1933 (*Alfa Romeo*)
39. Hans Ruesch, *Mille Miglia*, 1934 (*Alfa Romeo*)
40. Cortese/Guatto, *Mille Miglia*, 1937 (*Alfa Romeo*)
41. Giovanni Battista Guidotti and Ercole Boratto, 1937 (*Alfa Romeo*)
42. Franco Cortese, *Mille Miglia*, 1938 (*Alfa Romeo*)
43. Brudes/Roese, *Coppa Brescia*, 1940 (*BMW*)
44. *Mille Miglia*, 1957 (*Publifoto*)
45. Clemente Biondetti, *Mille Miglia*, 1949 (*Associated Press*)
46. Giannino Marzotto and Dorino Serafini, *Mille Miglia*, 1950 (*Publifoto*)
47. Stirling Moss and Bartecchi/Case, *Mille Miglia*, 1952 (*Publifoto*)
48. Giovanni Bracco, *Mille Miglia*, 1952 (*Publifoto*)
49. Juan Manuel Fangio, *Mille Miglia*, 1953 (*Alfa Romeo*)
50. Pietro Carini, *Giro di Sicilia*, 1954 (*Alfa Romeo*)
51. Umberto Maglioli, *Mille Miglia*, 1954 (*Publifoto*)
52. Alberto Ascari, *Mille Miglia*, 1954 (*Publifoto*)
53. Alberto Ascari, *Mille Miglia*, 1954 (*Publifoto*)
54. Hans Herrmann (*BP*)
55. Mercedes-Benz team, *Mille Miglia*, 1955 (*Porsche*)
56. Juan Manuel Fangio, *Mille Miglia*, 1955 (*Daimler-Benz*)
57. Anselmo/Peluso, *Mille Miglia*, 1955 (*Publifoto*)
58. Mercedes-Benz team, *Targa Florio*, 1955 (*Daimler-Benz*)
59. Peter Collins, *Targa Florio*, 1955 (*Daimler-Benz*)
60. Aosta–Gran San Bernardo hillclimb (*Fiat*)
61. Gregor Grant, *Mille Miglia*, 1957 (*Publifoto*)
62. Ak Miller, *Mille Miglia*, 1957 (*Publifoto*)
63. Peter Collins and Wolfgang von Trips, *Mille Miglia*, 1957 (*Louis Klemantaski/National Motor Museum*)
64. Piero Taruffi (*Daimler-Benz*)
65. *Carrera Panamericana de Mexico* (*Ford*)
66. Felice Bonetto, *Panamericana*, 1950 (*Alfa Romeo*)
67. Felice Bonetto, *Panamericana*, 1950 (*Alfa Romeo*)
68. Troy Ruttmann (*Indianapolis Motor Speedway*)
69. Karl Kling/Hans Klenk, *Carrera Panamericana de Mexico*, 1952 (*Daimler-Benz*)
70. Alfred Neubauer and John Fitch, *Panamericana*, 1952 (*Daimler-Benz*)
71. Chuck Stevenson (*Indianapolis Motor Speedway*)
72. Jack McGrath (*Indianapolis Motor Speedway/O'Dell-Shields*)
73. Jack McGrath and Consalvo Sanesi, *Panamericana*, 1954 (*Alfa Romeo*)
74. Walt Faulkner (*Indianapolis Motor Speedway/O'Dell-Shields*)
75. *Panamericana*, 1954 (*Alfa Romeo*)
76. *Targa Florio*, 1973 (*Chris Jones*)
77. Huschke von Hanstein, Paul Freré, Olivier Gendebien (*Porsche*)
78. Jo Bonnier and Wolfgang von Trips (*Porsche*)

MAPS

WHY ROAD RACING IS DEAD OR DYING

Motor racing has two main traditions. One, the European, is the tradition of racing on roads, or on tracks built to resemble roads, with corners to the left and the right. Races are held primarily for the benefit of car manufacturers, who want publicity for their products, and for sportsmen, who want to race and have fun. The second tradition, the American, is the tradition of track racing, on oval circuits. In this form of racing the key man is the promoter, who wants to draw a big crowd and make lots of money. In the early years they even went as far as fixing races so that the spectators could be sure of an exciting finish.

With a road race, held on real public roads, it can be extremely difficult, if not impossible, to charge people to watch the race, unless, as at Monaco, the circuit is short and the local community is united in pursuit of the tourist and his money. But in general road races—real road races—do not make any money. Most often the promoter, the car club, the town, the province, the country, will have to pay money out.

So if motor races are to be run on a strictly commercial basis they should be run in an enclosed stadium where every spectator will have to pay, and where every spectator will get his money's worth by getting a frequent, or even continuous, view of the cars. For it is unfortunately true that road racing, in its purest, wildest form, is a poor spectator sport. The toughest circuit still in use for Grand Prix racing, the Nürburgring in the Eifel hills of Germany, is also about the least interesting for the spectator, because even the fastest cars and drivers take more than seven minutes to get around those fourteen miles. You spend far more time sitting and waiting than you do watching. But the country is beautiful: many of the spectators go as much for the camping and picnicking as for the racing.

The *Targa Florio* in Sicily, which was held for the last time in 1973, was even more casual. The cars went by about every three-quarters of an hour. And since it was sports car racing, which has always attracted amateur drivers in large numbers, very few of the cars were really fast. Many were slow and driven by local men purely for sport, and often driven very badly. The spectators, mainly locals also, would give them a big cheer, but for the outsider it meant little. He would have to sit on his piece of grassy bank somewhere in the Madonie hills, drinking a bottle of beer bought from a stall under the trees by the roadside, and wait for a Ferrari or an Alfa Romeo or a Porsche, with a driver at the wheel who would give him that

feeling he would like to have all the time—a mixture of exhilaration and fear—as the narrow line is walked between perfection and disaster. Out of sixty cars only six or seven might give him this thrill. The rest were just clowns, like the horses in a bullfight. But the Madonie, like the Eifel, is beautiful country.

Of course, the distinction between the European and American traditions of racing is at times very blurred, and becoming more so. The USA has had road racing from the earliest times, but it was generally confined to the east coast, and organised by rich men who felt themselves to be as much European as American. After the early Vanderbilt Cup and Grand Prize races had faded away, these same men kept road racing alive, but as a very small sport, on about the same scale as a cricket match on a village green. It was not until after the Second World War that road racing in America, increasingly on artificial roads rather than real ones, began to become widely popular. For years it was run on a strictly amateur basis—the legacy of those rich pioneers—but in 1958 it turned professional, and its expansion on commercial lines was assured. The European tradition became Americanised.

In Europe the home of track racing was the Brooklands circuit in England, thanks entirely to the ban on racing on public roads in England. This cut British motor racing off from racing in continental Europe for many years. Britain also was the home of the amateur racing driver: on the Continent most leading drivers were employed by factories and were getting rich from racing even before the First World War, contrary to the common British belief that professionalism among racing drivers is a recent development, dating back to Stirling Moss at the earliest. In fact an old-timer like Giuseppe Campari would understand a modern professional like Jackie Stewart perfectly. Where professionalism has really increased in recent years is among promoters, not among drivers.

The beauty of a road race, held on real public roads, is that the circuit doesn't cost a bean. You just block the road off, pile up a few straw bales at obvious danger points, and perhaps put up a few barriers to keep spectators from wandering across the road. Up to the 'fifties, even into the 'sixties, numerous towns in Europe held their own little road races on short circuits. Nobody could have made any money, but at least losses were easy to control. Very few of them survive today (except for motorcycle races): costs have gone up; modern racing cars are faster; racing is closer; and the governing bodies of motor sport demand that safety barriers— miles of expensive steel barriers—be put up to protect both drivers and spectators. The cost of this is usually prohibitive on a circuit which, because it brings the whole district to a standstill, can only be used once or twice a year.

So, whether they like it or not, continental European promoters are forced, as the British have always been, to think of the American concept of the stadium circuit, although never to the extent of building an oval track. Land must be bought, the track laid, grandstands built—money, investment, shareholders, profit and loss. Again, the European tradition has been Americanised.

2. The urban road race. Brussels, 1961

So motor racing today is somewhere mid-Atlantic in style.

To some the fading of the European road racing tradition may seem a loss, and nothing but a loss, but this is not so. Permanent circuits have made club racing possible, and have thus brought racing within reach of many who, in the past, would not have been able to afford it. Club racing is the best training ground for future champions, as Britain, the first to have a thriving club racing scene, showed by its dominance of international motor racing in the late-'fifties and early-'sixties. The continental countries have only caught up since they began building permanent circuits themselves.

3. The modern autodrome, engineered for racing. Ricard, in the South of France

Vintage car-club members, and members of vintage car clubs, are fond of saying that racing today is dull and stereotyped. First, this is not true, for today a Lotus certainly looks as different from a Ferrari as a Ferrari did from an Alfa Romeo twenty-five years ago, or an Alfa Romeo did from a Bugatti twenty-five years before that. Second, the argument is irrelevant, because the vast majority of spectators go for the *racing*, not the cars. The cars are just tools, means to an end. And racing today is closer, faster, and better than it has ever been. It is no accident that the most popular form of motorised sport in Britain, where there must be more motor sport per square mile than anywhere else, is what used to be called dirt-track racing, and is now called, even more vaguely, speedway racing. It is motorcycle racing on loose-surface tracks of a quarter-mile or less. Twenty races are held in an evening, four laps and four riders per race, with spectacular sliding on the turns. All machines ridden look identical at thirty feet, but nobody is heard complaining. The race is the thing.

But road racing was not a stadium sport. In the greatest road races the spectator was not important. He paid nothing to watch, and sometimes got killed while doing so, which is to be treated very unimportantly indeed. Road races spanned whole countries, and sometimes whole continents. They crossed mountains, rivers, plains, valleys. Speedway racing is to road racing what a boxing match is to a war.

It was Aldous Huxley who called speed the only genuinely modern pleasure. This, of course, is untrue, but the invention of the horseless carriage did give a versatile new plaything to those who had had to be content with running, riding, chariot racing, sledging, ski-ing, or cycling. And it was road racing that took this ancient pleasure of speed, in its new, motorised, form, and blended it with the equally ancient pleasure of travel. Never before had men been able to travel so far so fast.

Road races—in their purest, wildest forms—are now dead or dying. This book is about these races, the longest and the toughest, the ones that are the most dead and the most near to dying.

Road racing began in France in 1895, and this first great era ended with the bloody Paris–Madrid race of 1903. This period has been dealt with by many other writers, so we will not waste our time by dealing with it again. Nor will we deal with Grand Prix races on short road circuits: this, too, is a well-documented field. We will look to some extent at hillclimbing, which in Britain is a specialised form of sprinting, but which in most other countries is a form of road racing. It can be argued that a hillclimb is not a race because competitors race against the clock, and not directly against each other, but most road races are run the same way— the cars start at intervals.

This book is set mainly in Italy, the undisputed home of road racing in Europe, where the obscure and poorly documented races of the 1890s led the way to the *Targa Florio* and *Mille Miglia*; in Argentina, the Italy of the Americas, where road racing still survives today; and in Mexico, where the Pan American road race was the most spectacular race in the world for five short, but well-remembered, years.

ITALY: 1895–1914

The Nineteenth Century

Motor sport began in Italy very soon after it began in France. On 18 May 1895 a reliability trial was run from Turin to Asti and back (see Map 1 for this, and other events in this chapter). There was then a two-year gap before Italy's first motor race was held, on 12 September 1897, from Arona to Stresa and back around the beautiful shores of Lake Maggiore. Six cars, two tricycles, and four motorcycles were entered. A Benz driven by Giuseppe Cobianchi completed the 22 miles (35 km) in 1 hr 34 min. to win at an average speed of 13.5 mph (22 km/hr). Another Benz was second, and the first tricycle, a De Dion Bouton, was third. All the motorcycles retired.

The next race, in July 1898, was more ambitious—119 miles (192 km) over a course Turin–Asti–Alessandria–Turin—and in it the men who were to create the future Italian motor industry began to emerge. The winner, driving a De Dion Bouton, was Luigi Storero, a close friend of the future founder of Fiat, Giovanni Agnelli. Storero was to become one of the first Fiat works drivers, and, more significantly, was to found a nation-wide sales and service network for Fiat cars, which was bought by Fiat in 1908 to form the basis for their own rapid expansion.

One of Agnelli's partners in Fiat, Count Carlo Biscaretti di Ruffio, also drove a De Dion Bouton in that second Italian road race, but retired. Another competitor was Giovanni Ceirano: the record shows that he retired a Prinetti & Stucchi tricycle; but that he did build both bicycles and light cars under the name Welleyes, working in a rented workshop in the courtyard of a house at 9 Corsa Vittorio Emanuele, Turin. The owner of the house was Giuseppe Lancia, whose 17-year-old son Vincenzo was soon to give up his accountancy studies and go to work for Ceirano. A year later Agnelli, Biscaretti & Co. were to take over Ceirano's firm to build Fiats, and Vincenzo Lancia was to find himself a Fiat works driver, before manufacturing cars under his own name from 1907 on. And the Ceirano family were to be responsible for many more cars, too: Rapid, Scat, Ceirano, and—most enduring—Itala.

Yet another competitor in that historic race was 16-year-old Ettore Bugatti, the

4. *Targa Florio*, 1907. Vincenzo Lancia (28/40 hp Fiat) leaving Petralia Sottana on his way to second place

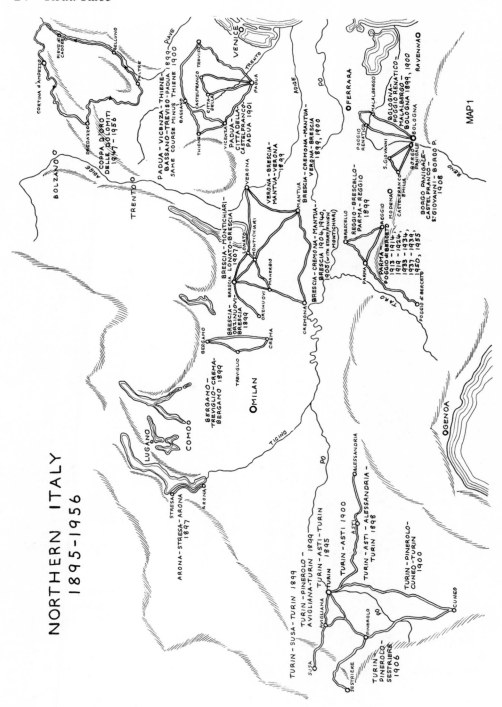

NORTHERN ITALY
1895-1956

MAP 1

son of Carlo Bugatti, a Milanese furniture designer, painter, sculptor, architect, and silversmith of the *Beaux Arts* school. Ettore had gone to art school to study sculpture, but had left to join Prinetti & Stucchi as a volunteer apprentice—much against the wishes of his father, whose only mechanical interest was in trying to build a perpetual-motion machine.

Ettore Bugatti retired from his first race, but in 1899, perched on the saddle of a special twin-engined tricycle he had built himself in the Prinetti & Stucchi workshops, he won four of the twelve road races held that year. He began the season by winning the Verona–Brescia–Mantua–Verona race, averaging 24.5 mph (39.5 km/hr) for the 100 miles (161 km), and beating Carlo Biscaretti (De Dion Bouton) by over two minutes. Fifth was a man soon to be famous as a racing driver, Victor Rigal, on a French Phebus tricycle. Giovanni Agnelli won the class for four-seaters with a Phénix—presumably one of the De Dion-engined cars built at the Prunel factory in France, which sold under various names.

The next road race, the Limone–Cuneo–Turin, was reserved for French cars and drivers, but the following race, the Turin–Pinerolo–Avigliana–Turin, was another win for Bugatti, who beat the all-French winner of two days before, de Gras (Peugeot), by over twenty minutes. Among the retirements were Luigi Storero (Phénix) and Giovanni Ceirano's brother Matteo, driving a Ceirano-built tricycle.

A week later, in early May, the circus moved south to Reggio Emilia, where a 53-mile (85-km) circuit did not venture into the Apennines, but stayed on the plain of the Po Valley, covering a roughly triangular course Reggio–Brescello–Parma–Reggio. Bugatti scored his third win, at a brisk 40.3 mph (64.9 km/hr).

So this busy season continued: a 50-mile (80-km) circuit out of Bologna on 22 May; a 108.5-mile (175-km) race Padua–Vicenza–Thiene–Bassano–Treviso–Padua on 19 June—Bugatti's fourth win; a track race at Mantua on 9 July; another at Piacenza on 12 August; a 62-mile (100-km) road race Piacenza–Cremona–Borgo Vercelli–Piacenza the day after that—with Luigi Storero winning on his Phénix on all three days; and so on. A race for motorcycles on 10 September from Brescia to Orzinuovi, on the road to Crema, was won by Carlo Maserati, the eldest of six sons of Rodolfo Maserati, an engine driver from Voghera. Carlo rode a Carano machine he had built himself. Later the Maserati brothers—Carlo, Bindo, Alfieri, Mario, Ettore, Ernesto—were to work for Fiat, Bianchi, Junior, Isotta Fraschini, and Diatto, before building their own cars under the name of Maserati, and after the Second World War under the name Osca.

The day after Maserati's win the first race was held over a course that was to see some of the most important Italian races of the pre-1914 era: Brescia–Cremona–Mantua–Verona–Brescia. At 138 miles (223 km) it was the longest circuit used until then in Italy, and the field was the biggest so far seen: thirty-six starters. The winner was Luigi Storero (De Dion Bouton) at 25.5 mph (47.6 km/hr). Bugatti was third.

The season ended with a more modest road race, the 50-mile (80-km) Bergamo–

Treviglio–Crema–Bergamo, and with a speed weekend at Treviso—two track races and another 50-mile road race.

The summer of 1899 laid a very firm foundation for Italian motor sport—and, indirectly, for French motor sport, too, with the rise of Ettore Bugatti—and in 1900 the good work went on, although there were only six road races that year. There had, of course, to be setbacks. It was on 10 September 1900, in the *Coppa Brescia*—later to become the *Coppa Florio*—over the Brescia–Cremona–Mantua–Verona–Brescia circuit, that Attilio Caffaratti, born in Pinerolo 1877, crashed and fractured his skull against a tree—the first death in an Italian motor race.

There were other firsts in 1900. On 21 April was the first Italian hillclimb—a form of motor sport that was to become an Italian speciality. This first climb was the 3.1-mile (5-km) Madonna del Pilone–Pino Torinese, and was won by Carlo Biscaretti (Phénix).

April 23 1900, saw the first competition appearance by a Fiat, in the 80.6-mile (130-km) Turin–Pinerolo–Cuneo–Turin race. The driver was Federico della Ferrara, driving under the name 'Robur', and he finished third—to be disqualified for going off course. Honour was partially saved by a Cook, a licence-built Fiat, finishing third and winning the light-car class. The driver, calling himself 'Iris', was the Marquess César Carano, the money behind the Maserati-built Carano motorcycles.

The same year saw the last competition appearances of Ettore Bugatti and his Prinetti & Stucchi cars: he won a 46.5-mile (75-km) road race out of Bologna on 28 May; and was second in the 136-mile (220-km) Padua–Vicenza–Bassano–Treviso–Padua race on 1 July; on the latter occasion driving a four-wheeler. After that Prinetti & Stucchi stopped car production to concentrate on sewing machines. Bugatti, still in his teens, set up his own company to build a one hundred per cent Bugatti car; although the fruits of his labours were not to be felt in motor racing for another twenty years.

The Padua race saw the first appearance of Vincenzo Lancia and of Felice Nazzaro, born in the same year as Lancia and Bugatti, the son of a coal merchant, who was to become a truly great driver, but only a moderate success, compared with his two contemporaries, as a manufacturer. Driving Fiats, Lancia won the Padua race, and Nazzaro was third; splitting them was Gaste on a Perfecta Soncino tricycle, a car apparently derived from the French Soncin. The Italian driver calling himself Soncino was, it seems, only a red herring to try to hide the French origins of the car.

1901–05

So far the road races of Italy had been pale shadows of those of France. In 1901 the Italian touring club tried to rectify this. At the suggestion of Carlo Biscaretti and with financial help from the Milan newspaper *Corriere della Sera* they organised the *Giro Automobilistico d'Italia*. The name was too grand: it was not a circuit of Italy like the one that was to be held in 1934. That did circle virtually the whole of Italy—a distance of 3,526 miles (5,687 km). The 1901 *Giro* was of 1,018

5. Two Fiats before the start of the 1901 *Giro d'Italia*. The 12 hp
car on the right is that of Count Biscaretti

miles (1,642 km), and was nearer to the *Mille Miglia*—the Thousand Miles—
which was to start twenty-six years later.

From Turin the route went east to Alessandria, south to the coast at Genoa,
followed the coast to Pisa, went inland to Florence—the first time there had been
racing south of the Apennines—then over the hills to Siena, back to the coast at
Grosseto, and then along the coast to Rome. From Rome it turned north to Terni
and Perugia, and on over the Apennines to the Adriatic coast. North of Rimini it
turned inland again for Bologna, Padua, Brescia, and, finally, the finish at Turin.

It was a bold experiment, and if it had drawn works teams from abroad it might
have succeeded. But there were only thirty-two entries—far too few for a
thousand-mile course, even one divided into fifteen stages. Fiat entered nine cars,
and, under conditions that did not favour the light tricycles, won. Felice Nazzaro
drove the winning car, a 3.8-litre, 4-cylinder car built on Mercedes lines.

Track racing, over a short, closed circuit, usually a horse track, is almost as old as road racing. Races were held around a one-mile track at the Rhode Island State Fair, Providence, USA, in 1896. But the use of closed road circuits, lapped several times, from which the modern racing circuit has developed, is usually held to have started with the *Circuit des Ardennes* in Belgium in 1902.

This is unjust to Italy. On 30 June 1901 the *Coppa Italia* was run over four laps of a 46.5-mile (75-km) circuit Padua–Cittadella–Castelfranco–Padua. It was dominated by Panhards from France: Guido Adami won on a 5.3-litre, 16 hp model, covering the 186 miles (300 km) at 36 mph (58 km/hr).

After the *Giro* and Padua races there was little road racing in Italy in 1901, although Nazzaro did win a 50-mile (80-km) race from Piombino to Grosseto on the Tuscany coast, and also a private challenge race from Turin to Bologna against Garibaldi Coltelletti and the Duke of Abruzzi.

The 1902 season was equally poor. In June that year there was at least the first running of an event that was to survive until 1964—the *Coppa della Consuma* hill-climb. It started from Pontassieve, east of Florence, and climbed the Consuma Pass, a distance of 9.4 miles (15.1 km). Over the following sixty-two years the Consuma Cup was to be won by, among others, Felice Nazzaro, Vincenzo Lancia, Antonio Ascari, Giulio Masetti, Clemente Biondetti, Tazio Nuvolari, Giulio Cabianca, and Ludovico Scarfiotti. The first winner, in 1902, was Ugobaldo Tonietti (Panhard 16 hp), who had been second in the *Coppa Italia*.

Two other hillclimbs were founded that year, and both were won by Vincenzo Lancia on 24 hp Fiats. One was within the city of Turin, 2.8 miles (4.5 km) from Sassi up to the Superga, the church and convent overlooking the city—this event was to survive, off and on, until 1960. The other was the Susa–Moncenisio climb, a short road race of 14 miles (22.6 km) on the road from Turin to Val D'Isère and Grenoble—this was to survive until 1953, and among the winners would be Ferdinando Minoia, Alfieri Maserati, Giuseppe Campari, Achille Varzi, Umberto Borzacchini, Piero Taruffi, Giovanni Bracco, and Willy Daetwyler.

These three hillclimbs were the nearest 1902 came to real road racing. All other events were flat sprints. In 1903 it was even worse: apart from the Consuma hill-climb all the events were flat sprints.

The next year, 1904, the Brescia circuit was in use again, in a shortened version excluding Verona. Racing cars competed over two 115-mile (185-km) laps; touring cars over one lap. The racing car winner was Vincenzo Lancia (14.1-litre Fiat 75 hp); from Louis Teste (15.4-litre Panhard 80 hp); Vincenzo Florio (9.2-litre Mercedes 60 hp), the immensely rich young Sicilian who was to donate a cup to the race a year later; Victor Hémery (5.7-litre Darracq), Florio's opposite, a professional driver and tough ex-seaman from Le Mans; and Arthur Duray (11.3-litre Darracq), a New York-born Belgian. This race marked the real beginning of international racing in Italy, on 5 September 1904. The monster cars that now dominated motor racing had a top speed of around 90 mph.

For the first *Coppa Florio*, on 9 September 1905, the Brescia circuit was altered

6. Vincenzo Lancia (24 hp Fiat) winning the 1902 Susa–Moncenisio hillclimb in the mountains twenty-five miles west of Turin

7. Vincenzo Lancia (75 hp Fiat) winning the 1904 Brescia–Cremona–Mantua–Brescia race. A year later this event became the *Coppa Florio*

again, the start/finish line being moved to Montechiari, on the Mantua road, the circuit being shortened to 103.6 miles (167.1 km), to be lapped three times. This race was a triumph for Matteo Ceirano: one of the new 15.5-litre cars from his Itala factory was first, driven by G. Battista Raggio, almost ten minutes ahead of Arthur Duray's 17-litre De Dietrich. Third was Lancia (16.3-litre Fiat); fourth, Hémery (9.9-litre Darracq); fifth, Henry Rougier (De Dietrich); and sixth, Nazzaro, back in the Fiat team after a spell working for Vincenzo Lancia in Sicily.

La Madonie

It was Henri Desgrange, editor of the Paris daily *L'Auto* and founder of the greatest of all cycle races, the *Tour de France*, who suggested to Vincenzo Florio that a motor race should be held in Sicily. Florio, who was generally indifferent to his native island, said it was impossible: Sicily had no roads.

But, on closer examination, it was found that Sicily did have roads, and Florio and his friends set about looking for a suitable circuit. They found what they wanted thirty miles east of Palermo, in the hilly country known as *la Madonie*, where a narrow dirt road twisted its way into the hills, through fields and olive groves at first, then among the crags and perched villages and 5,000-feet peaks of the

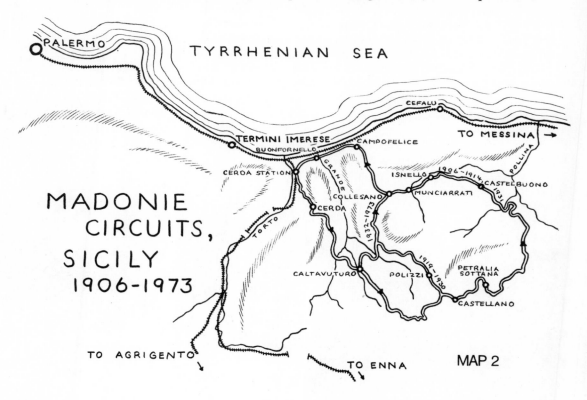

highlands, and finally back to the coast, where there was a long, narrow straight to complete the circuit (see Map 2). The distance was 92.5 miles (149 km), and, despite the long coastal straight, there was an average of more than a dozen corners to the mile. There was no relaxing on the straight, either: in the 67-year history of the Madonie circuit the roads were improved from cart-tracks into modern motor roads, but right to the end drivers had to sweat blood to keep their bucking cars out of the gutters and away from the walls on that long, full-throttle straight.

The first race on the Madonie circuit was on 6 May 1906. There were many problems in organising it. The start/finish line was put at Cerda railway station, the one point where the railway touched the circuit. Cerda itself, several miles up the road, was a tiny village wihout garage or hotels, so the drivers were based at the ancient town of Termini Imerese, back along the coast towards Palermo. The management of the Hotel Igiea in Palermo were given the job of organising accommodation in Termini for the twenty-two sportsmen who were to compete for the first *Targa Florio*. In the event, strikes in France and a shipping delay in Genoa cut the number of starters to ten.

The centre point of Termini Imerese, was the Grand Hotel des Thermes, complete with hot springs where the drivers could soothe their aching muscles after a bone-jarring drive into the Madonie. It was from the marble-walled luxury of the des Thermes that the drivers had to leave before dawn to make the six o'clock start on that Sunday in 1906.

The first *Targa Florio* was unlike any race the ten drivers had competed in before. [Vincenzo Lancia, for example, was now a veteran of the 1903 Paris–Madrid, but Cerda was a very different place from Paris.] In the Paris–Madrid he knew that all of France was following him, that tens of thousands were lining the course to cheer him on, that on the outskirts of every town he would check into a control point, and be guided through at a safe speed by a cyclist before being checked out and let loose again on the open highway.

But in Sicily there were no highways. Unlike France, it had had no Napoleon to build them, and no cyclist lobby to improve them (although Florio had been a keen cyclist before he turned to cars). The bumpy cart-tracks led through medieval villages, none of which had telegraph. The race officials were all back at Cerda railway station, waiting for the drivers to return, ready to send out a search party. And the search party had just as good a chance of breaking down and getting stuck. There was also the fear of bandits: fortunately it remained a fear only. No Madonie competitor was ever shot at or in any way threatened by bandits.

The entry for 1906 was limited to production cars, of which at least ten had to have been built. The full list of starters was as follows: Vincenzo Lancia, still two years away from founding his own firm, drove a 7.4-litre Fiat; the brothers Henri and Maurice Fournier from Le Mans, ex-cyclists, both drove 3.8-litre Clément-Bayards; Paul Bablot drove a 6.3-litre Berliet, from a firm that still makes heavy vehicles today; a touring Hotchkiss, a name better known for guns, was shared by

8. Alessandro Cagno, winner of the first *Targa Florio* in 1906

Monsieur le Blon and his wife; and the most popular make was the 6.7-litre Itala—drivers were Alessandro Cagno, Baron Pierre de Caters, Ettore Graziani, H. R. Pope (Itala's British agent, who started the race smoking a cigar), and

Florio's own driver, taking over Nazzaro's job, Victor Rigal.

The race was over three laps, 277.4 miles (446.4 km), and could not have been very exciting by the standards of today for the watchers who were still at Cerda station 9 hrs 32 min. 22 sec. after the start when Cagno took his Itala across the line to win. The second finisher, Ettore Graziani, was over half an hour behind, and it was another two hours before the rest of the finishers had all come home. Maurice Fournier was too late to be classified. Pope and Lancia were let down by their cars; Henri Fournier let down his by thumping a roadside boundary stone and damaging the Clément-Bayard's rear axle. Light relief was given by Bablot and Rigal, who accidentally refuelled with water. Both got going again to finish third and fourth. Ten starters; six finishers—Cagno, Graziani, Bablot, Rigal, de Caters, M. and Mme. le Blon. Cagno's speed was 29 mph (46.8 km/hr).

On the Italian mainland 1906 was a poor year: the emphasis was on long-distance trials. One interesting road race was the *Criterium Colle del Sestriere*, 54 miles (87 km) Turin–Pinerolo–Colle del Sestriere. It was limited to cars of under one litre, and was won by a little air-cooled, single-cylinder Otav, built in Milan and driven by a young ex-cyclist named Ugo Sivocci, a future winner of the *Targa Florio* and member of the Alfa Romeo works team.

Meanwhile, back in Sicily Florio organised a light-car race. Cars were a problem, so he imported a fleet of single-cylinder De Dion Boutons from France, making it almost a one-make race. Florio himself drove, and won, averaging 21 mph (33 km/hr) over a course that started in Palermo, went along the coast to complete a circuit of the Madonie course, then returned to Palermo, a distance of 152.5 miles (246 km).

1907

The light cars were back again in April 1907, five days before the second *Targa Florio*, for a two-lap race around the Madonie circuit. This time Louis Naudin, in a Sizaire-Naudin he had built himself, beat Florio (De Dion Bouton) by sixteen minutes, averaging 24 mph (38.6 km/hr). The Sizaire-Naudin had independent front suspension, a very unusual feature in 1907.

Forty-five cars started in the *Targa*. The leader at the end of the first lap was Vincenzo Lancia (Fiat), ahead of Alessandro Cagno (again on Itala), Vincenzo Trucco (Isotta Fraschini), Felice Nazzaro (Fiat), and the Alsatian Louis Wagner (Darracq). Trucco retired on the second lap, while Nazzaro and Wagner both moved ahead of Lancia. Cagno also passed Lancia, but then slipped back. Finally, Wagner's Darracq failed in the third and last lap, leaving the two Fiats, Nazzaro and Lancia, to come home first and second, Nazzaro's speed being 34.2 mph (54.1 km/hr). Following them were Maurice Fabry (Itala), Arthur Duray (Lorraine Dietrich), Cagno (Itala), and Fernand Gabriel (Lorraine Dietrich). Back in tenth place was an Isotta Fraschini driven by a 22-year-old Italian, Ferdinando Minoia.

In 1907 Nando Minoia had been racing for three years, and he would race for

9. Vincenzo Florio (28/40 hp Fiat) before finishing second in the 1907 *Targa Florio*. The riding mechanic is 17-year-old Pietro Bordino. He began driving in 1908 and became, in the opinion of Sir Henry Seagrave, 'the finest road race driver in the world'

10. The winner of the 1907 *Targa Florio*, Felice Nazzaro (28/40 hp Fiat), passing through Petralia Sottana

11. Felice Nazzaro after winning the 1907 *Targa Florio*. Beside him is Vincenzo Florio

twenty-five more. Twenty years later, in 1927, he would win the first *Mille Miglia*. He became European Champion in 1931, a few months before his retirement, and was knighted by the Italian monarchy. He died in 1941, aged 56. In the English-speaking world Minoia is a forgotten man, but his contemporaries had high praise for his cool, precise driving.

Nazzaro's winning time was a full 1 hr 14 min. faster than Cagno's in 1906. The half-hour gap between first and second had been cut to twelve minutes. Minoia, in tenth, was only thirty-six minutes behind Nazzaro.

Florio again organised the Palermo–Madonie–Palermo light-car race, and again won on a De Dion Bouton, cutting thirty minutes off his 1906 time. The Madonie circuit was used for a fourth time that year, in late-October, for a three-lap light-car race, won by Paolo Tasca (De Dion Bouton), who beat Naudin's time of earlier in the year.

Meanwhile, on the mainland Nando Minoia (8-litre Isotta Fraschini) had won the *Coppa Florio* over eight laps of a 37.8-mile (60.7-km) circuit Brescia–Montichiari–Castiglione–Lonato–Brescia. He averaged 64.8 mph (104.5 km/hr) to beat Victor Hémery (Benz) by ten minutes. Among the other finishers was Vincenzo Trucco (Isotta Fraschini) in fifth, and Carlo Maserati (Darracq) in tenth.

1908

Light-car racing became increasingly popular. Over five laps of a 22.3-mile (36-km) circuit south of Turin, Giosuè Giuppone won on one of the very fast new Peugeots. Over two laps of the Madonie circuit in May Giuppone again won. Vincenzo Florio (De Dion Bouton) was among the retirements, as were Louis Naudin and Maurice Sizaire (both Sizaire-Naudin), and Giuppone's Peugeot team-mate Georges Boillot.

The third *Targa Florio*, on 18 May, had only thirteen starters—the beginning of a dull period that was to last until the war. At the end of the first lap the Fiat twins, Nazzaro and Lancia, were hard at it again, with Nazzaro only sixteen seconds in front. On the second lap Nazzaro was forced out with broken steering, while Lancia stopped to change tyres (unnecessarily, it was alleged), allowing Vincenzo

12. *Corsa Vetturette*, Madonie, 1908. Duvernoy (Lon Peugeot) crosses the line to finish sixth. His team-mate, Giuponne, was the winner

Trucco (Isotta Fraschini) to win by fourteen minutes. Third, behind Lancia, was Ernesto Ceirano, brother to Giovanni and Matteo, driving a Spa built in Matteo's factory. Fourth was Porporato (Berliet).

The *Coppa Florio* deserted Brescia for Bologna, where a 32.7-mile (52.8-km) circuit started and finished at Borgo Panigale, just west of the town. From there it took the road to Modena as far as Castelfranco, then it looped north to pass close to Nonantola and San Giovanni in Persiceto, before returning to Borgo. Nazzaro won the ten-lap race at 74 mph (119.4 km/hr), beating Trucco (Lorraine Dietrich) by almost ten minutes. Cagno (Itala) was third, Demogeot (Mors) fourth, Lancia (Fiat) fifth, and Florio (Fiat) sixth. Lancia's riding mechanic was a man with a future: Pietro Bordino. Minoia, the winner the year before, retired his Lorraine Dietrich. Other retirements were Louis Wagner (Fiat), Arthur Duray (Lorraine Dietrich), and Charles Faroux (Monobloc), the man who was to become one of the best-loved father figures of French motor sport.

The day after the *Coppa Florio*, a minor race, the *Targa Bologna*, over the same circuit, was won by Porporato (Berliet).

Florio did not again hold his end-of-season light-car race on the Madonie circuit, but he did organise a hillclimb—and won it himself on a De Dion Bouton.

1909

The Madonie light-car race a week before the *Targa* looked like being another win for Giuppone and his Peugeot. He lapped twenty minutes faster than his team-mate Jean Goux—but then ran out of petrol and had to walk three miles to fetch more. A borrowed bicycle sped him back to the Peugeot, and he managed to close within four and a half minutes of Goux by the finish. The use of the bicycle was contested by third finisher Norman Olsen, who had been almost an hour behind, and the judges relegated Giuppone to third. There were only three finishers.

The Messina earthquake of that year, which had caused heavy loss of life in the town, had affected the whole island, and the *Targa* suffered too. There were only eleven starters, four of them light cars, and Florio himself helped to make up the numbers by driving a Fiat. He finished second to Francesco Ciuppa (Spa), ahead of Guido Airoldi (Spa). The race was of one lap only.

Even without the earthquake it would have been a poor *Targa*. Motor sport was suffering badly from competition from aviation, which was drawing away men and machines. There were no French Grands Prix in 1909 and 1910. Blériot had flown the English Channel, and all the world, it seemed, wanted to fly. Daring young men found it more fun in the air than on the ground. Florio organised flying meetings, and devoted more time to an old family interest, boating. It was even widely supposed that motor sport was finished.

1910–11

Entries for the 1910 *Targa* were so poor that one race was held for both light cars and the bigger racing machines. The light Peugeots dominated completely, finishing one-two-three, Georges Boillot leading home Giuppone and Goux. The bigger cars, all second-rate, were hours behind.

Only two events were run on the Italian mainland that year: a sprint around a stadium at Verona; and a flying-mile sprint at Modena.

In 1911 things were only marginally better. There were only fourteen starters in the *Targa*, of which five finished. Ernesto Ceirano (Scat) won, from Mario Cortese (Lancia). The event is perhaps best remembered as the first major event in which Alfa Romeo cars appeared—although both entries retired.

1912

By now Vincenzo Florio, one of the richest and most powerful men in Sicily, was being criticised: it was said that too much of the island's meagre public funds was being used to maintain the roads of the Madonie circuit, and not enough was being used on the other roads of the island. The solution was simple: the next *Targa Florio*, starting on 25 May 1912, was made the first *Giro di Sicilia*—a race circling the whole of the island (see Map 3). This race was to survive, on and off, until 1957, making it the most enduring Italian road race after the Madonie and Mugello events.

The first *Giro* was possibly the most punishing race ever held. The Madonie circuit had already proved an admirable breaker of cars and bruiser of men, with race distances of less than 300 miles. Now cars and drivers were being asked to go more than twice the distance, 605 miles (975 km). In the event, this meant that they were on the road for more than twenty-four hours. In the past longer races had been held, but always they had been divided into stages. Today, twenty-four hours in a rally car is not unusual—but twenty-four in a cart-sprung car of 1912, with no protection from heat or cold, wind or rain, was hell.

There were twenty-six starters, fourteen finishers, and the brave winner was Cecil Snipe on a 4.5-litre Scat. He took 24 hrs 37 min. 9.8 sec. for the course, an average of 26.3 mph (32.6 km/hr). Snipe, the nephew of the British backer of Scat, was their works driver and tester. His speed would have been better had he not had to stop and lie down on a bank for an hour to sleep. Fortunately he had a two-hour lead, and after riding mechanic Pedrini had woken him with a bucket of water—his coma was so deep—they continued, to win by over half an hour from the Lancia of Garetto/Gugliel/Minetti.

Among the retirements was the Florio/Airoldi Mercedes, which got stuck in the tramlines near Messina and went straight ahead where the road bent.

1913

The same route was retained for the second *Giro*, but with a break at Agrigento, after 406 miles (655 km). The field had improved: Felice Nazzaro drove one of his own 4.4-litre Nazzaros; Nando Minoia a 4.4-litre Storero; Ugo Sivocci a De

Vecchi; and Pietro Bordino a Lancia. Cecil Snipe and Ernesto Ceirano both drove Scats.

But the hero of the race turned out to be an amateur who had been around since 1902 without scoring any real success: Vincenzo Marsaglia. Driving a 4.2-litre Aquila Italiana, a 6-cylinder car developing 60 bhp at the then very fast 3,600 rpm, he won the first stage, beating Nazzaro by twenty minutes after more than thirteen hours on the road. Nazzaro, in turn, was over twenty minutes in front of Pietro Bordino. Of thirty-three starters, sixteen completed this stage.

Nazzaro's chance came during the final 200 miles, when Marsaglia was slowed by repeated trouble with his lights. One oil lamp got broken, the other would not burn properly.

Felice Nazzaro won in 19 hrs 18 min. 40.6 sec., an average of 33.7 mph (54.4 km/hr). Vincenzo Marsaglia was a gallant but distant second, in 20 hrs 43 min. 49.2 sec. Third was De Vecchi's Padua agent, Alberto Marani, who raced under the name 'Gloria'. Sivocci on the other De Vecchi was sixth; Bordino was tenth on a Lancia.

The dismal state of Italian motor sport—which most of Europe shared—was enlivened slightly in late-September by the first hillclimb from Parma up the Taro Valley to the Poggio di Berceto—the hill of Berceto—a distance of 33 miles (53 km). This little road race was to survive, on and off, until 1955. The first winner, at 45 mph (72.3 km/hr), was Vincenzo Marsaglia (Aquila Italiana), who beat Nino Franchini (Alfa Romeo), Mario Negri (Itala), Lorenzo Valenti (Fiat), and, in an Alfa Romeo, a well-fed young man named Giuseppe Campari.

1914

In 1914 the *Giro di Sicilia* was again divided into two stages, although this time the rest came at Syracuse, making the second stage longer than the first. The entry was slightly better than the year before: there were past winners Cecil Snipe (Scat) and Felice Nazzaro (Nazzaro), Marsaglia (Aquila), Sivocci and 'Gloria' (both De Vecchi), Campari (6.1-litre Alfa Romeo), and a young Venetian, Meo Costantini (Aquila), who was to become famous after the war as driver and team-manager for Bugatti.

But one entrant, Ernesto Ceirano, had a secret weapon: Houdaille hydraulic dampers fitted to his Scat. They proved much superior to the friction dampers then normal, and he won both stages convincingly. On the first he was followed home by Sivocci and Nazzaro, but both retired in the second. Ceirano averaged 36 mph (58 km/hr) to win in just under seventeen hours. 'Gloria'—Alberto Marani—was second, followed by Luigi Lopez (Fiat). Only eight finished from thirty-one starters. Marsaglia, Campari, and Costantini were among the retirements.

A week later, at the end of March, the Madonie circuit was used for the first time in two years, this time for the *Coppa Florio*. Nazzaro won from Ceirano and the Alfa Romeos of Nino Franchini and Giuseppe Campari. Nobody succeeded in going as fast as the light cars had in 1910.

13. Nando Minoia. Photograph taken in Fanø, Denmark, in 1919.
The car is a 1914 GP Fiat, of the type that Count Masetti used
to win the 1921 *Targa Florio*

Three months later road racing returned to Tuscany for the first time since 1901. The new race, on 21 June, over four laps of a 40.3-mile (65-km) circuit, was won by Giovanni Negro on a Caesar, a Turin-built car also known as a Scacchi. The circuit started at San Piero a Sieve, in the Apennines above Florence, headed north to Firenzuola, then west and south over the Futa Pass back to San Piero. This will sound familiar to some, and it should. This circuit was used until 1970, and was usually named after the district—Mugello (see Map 4).

Four days later the Parma–Poggio di Berceto hillclimb attracted an all-star cast. Ernesto Ceirano (Scat) won, beating Campari (Alfa Romeo), Marsaglia and Costantini (both Aquila). Nando Minoia (Peugeot) could only manage seventh, just in front of Sivocci (De Vecchi), but he won the last event, the Susa–Moncenisio hillclimb.

By now, however, it was too late. The Archduke Franz Ferdinand was dead, and soon the Austrian guns would shell Belgrade.

RUSSIA AND THE USA

Italy was not the only European country to keep road racing alive after the 1903 Paris–Madrid disaster. Russia played a small part.

A race from Moscow to St Petersburg was held on 7 June 1907, to coincide with the first motor show in St Petersburg. The route was 422 miles (680 km) long, with controls at Klin, Kalinin, Vyshniy-Volochek, Kresttsy, Novograd, and Chudovo. The finish was at Tsarsko-Selo—now called Pushkin—where the Tsar had a residence, twelve miles short of St Petersburg. From there the survivors were escorted in convoy into the motor show in the city.

There were twenty-six starters, ten of them motorcycles, and the start was at 2 a.m., under the midnight sun. The only established racing driver present was Arthur Duray (De Dietrich), and he won, after leading all the way, in 9 hrs 22 min. —beating the express train by 2 hrs 38 min. The only trouble he had was that he hit a dog. Up until Novograd second place was held by Landon (Mors), but mechanical troubles dropped him to fourth. Second at the finish was Champoiseau (Charron), over two and a half hours behind Duray, and third was Folkin (Fiat), almost two hours farther back still.

It has often been said that the early Russian road races were held over atrocious roads, but Arthur Duray said after his win that they were not as bad as the evil reputation they had even then. They were wide and straight, with few difficult bends. The race organisation, with Cossacks for crowd control, was good.

Seven weeks after the Moscow–St Petersburg race there arrived in Moscow an Itala driven by Prince Scipione Borghese from Italy. He had driven from Peking, and he was bound for Paris.

With so much written about the great Peking–Paris Trial of 1907, it is surprising that it is still repeatedly called a race, but even if speed was not the objective it certainly deserves its reputation as one of the greatest of all motoring adventures. It has been well recorded by Luigi Barzini, one of Prince Borghese's crew, and by many writers since.

The Peking–Paris Trial was the inspiration for the 1908 New York–Paris event, which was a genuine race, over a distance of 12,116 miles (19,500 km). It was won in 170 days by a Thomas Flyer driven by George Schuster and Montague Roberts. It has never had quite the fame, in Europe, anyway, of the Peking–Paris, but enough legends have grown up around it. For example, it is said that one

14. Prince Scipione's Itala being recovered after falling through a
bridge in Siberia during the 1907 Peking–Paris Trial

competitor was chased by wolves in the Rocky Mountains—a story no more true
than the ones about Madonie competitors being shot at by bandits.

In 1908 the Russians organised another race, this time from St Petersburg to
Moscow. There were more foreign entries this time, and it was won by Victor
Hémery (Benz), from Demogeot (Darracq) and H. R. Pope (Itala). Hémery
averaged 52.4 mph (82.7 km/hr). In 1910 Isajeff (Benz) won a race over the 220-odd
miles (360 km) from Moscow south to Orel. Second was George Gass (Benz),
who afterwards sold his car to the Russian War Ministry. Various long-distance
trials also were held in Russia in the years before the First World War, and in 1914
there was a Grand Prix over a fast 20-mile (32-km) road circuit south of St
Petersburg, won by V. Soll (Benz).

After the war motor sport began in Soviet Russia in 1923, with the long-distance
All-Russia Trial, won by Heusler in a Praga Grand, a very solid and successful
Czech car which had first appeared in 1912, doing well in the Austrian Alpine
Trials. Long-distance trials—what we would now call rallies—have always been
popular in Eastern Europe.

If the terrain is rugged enough the distinction between rally and race can become blurred: if your car is up to its hubs in mud you will be too exhausted trying to free it really to care about race positions—you just try to keep going. In character the New York–Paris was more of a trial than a race, and so too was an event inspired by it, the 1909 New York–Seattle race.

This event, sponsored by Robert Guggenheim, who wanted publicity for the Alaska–Yukon–Pacific Exposition in Seattle, ran from New York via Syracuse, Buffalo, Cleveland, and Chicago to St Louis in six stages, the longest only 296 miles (477 km). From St Louis to Seattle there were no organised stops; just nineteen checkpoints to keep the cars on course.

The American motor industry showed little interest: at that time manufacturers in the USA confined their competition to courts of law, where they sued each other over patent rights. But Henry Ford, knowing good publicity when he saw it, entered two Model Ts to race against the three other entries: one Itala, one Acme, and one Shawmut.

It was Peking–Paris and New York–Paris all over again: breakdowns, exhaustion, mud, still more mud, heroic effort, cheap tricks. A Ford won, driven by Bert Scott and Jimmy Smith, covering the 4,106 miles (6,610 km) in 22 days 55 minutes—an average of 7.75 mph (12.74 km/hr). The Shawmut was second, its crew accusing Scott and Smith of holding them up by bribery of ferry operators and other dubious practices.

The New York–Paris and New York–Seattle were not the only road races in the USA. From 1904 until 1916 there were the Vanderbilt Cup races and the American Grand Prizes, but these belong to a history of Grand Prix racing. In 1913 a race was run from Los Angeles to Sacramento, and was won by Frank Verbeck in a stripped Fiat tourer. There were also races from Los Angeles to Phoenix, and from El Paso to Phoenix, both finishing at the Arizona State Fair. Had they been organised on an international scale they would have been among the greatest road races ever run, instead of just curiosities.

But road racing was never in the mainstream of American races. The nearest one can find there to a vernacular tradition of road racing is the Pikes Peak hillclimb in Colorado, which began in 1916, making it the second most enduring event in the USA, after the Indianapolis 500. Prohibition did breed some fine competitive motoring between bootleggers and revenue officers in the south-eastern states, but these drivers preferred to turn their talents towards stock car races on oval circuits rather than road races. A wonderful opportunity was lost. And later, when rallying became popular in the USA, it developed along British, not continental European lines: a test of navigator rather than of driver. American road laws are too strict to allow any sort of speed event, except on special stages. Americans take their everyday motoring very seriously. They don't like a lot of crazy racers fooling about.

ITALY: THE 1920s

1919

Racing began again in 1919. The old races were held, but many of the drivers were new. The Parma–Poggio di Berceto in October was won by Antonio Ascari, a garage owner from Milan, on his own 4.5-litre 1914 Grand Prix Fiat. Second was Guido Meregalli (4.4-litre Nazzaro). Also competing, making his competition début, was a 21-year-old test driver for the CMN works named Enzo Ferrari.

Ferrari also raced in the *Targa Florio*, run on 23 November over a shortened 67.1-mile (108-km) version of the Madonie circuit. The old long circuit was to be used only once more, in 1931. For Ferrari and his team-mate, Ugo Sivocci, the 1919 *Targa* was to prove an adventure before the race even started: driving from Milan to Naples, from where they were to take ship to Palermo, they were chased by wolves in the Abruzzi Mountains.

The competition in Sicily was tough. Two 1914 Peugeot Grand Prix cars were entered: one a works car for André Boillot, younger brother of Georges Boillot, who had been killed in the war; the other owned and driven by Rémy Réville, the son of a French Senator, who had paid the then huge sum of £4,000 for it in 1914. These cars were designed by Ernest Henry, who had designed also the sole post-war car competing, the straight-eight 4.9-litre Ballot, which had been built for Indianapolis. Ernest Ballot's driver was René Thomas, a Frenchman who had been racing since 1906.

It was Thomas who led on the first lap, on roads made slippery by rain. When Thomas led things looked good, for he was not one to take risks.

But André Boillot *was* one to take risks: death or glory was his slogan. Eventually, thirteen years later, death was to win, but in the 1919 *Targa* glory won by a short head. He crashed once, got started again, crashed again, recovered, crashed again—and again recovered. He did not crash as badly as, for example, Antonio Ascari, who went down a ravine and had to be winched out, unharmed, hours later by a search party. Boillot kept his crashes within reason: riding up banks, skidding into ditches, bouncing off stone walls. The sun came out, the road dried, and as he started the last lap with seven minutes lead over Thomas he had the

15. Giuseppe Campari (40/60 hp Alfa Romeo) on his way to eleventh place in the 1922 *Targa Florio*

16. Parma–Poggio di Berceto, 1919. Franchini/Marinoni (20/30 hp Alfa Romeo) on their way to fourth place

sense to stop to change his knobbly tyres for smooth-treaded ones for maximum speed on the hard clay road.

He was approaching the finish line, with six crashes to his credit, still in the lead, when he made another slight error. Exhausted, he braked too suddenly, spun three times, and the Peugeot disappeared nose first into a wooden grandstand. This created a problem, for the car was still a few yards short of the finish line, but willing hands dragged it clear. Boillot, who had been thrown out, was retrieved from a puddle of mud and put back in the driving seat. The car was facing the wrong way, so he jammed the gears into reverse and backed across the line.

He was greeted as a hero until cries went up that he should be disqualified for finishing in reverse. There were no regulations to support this view, but in the heat of the moment nobody thought of that. Ernest Ballot, Peugeot's rival, put the punch-drunk Boillot back in the driving seat again and demanded that he drive a few metres up the road, turn around, and finish in the correct manner. Which he did, saying before he fainted from exhaustion, *'C'est pour la France.'*

Meanwhile, René Thomas, trying to catch up, had crashed his car out of the race.

There is a strange story about Boillot's finish. Enzo Ferrari, writing in his autobiography, said that Boillot ran over and killed a man at the finish, and that this was his, Ferrari's, first encounter with death in motor racing. Yet, also according to Ferrari, he lost forty minutes early in the race with a loose fuel tank, lost even more time when he found the road blocked at Campofelice by a crowd listening to a speech by President Orlando of Italy, and that when he arrived at the finish line the timekeepers and everyone else (including, presumably, the corpse) had taken the last train back to Palermo.

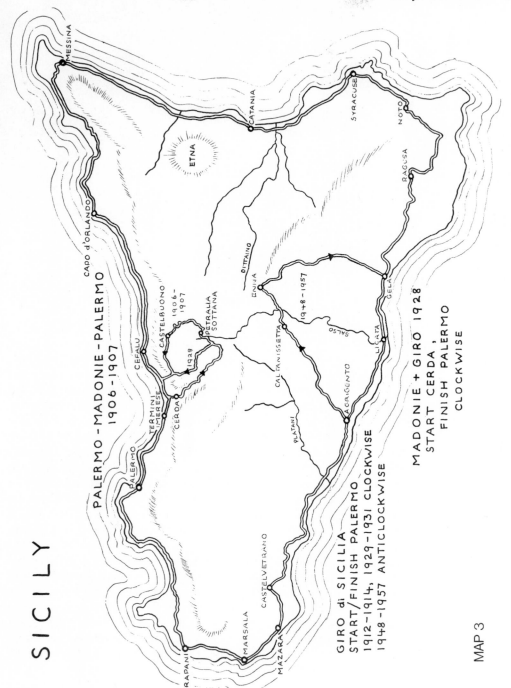

SICILY

PALERMO - MADONIE - PALERMO
1906 - 1907

GIRO di SICILIA
START/FINISH PALERMO
1912-1914, 1929-1931 CLOCKWISE
1948-1957 ANTICLOCKWISE

MADONIE + GIRO 1928
START CERDA,
FINISH PALERMO
CLOCKWISE

MAP 3

MESSINA
CAPO d'ORLANDO
CATANIA
ETNA
SYRACUSE
NOTO
RAGUSA
DITTAINO
ENNA
1948 - 1957
CASTELBUONO
1906 - 1907
PETRALIA SOTTANA
CEFALU
1928
TERMINI IMERESE
CERDA
PALERMO
CALTANISSETTA
SALSO
LICATA
GELA
AGRIGENTO
PLATANI
CASTELVETRANO
MARSALA
MAZARA
TRAPANI

17. Enzo Ferrari, at the wheel, with Giulio Ramponi in an Alfa
Romeo RL, Modena, 1923

1920

The season began well for Giuseppe Campari and the fast-rising firm of Alfa
Romeo. This combination, using a 4.2-litre pre-war car, won the Parma–Poggio di
Berceto, beating the Florentine amateur Count Giulio Masetti (4.5-litre Fiat) and
Enzo Ferrari (6-litre Isotta Fraschini straight-eight), and then won the second
Mugello race, easily beating Augusto Tarabusi (3-litre Diatto) and Eduardo
Weber, in a car of his own manufacture. Weber's cars never made much impres-
sion, but his firm's carburettors are still regarded as the best in the world.

Rémy Réville had some success with his expensive Peugeot, winning the Susa–
Moncenisio hillclimb. A new long climb was introduced that year, the 19-mile
(30.5-km) Aosta–Gran San Bernardo, on the road from Turin into Switzerland.
The winner was Count Alberto Conelli driving a 3-litre Fast, a short-lived fast
tourer built in Turin. Second was Felice Nazzaro (Nazzaro), in what was probably
his first post-war event. The Aosta–Gran San Bernardo hillclimb survived until
1957, and was one of the very rare European speed events, outside of rallying, to be
held on an unpaved road long after the Second World War.

The *Targa* was poor: only sixteen starters, with Campari the only star, and
race day, 20 October, made miserable by wind and rain. Campari retired his works
Alfa Romeo, leaving Guido Meregalli (Nazzaro) to win. Enzo Ferrari, a new
recruit to Alfa Romeo, was second, Luigi Lopez (Darracq) was third.

1921

The last French Grand Prix before the war, in 1914, had been dominated by Mercedes, who finished one-two-three. Now, three years after Germany's defeat, they made a cautious comeback. One car was entered for the *Targa Florio*, a 7.25-litre, 6-cylinder monster dating from 1913—in the Indianapolis 500 that year Ralph de Palma had found it undriveable due to a vicious vibration, but the engine had been used in fighter aircraft during the war, and this fault eradicated. Now the driver was Max Sailer, a veteran company man who was later to become race chief of Mercedes-Benz.

Sailer's main rival was his exact opposite: the wealthy amateur Giulio Masetti, who had a smaller, more easily handled car, a 4.5-litre 1914 Grand Prix Fiat. Alfa Romeo also entered a strong team, with Ascari, Campari, Sivocci, and Ferrari driving.

The race was over four laps, and at the end of the first Sailer came through with twenty-one seconds on Masetti. On the second lap it was even closer: Masetti got past and led by 2.5 seconds. The Alfa Romeo team, despite its greater experience of the circuit, could do nothing about the leading pair.

Masetti won, at 36.1 mph (58.2 km/hr): on lap three he had pulled out fifty-eight seconds on Sailer—still very close in a race of more than seven hours—and at the end he was over two minutes ahead. The defeated Alfa Romeo team was not disgraced: Campari was less than three minutes behind Sailer, with Sivocci and Ferrari close behind. Less than ten minutes covered the first six cars. The sixth finisher was an Itala touring car driven by British-resident Italian Giulio 'Jules' Foresti. His riding mechanic was a little Cockney of Swiss descent named Leo Villa, who was later to be mechanic to Sir Malcolm Campbell, and to Sir Malcolm's son, that Don Quixote of speed, Donald Campbell.

The Mugello race, two months after the *Targa*, was completely dominated by Alfa Romeo, Campari leading home Ferrari and Sivocci at 38.8 mph (62.6 km/hr). The Susa–Moncenisio saw the first of three straight wins by Alfieri Maserati, who had been racing since 1908. On this occasion he drove an Isotta Fraschini, beating the winner of the year before, Rémy Réville (Peugeot).

1922

Mercedes's good showing in the 1921 *Targa* encouraged them to enter a full team the following year. Six cars were entered: two developed versions of the 1914 4.5-litre Grand Prix car for Christian Lautenschlager (winner of the 1914 French Grand Prix) and Otto Salzer; two supercharged 7.25-litre cars for Max Sailer and Christian Werner; and two little supercharged 1.5-litre cars for Nando Minoia and Scheef. A third 1914 Grand Prix car was privately entered by Giulio Masetti.

And it was Masetti who led at the end of the first lap, from Jean Goux, winner of the 1909 light-car race, who this year had a 2-litre Ballot. Third was a surprise: Biagio Nazzaro, nephew of Felice, on a Fiat straight-eight. The works Mercedes,

18. Giulio Masetti (Mercedes) winning the 1922 *Targa Florio*

all six of them, were being well beaten.

On lap two Biagio Nazzaro crashed, hurting himself slightly. Reporters quickly announced to the world that the great Felice Nazzaro had been killed in Sicily. Felice heard about this when telegrams of sympathy began arriving for his wife. Biagio Nazzaro was, however, soon to die: a rear axle failed on his works Fiat in the 1922 French Grand Prix at Strasbourg.

Meanwhile Goux had overtaken Masetti. Entering the last lap he was sixty-seven seconds ahead. But his brakes were failing: he crashed and staggered on, frame broken and radiator leaking. He might still have won had he not had to stop to change a punctured tyre, and drive carefully to preserve his remaining tyres. Still, he was less than two minutes behind Masetti, who finished first with a speed of 39.1 mph (63.1 km/hr). Third was Giulio Foresti (with Leo Villa beside him) in another works Ballot.

For the 72 bhp Ballots it was a moral victory over the 115 bhp Mercedes, the first of many occasions when good handling would beat power on the Madonie circuit. But it was a great personal triumph for Masetti: he won; yet the best works Mercedes, Sailer's, was sixth.

Among the other finishers, back in nineteenth, was a 1.1-litre Austro-Daimler driven by Alfred Neubauer, who was soon to move across the border to the parent Daimler company in Stuttgart and become the legendary team-manager for Mercedes-Benz. Among the drivers who did not finish was Tornaco, driving the first Bugatti to appear on the Madonie circuit. It would not be the last.

That year, 1922, was the year that the Monza autodrome was opened, Italy's first permanent motor racing circuit, but road racing still thrived. It was Alfieri Maserati's year: he had built a special car, using one half of a V8 Hispano-Suiza aero engine mounted in a shortened Isotta Fraschini chassis. He won at Mugello, beating Gastone Brilli-Peri (Fiat) and Carlo Masetti (Bugatti), brother of Giulio; at Susa–Moncenisio, beating Nando Minoia (O M); and at the Aosta–Gran San Bernardo, beating Count Conelli (Ballot) and Giuseppe Campari (Alfa Romeo). Conelli in the Ballot won the Parma–Poggio di Berceto, beating the Fiats of Biagio Nazzaro and Gastone Brilli-Peri.

A road race was also held in Sardinia, over a 51.5-mile (83-km) circuit out of Cagliari. The winner was Ernesto Ceirano (3-litre Ceirano). The total length of the race seems not to have been recorded, but Ceirano spent over six hours on the course.

Late in the year, on 19 November, the *Coppa Florio* was contested over the Madonie circuit. The winner, at 37.5 mph (60.4 km/hr), was André Boillot, driving a 1914 Grand Prix Peugeot fitted with a 3.8-litre sleeve-valve engine. A poor second was the works Sunbeam of Henry Seagrave, who was not yet started on his great record-breaking career.

The Sunbeam team had come from England, cars and all, on the steam yacht of Kenelm Lee Guinness. Seagrave found the Madonie hills wild and inhospitable: during practice one evening he broke down and had to take shelter, with his mechanic, in a peasant's house. The owner was suspicious, and his suspicion turned out to be well justified when Seagrave, having no money in his overalls, paid for his lodgings with some gaudy and worthless Spanish raffle tickets.

1923

A poor year. There were only fifteen starters in the *Targa Florio*: Sivocci won from Ascari, both on works Alfa Romeo; Nando Minoia was third on Steyr; and Giulio Masetti fourth on Alfa Romeo.

On 6 May a new road race was introduced, run over a 39-mile (63-km) circuit starting and finishing at Cremona, and passing through Piadena and Palvareto. Antonio Ascari (Alfa Romeo) won, at 83 mph (134.2 km/hr), from Alfieri Maserati in a works Diatto he had developed himself. With this car Maserati won the Susa–Moncenisio and Aosta–Gran San Bernardo hillclimbs later in the year. Parma–Poggio di Berceto fell to Gastone Brilli-Peri (4.5-litre Fiat), Mugello to Giulio Masetti (Alfa Romeo), with Brilli-Peri, this time on Steyr, second, and

19. Refreshments. Giulio Masetti, Ugo Sivocci, and Antonio Ascari at the 1923 *Targa Florio*

20. Mugello, 1923. Antonio Ascari, with mechanic Giulio Ramponi, on his way to third place in an Alfa Romeo RL

Ascari (Alfa Romeo), third. Another new road race that year was run over the 27.6-mile (44.6-km) Savio circuit south of Ravenna. Enzo Ferrari (3-litre Alfa Romeo) won at 57.7 mph (93 km/hr) from Eduardo Weber (1.5-litre Fiat).

1924

The *Coppa* and *Targa* races were now combined: the winner of five Madonie laps was to win the *Coppa*; the leader at four laps was to win the *Targa*. Rather pointless, but the manufacturers and drivers flocked back that year.

Mercedes had three cars for Werner, Lautenschlager, and Neubauer, with designer Ferdinand Porsche in attendance. Alfa Romeo entered Campari, Ascari, and Louis Wagner, the Alsatian who had raced in the *Targa* back in 1907. Masetti had a private Alfa Romeo, Goux a fast little Ballot, while Boillot and Foresti had sleeve-valve Peugeots. Felice Nazzaro was on the sidelines, but when Carlos Salamano crashed a works supercharged Fiat, hurting himself more than the car, Nazzaro offered to drive it. But he disliked the handling and decided not to start, leaving Pietro Bordino to race the sole supercharged Fiat.

The racing was good: after the first lap half a minute covered the first five cars.

21. *Coppa* and *Targa Florio* races, 1924. A pit stop for André
Boillot's Peugeot. This car is a 1914 GP model re-engined with
a 3.8-litre sleeve-valve unit

In the lead was Masetti's Alfa Romeo, and second, to everyone's amazement, was a big 6.6-litre Hispano-Suiza driven by a French aperitif manufacturer who had been racing only three years, André Dubonnet. Eating his dust were Werner, Boillot, and Ascari. But Dubonnet could not hold the pace, and he dropped back, as did Masetti, giving one-two to Werner and Ascari on lap two.

And that was the way they stayed until within sight of the finish, when Ascari's Alfa Romeo engine seized. So Christian Werner in the Mercedes won comfortably, at 40.4 mph (65.2 km/hr), from Masetti (Alfa Romeo), Campari (Alfa Romeo), Boillot (Peugeot), who had been off the road and had tyre problems, and Dubonnet (Hispano-Suiza), the hero of the day. Most disappointed man was Bordino (Fiat), who had been third the lap before, thus getting into the *Targa* record book, but had then stopped in the pits and collapsed from heat exhaustion. Nazzaro had taken over the car and crashed it. Also very annoyed was Nando Minoia (Steyr), who was forced to retire when his mechanic collapsed.

Mugello was dominated by OM cars from Brescia, who had a fast new 6-cylinder 2-litre model. Giuseppe Morandi won, at 40.7 mph (65.7 km/hr), from Renato Balestrero—two names that were to become famous throughout Italy. Ascari on Alfa Romeo had a good year, winning at Cremona and the Parma–Poggio di Berceto. The Parma hillclimb was now a fast event for its type: Ascari averaged 55.2 mph (88.9 km/hr).

1925

So far eighteen races had been held on the Madonie circuits, and they had been won by eleven different makes of car. Itala, Sizaire-Naudin, De Dion Bouton, Isotta Fraschini, Spa, Scat, and Alfa Romeo had won one each; Fiat, Nazzaro, and Mercedes had won two each; and Peugeot had been by far the most successful, with five wins. Now another French make, Bugatti, was to equal and eclipse Peugeot by winning the *Targa Florio* five times in a row, from 1925 to 1929.

After leaving Prinetti & Stucchi in 1900, Ettore Bugatti had built his own car, which promptly won him a contract with De Dietrich in Alsace. He was just twenty-one. In 1904 he designed the Hermes cars, also in Alsace; in 1906 he moved to Deutz of Cologne; and in 1909 he moved back to Alsace—to Molsheim, near Strasbourg—to produce cars under his own name. He was still as interested in racing as ever, although no longer as a driver, and he sent a car to Indianapolis as early as 1914. But racing successes did not come until after the war.

Despite all that has been written about Bugatti cars, they cannot, on their record, be considered one of the real greats of motor racing—they did not have the successes of Mercedes-Benz, or Alfa Romeo, or Ferrari, or Lotus—but are on about the same level as Cooper. Both Bugatti and Cooper gained their early successes with light cars; both sold their cars to the public, thus gaining the gratitude and affection that a manufacturer such as Mercedes-Benz, whose racing cars are remote and unobtainable, can never have; both had a brief peak in Grand Prix racing followed by rapid stagnation and decline. Bugatti gained their Grand Prix wins over a period of eight years; Cooper over nine.

In 1925 the combined *Coppa/Targa* race was again run over five laps. Two works teams appeared: Peugeot with their sleeve-valve cars driven by Boillot, Wagner,

22. Giulio Foresti (Peugeot) just past the start/finish line during
    the 1924 *Coppa* and *Targa Florio* races

Christian Dauvergne, and Louis Rigal (a Frenchman, not to be confused with Victor Rigal); and Bugatti, the new challenger, with Meo Costantini and the brothers Pierre and Fernando de Vizcaya.

Peugeot were quickest: at the end of the first lap Boillot led from Dauvergne and Wagner, followed by Costantini's Bugatti and the other Peugeot of Rigal. Boillot, as usual, was burning up his tyres and had to drop back, but the Peugeots of Wagner and Dauvergne took over the lead, with Costantini fourth. All looked settled until Dauvergne crashed: his mechanic was thrown clear, stunned, and Dauvergne himself was trapped under the car, which began to burn. The mechanic aroused himself and, with help from spectators, tried to free Dauvergne. Wagner, behind on the road and ahead on time, stopped to help. Dauvergne was free at last, badly burned, and began a seemingly endless wait for an ambulance.

Louis Wagner raced on, but it was too late. Costantini in the Bugatti was first, at 44.4 mph (71.6 km/hr), with Wagner and Boillot second and third. Pierre de Vizcaya was fourth on another Bugatti, and Renato Balestrero (OM) was fifth.

Mugello that year, and the next, was run over a short circuit. Both years it was won by Emilio Materassi (2-litre Itala).

In 1925 the Cuneo automobile club introduced a new, long hillclimb over a 41.5-mile (66.8-km) course starting in Cuneo and taking the road south-west to Borgo San Dalmazzo and Vinadio, before climbing the winding road to the Colle della Maddalena. It was held four times, in 1925, 1926, 1927, and 1930, generally not attracting the best drivers, although Nuvolari (Alfa Romeo) won in 1930, beating Luigi Fagioli (Maserati) and Luigi Arcangeli (Alfa Romeo).

1926

Three works teams contested the *Targa Florio* this year with good chances of success: Peugeot had Boillot and Wagner; Bugatti had Costantini, Jean Goux, and Nando Minoia; Delage, with their complex but very powerful 2-litre V12s, had René Thomas (back for the first time since his defeat by Boillot in 1919), Robert Benoist, Albert Divo, and Giulio Masetti—Masetti's car, as usual, entered by himself.

The Delages were not at home in the hills: they handled badly, and the brakes were spongy. It took all Masetti's skill to be quickest in practice, and even that skill was not enough. On the first lap of the race Masetti's Delage hit a bank and rolled over, killing the driver. His body remained there, guarded by a *carabiniere*, throughout the race, a sombre warning. The Delage team all withdrew.

The Bugatti team finished one-two-three: Costantini first, at 45.6 mph (73.5 km/hr), Minoia second, Goux third. Next came a big Itala powered by a Hispano-Suiza engine and driven by Emilio Materassi. Behind him, fifth, was that old Hispano exponent, André Dubonnet, this time driving a Bugatti, leading the only Peugeot to finish, Wagner's. Balestrero (OM) was seventh.

In ninth place was a new car making its début: the first-ever Maserati, driven

23. The 41-mile hillclimb from Cuneo, south of Turin, to the Colle della Maddalena: Giulio Ramponi (1.5-litre Alfa Romeo) on his way to third place in 1927

by Alfieri Maserati. It won the 1.5-litre class, but there were too few finishers to make this an achievement of much note. There was also a 1.1-litre class, won by a Salmson driven by young Umberto Borzacchini.

On 20 June, in Calabria, a new road race was run over two 106-mile (170-km) laps starting and finishing at Cosenza (see Map 6). This event, the *Coppa della Sila*, was run as a rally in 1924 and 1925, but was now an unrestricted race. Saverio de Bartolo (Ansaldo) was first, averaging 30.3 mph (48.8 km/hr), from Guido d'Ippolito (Ceirano) and Renato Balestrero (OM).

Late in 1925 a hillclimb was held from Bologna up to the Raticosa Pass, on the road to the Mugello and Florence. It did not attract top competitors, and was won by Antonio Testi (Diatto). What was more important, in hindsight, was the winding stretch of road itself. Starting on 26 March 1927, it was to be used twenty-three times in thirty years in the greatest of all road races, the *Coppa della Mille Miglia*.

24. The first *Mille Miglia*, 1927: the Gastone Brilli-Peri/Bruno Presenti Alfa Romeo, which led in Rome before retiring, crosses the Futa Pass in the Apennines between Bologna and Florence. This was also part of the Mugello circuit

Mille Miglia

The *Mille Miglia*—the Thousand Miles—was unique. It was longer even than the *Giro di Sicilia*, and, unlike the *Giro*, it ran through the heartland of Italy: through Rome, Florence, Bologna, Verona. Some years it went to Milan, Turin, Perugia, Pisa, Venice. It crossed the Apennines, the Abruzzi, the plains of Lombardy. It used the Via Aurelia, the Via Flaminia, the Via Cassia, the Via Tiburtini, the Via Emilia. The race was run twelve times before the Second World War, and eleven times after. The complete list of winners looks like this:

Clemente Biondetti—*four wins*
Giuseppe Campari, Tazio Nuvolari, Carlo Pintacuda, Giannino Marzotto—*two wins each*
Nando Minoia, Rudolf Caracciola, Umberto Borzacchini, Achille Varzi, Antonio Brivio, Luigi Villoresi, Giovanni Bracco, Alberto Ascari, Stirling Moss, Eugenio Castellotti, Piero Taruffi—*one win each*

For the reader from the English-speaking world, and perhaps for any non-Italian, the response is likely to be: who was Clemente Biondetti? Who was this driver who managed to outshine such acknowledged greats as Campari, Nuvolari, Caracciola, Varzi, Ascari, and Moss? Finding the answer is not easy. Two encyclopedias of motor sport have been published in English in recent years, but neither lists Clemente Biondetti—nor do they mention Nando Minoia, Carlo Pintacuda, Giovanni Bracco, and Giannino Marzotto.

All of them were, of course, Italians, and the *Mille Miglia*, far more than the cosmopolitan *Targa Florio*, was very much an Italian race. Only two foreigners, Rudolf Caracciola and Stirling Moss, ever won it, although a handful of others did show the necessary skill around that vast 1,000-mile lap, notably Juan Manuel Fangio, Karl Kling, Peter Collins, Olivier Gendebien, and Wolfgang von Trips.

The Italian dominance may be due to the difficulty in learning a course a thousand miles long—a feat that may seem impossible at first glance, but that is probably no more difficult than learning a new language. Obviously a local driver has more time for private practice. It can be argued that it is not surprising that a Roman, Piero Taruffi, won the last *Mille Miglia* in 1957, for he not only lived on the course but had also first competed in the race in 1930. By 1957 he should have known his way around blindfolded.

But this argument is not so overwhelming if one remembers that the *Mille Miglia* course was changed thirteen times. Taruffi raced on eleven different circuits, with radical changes in 1938, 1947, 1949, 1950, 1951, and 1953. Clemente Biondetti's four wins were on three different circuits. The only sections of road that were used in all twenty-three races were on the northern plains: Brescia to Vicenza, and Padua to Ferrara—and these sections were covered in both directions. The maps, 5 and 7, should make it clearer.

1927

The first *Mille Miglia* attracted seventy-seven entries. It was not a brilliant field: the only top Grand Prix driver present was Gastone Brilli-Peri, crewed by Ugo Presenti, on Alfa Romeo, but there was the veteran Nando Minoia, with Giuseppe Morandi, on OM. One of the founders of the race, Count Aymo Maggi, shared a big Isotta Fraschini with Bindo Maserati, the second of the Maserati brothers, born between Carlo and Alfieri. Among the up-and-coming drivers present were Tazio Nuvolari on Bianchi and Luigi Fagioli on Salmson.

Brilli-Peri was the quickest: he reached Rome in 7 hrs 11 min., fourteen minutes ahead of Minoia. But at Spoleto, on the way north from Rome to Perugia, the Alfa Romeo failed. The race became an OM benefit: Minoia/Morandi led home two other OMs driven by Timo Danieli/Renato Balestrero and Mario Danieli/Archimede Rosa. Two Lancia Lambda touring cars were fourth and fifth. Sixth was the Maggi/Maserati Isotta Fraschini. Nuvolari and Fagioli both failed to finish.

The winning car had left Brescia at 8.58 on the morning of 26 March, and had arrived back in Brescia at just after five o'clock the following morning, averaging 48 mph (77.2 km/hr).

In the weeks before the 1927 *Targa Florio* residents of the Madonie saw a small woman, obviously respectable, walking around the racing circuit at a rate of about twelve miles a day. She was Czech, and the man with her was her husband, a banker from Prague. They owned a Bugatti and had entered it in the *Targa*. After walking around the circuit Elizabeth Junek began practising in the car, doing up to five laps a day.

Bugatti again dominated the entry: at the end of the first lap they were solidly in the lead, Nando Minoia leading André Dubonnet, Emilio Materassi, and little Mrs Junek. On the second lap the steering of the Junek Bugatti broke, putting the car off the road, without injury to the driver. Minoia's Bugatti suffered collapsed suspension, and Dubonnet also dropped back, eventually finishing sixth. This left Materassi to win, at 44 mph (71 km/hr), from Count Alberto Conelli, also on Bugatti, Alfieri Maserati (Maserati), and the faithful André Boillot on Peugeot.

1928

The second *Mille Miglia* saw the number of entries up to eighty-eight. Nando Minoia was back, but with little chance of an outright win at the wheel of a big La Salle touring car, a product of the Cadillac Motor Company. Beside him was Renato Balestrero. Mario Danieli/Corrado Lotti had another La Salle, and there were four Chryslers, one driven by Emilio Materassi/Rodolfo Caruso. The favourites for outright victory were the Alfa Romeo team, with Giuseppe Campari/Giulio Ramponi and Attilio Marinoni/Battista Guidotti their quickest drivers, and the Bugatti team, with Tazio Nuvolari/Amedeo Bignami, Achille Varzi/Tabacchi, Brilli-Peri/Arturo Lumino, and the ex-Fiat driver Pietro Bordino, with de Giovannini.

Some of these co-drivers were to prove durable. Guidotti, a faithful Alfa employee, was to be rewarded after the Second World War with Grand Prix drives. Bignami, although with Nuvolari in this race, was to become Varzi's regular mechanic, and, after Varzi's death, was to work for Juan Manuel Fangio. Ramponi, also a driver, moved to London in 1936: a tuning firm bearing his name still operates in a Bayswater mews, while Ramponi himself lives in retirement in South Africa.

It was Ramponi, alongside Giuseppe Campari, who took the chequered flag in the 1928 *Mille Miglia*, having led all the way—the first of eight winners to disprove Clemente Biondetti's famous statement: 'He who leads in Rome will not lead in Brescia.' Campari/Ramponi (Alfa Romeo) did win, at 52.8 mph (84.1 km/hr), from Archimede Rosa/Mazzotti (OM), and, doing even better than the year before, the touring Lancia Lambda of Ermenegildo Strazza/Alfieri Varallo. The Lancia beat the two Alfa Romeos of Marinoni/Guidotti and Alfredo Bornigia/Angelo Guatta, and the Bugatti of Brilli-Peri/Lumino. Nuvolari was thirteenth; Varzi retired.

Bugatti were never to do well in the *Mille Miglia*, although it was a race that seemed well-suited to their cars. If they could survive and win events such as the

25. Elizabeth Junek at the 1928 *Targa Florio*. Sitting beside her is
Vincenzo Florio

Targa Florio and the *Marathon de la Route*, the toughest of all rallies, there is no
reason why they could not have won the *Mille Miglia*. More entries would, no
doubt, have brought better results.

Of the six American cars entered in the 1928 *Mille Miglia*, four finished, the
fastest being the Minoia/Balestrero La Salle, fifteenth out of thirty-eight finishers,
and winner of the 5-litre class. It was not until 1953 that another US car, a
Chrysler Saratoga driven by Paul Frère, was to score another class win.

Year Four of the Bugatti era of the *Targa Florio* saw no less than ten cars from
Molsheim entered: Materassi (who was soon to die at Monza, taking twenty-two
spectators with him); Minoia (still trying to win); Giulio Foresti; Pietro Bordino;
Elizabeth Junek; another woman driver, Countess Margot d'Einsiedel; Count
Gastone Brilli-Peri; Count Conelli; and two newcomers to the *Targa*, Louis
Chiron, and Tazio Nuvolari—beauty and the beast.

Opposing them were the Alfa Romeo team of Campari and Marinoni, and the
Maserati team of Borzacchini, Ernesto Maserati, and Luigi Fagioli.

At the last moment Bordino's Bugatti was taken over by Alberto Divo, who had
raced one of the Masetti-killing Delages two years before—and it was Divo who
won. What happened to all the formidable talent mentioned above? They not

26. Sicilian driver Carlo Gasperin (1.5-litre Alfa Romeo) in the 1928
Giro di Sicilia. In 1930 he was second in this event, sharing an
Alfa Romeo with Luigi Arcangeli

only were beaten by Divo—they were humiliated by Elizabeth Junek as well. Her race went like this: First lap—fourth. Second lap—first. Third lap—second. Fourth lap—second. Fifth lap—exhausted—fifth. The final results looked like this: Divo, Campari, Conelli, Chiron, Junek, Minoia, Fagioli, and René Dreyfus.

It is often said that Elizabeth Junek was the greatest of all woman racing drivers. If she wasn't, the only possible rivals for that position are Pat Moss—who reached her peak in winning the 1960 *Marathon de la Route*—or Ewy Rosqvist, who won the 1962 *Gran Premio Standard* in Argentina.

Three weeks after the 1928 *Targa Florio* the first *Giro di Sicilia* since 1914 was held, run over a course that combined the Madonie circuit with a complete circuit of the island—a distance of 643.6 miles (1,038 km). Unfortunately there were only eighteen starters, of whom ten finished. Costantino Magistri (1.5-litre Alfa Romeo) won, in sixteen and a half hours, at a speed of 39.2 mph (63.3 km/hr).

That year the Mugello race returned to its original long circuit. The prize was now the *Targa Masetti*, in honour of the late Count Guilio Masetti. Emilio Materassi (1.5-litre Talbot) won at 43.8 mph (70.7 km/hr) from Bruno Presenti and Enzo Ferrari on 1.5-litre Alfa Romeos. Campari (Alfa Romeo) retired after setting fastest lap.

Talbot also won at Cremona, the race being revived for the first time since 1924. It was won by Luigi Arcangeli, on a 2-litre Talbot, at 101.1 mph (163 km/hr). Nuvolari (2-litre Bugatti) was second, and Materassi (1.5-litre Talbot), third.

Campari again set fastest lap before retiring.

Just over a month later a new circuit of almost exactly the same length as Cremona, 39.2 miles (63 km), was used for the first time. The *Circuito della Val d'Elsa*, with start and finish at Siena in Tuscany, ran south-west from the town through Costalpino and Rosia to the Elsa Valley, which it followed north as far as the Colle di Val d'Elsa, where it turned south through Monteriggioni and back to Siena. The race, over five laps, 195.3 miles (315 km), was won by Bruno Presenti (Alfa Romeo), from Renato Balestrero in the big *Mille Miglia* La Salle, and Aldo Bassi (Lancia Lambda). Luigi Arcangeli (Bugatti) set fastest lap, at 53.6 mph (86.5 km/hr). Presenti's winning average was little slower: 53.1 mph (85.7 km/hr).

On the same day as the Siena race Alfa Romeo scored another win, down in Calabria, where Guido d'Ippolito in a 1.5-litre car won the *Coppa della Sila* at Cosenza.

Another long-circuit road race was introduced, but this one, like the Siena event, did not last. Start and finish was at Rimini, and the distance of the triangular circuit was 31 miles (50 km). Luigi Fagioli (1.1-litre Salmson) won, covering six laps at 60.6 mph (97.8 km/hr).

1929

On paper the *Mille Miglia* looked like another Alfa Romeo win, with OM perhaps challenging. But from the start it was the lone 1.7-litre Maserati of Umberto Borzacchini/Ernesto Maserati that led. In Rome they still led, three minutes in front of the Campari/Ramponi Alfa Romeo. At Terni, the birthplace of Borzacchini, the Maserati finally let him down, and Campari inherited a secure lead.

Campari's winning average was 55.7 mph (89.7 km/hr). Second were Giuseppe Morandi/Archimede Rosa (2-litre OM), third Achille Varzi/Colombo (1750 Alfa Romeo), and fourth the inevitable Lancia Lambda of Strazza and Varallo.

During the race the Alfa Romeo of Nando Minoia/Attilio Marinoni stopped to have its front axle and springs changed, its tank refuelled, and shock absorbers tightened, all in seventeen minutes—the sort of rebuilding operation that is common today in rallying. They finished sixth, almost an hour behind Campari.

Back in ninth place was another 1750 Alfa Romeo driven by Franco Cortese/Angelo Guatta. (After the Second World War Cortese was to have the honour of driving the first Ferrari in its first race.) In twenty-fifth place was the Fiat 521 touring car of Ambrosini/Dusio—the Piero Dusio who was to manufacture Cisitalia cars after the war. The most photogenic finisher was the Italian actress Mimy Aymler, who was twenty-ninth out of forty-two finishers after almost twenty-five hours in her Lancia. She was an unusual woman in several ways: she was a former mistress of an ambitious young diplomat named Galeazzo Ciano, who, in 1930, was to become Benito Mussolini's son-in-law, and swiftly rise to become Foreign Minister of Italy.

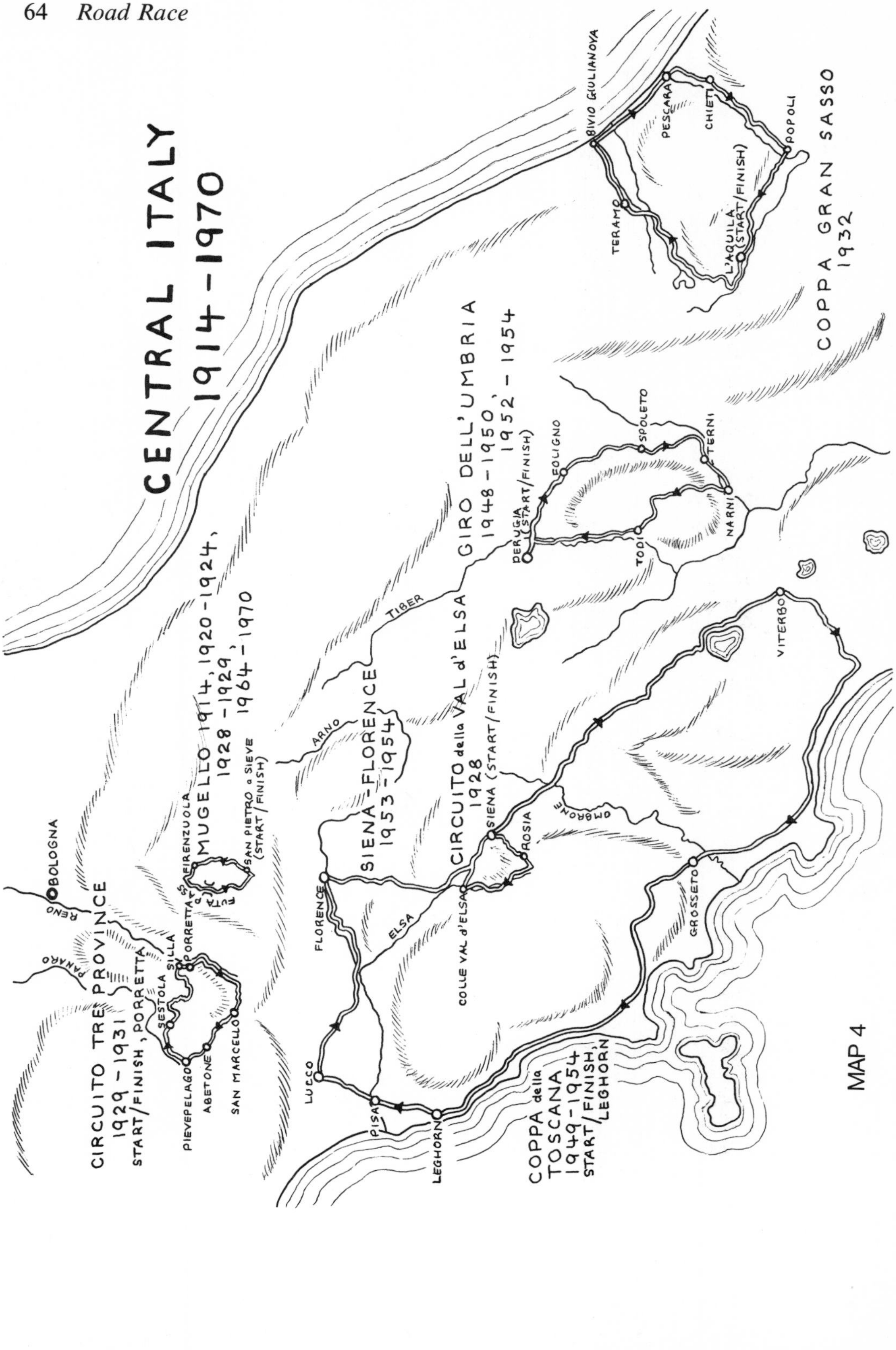

CENTRAL ITALY 1914-1970

CIRCUITO TRE PROVINCE
1929-1931
START/FINISH, PORRETTA

BOLOGNA

RENO

PANARO

SESTOLA SILLA

PORRETTA

FUTA

FIRENZUOLA

MUGELLO 1914, 1920-1924, 1928-1929, 1964-1970

SAN PIETRO a SIEVE (START/FINISH)

PIEVEPELAGO

ABETONE

SAN MARCELLO

LUCCA

PISA

LEGHORN

COPPA della TOSCANA
1949-1954
START/FINISH, LEGHORN

FLORENCE

ARNO

ELSA

SIENA-FLORENCE
1953-1954

CIRCUITO della VAL d'ELSA
1928

COLLE VAL d'ELSA

SIENA (START/FINISH)

ROSIA

OMBRONE

GROSSETO

TIBER

GIRO DELL'UMBRIA
1948-1950,
1952-1954

PERUGIA (START/FINISH)

FOLIGNO

SPOLETO

TERNI

TODI

NARNI

VITERBO

BIVIO GIULIANOVA

TERAMO

PESCARA

CHIETI

L'AQUILA (START/FINISH)

POPOLI

COPPA GRAN SASSO
1932

MAP 4

27. Nando Minoia (Bugatti) on his way to second place in the 1929
Targa Florio

For the *Giro di Sicilia* the *Giro*-plus-Madonie experiment was abandoned, and the plain circuit of the island, as in pre-war years, was reintroduced. The field was bigger than in 1928, forty starters, but still the stars kept away. Archimede Rosa/ Trombetta (OM) won, at 42 mph (67.7 km/hr), from Giuseppe Morandi/Giulio Foresti (OM).

In 1929 it was decided to reintroduce the *Coppa Florio*—not as a separate race, but as a fourth-lap award in the *Targa Florio*, in the way that the *Targa* had been awarded in the *Coppa Florio* from 1924 to 1926. Whatever this was meant to achieve, it evidently failed. It was a much poorer entry than the year before, and only four cars succeeded in finishing officially, although a couple more arrived hours late. Albert Divo (Bugatti) won again, at 46.1 mph (74.4 km/hr), from Minoia (Bugatti), Brilli-Peri (Alfa Romeo), and Campari (Alfa Romeo). Achille Varzi, making his Madonie début on Alfa Romeo, failed to finish, as did Louis Wagner (Bugatti), who, according to a history book the author has before him, retired from racing two years before.

The rest of the long-circuit races in 1929 were won by either Gastone Brilli-Peri or Giuseppe Morandi.

Brilli-Peri won at Mugello on a 1.5-litre Talbot, beating Morandi (3-litre OM). This was the last time the Mugello circuit was used until 1964, although a short-circuit race was held in 1955. At Cremona Brilli-Peri won again, this time on Alfa Romeo, averaging 114.2 mph (184.1 km/hr), beating Varzi (Alfa Romeo) and Ernesto Maserati (Maserati). This was the last time that the Cremona race was held, which is ironic, since it attracted far better entries than the more enduring races farther south—the *Targa* excepted, of course.

Morandi, again on 3-litre OM, won the Cosenza auto club's *Coppa Michele Bianchi*, formerly the *Coppa della Sila*, beating Ermenegildo Strazza (Lancia), the Brescia driver making a rare visit to the south, and Guido d'Ippolito (1750 Alfa Romeo). Morandi also won a new race, the *Circuito Tre Province*. The course was a single 79.7-mile (128.5-km) lap in the Apennines, starting and finishing at Porretta Terme, in the hills above Pistoia, west of Florence (see Map 4). Averaging 37.6 mph (60.7 km/hr), Morandi (OM) led home Luigi Fagioli (Maserati) and Mario Tadini (OM).

1930

Up until 1929 the *Coppa* and *Targa Florio* events were the only Italian road races to attract entries from abroad in any number. The *Mille Miglia* was still almost exclusively an Italian race. Italy was a major force in motor racing, but neither Nuvolari nor Varzi had won a Grand Prix outside Italy. The only Italians to have done that since the war were Campari, in 1924, and Ascari, in 1925. The internationalism that we today take for granted in motor sport was then a very weak force.

In the 1930 *Mille Miglia* there came a sign that the national barriers were beginning to crumble: a works Mercedes-Benz was entered. Appropriately, the driver was a man who had always been an anti-nationalist: Rudolf Caracciola, a Protestant Rheinlander of Italian descent who lived in Switzerland.

From the start at Brescia Luigi Arcangeli (Maserati) led across the plains to Bologna, followed by Nuvolari (1750 Alfa Romeo), with Caracciola and Varzi (1750 Alfa Romeo) dead-heating for third. Over the Apennines Arcangeli crashed, and Caracciola had slipped to seventh by Florence—the massive Mercedes-Benz was proving clumsy on the mountain roads. Nuvolari and Varzi were left fighting for the lead. In Rome they dead-heated. Varzi had started ten minutes ahead of Nuvolari, which gave Nuvolari a tactical advantage: if he could catch Varzi and keep him in sight he would be sure of winning. This he did: in one of the most famous acts of gamesmanship in the history of motor racing, he crept up behind Varzi in the dark, driving without lights. Varzi did not know Nuvolari was there until his arch-rival turned on his lights and roared by. By then it was too late for Varzi to recapture the lost ten minutes. Nuvolari came home with an average of 62.3 mph (100.5 km/hr). Third was Campari/Marinoni (Alfa Romeo); fourth,

28. Eugenio Siena, Tazio Nuvolari, and Luigi Arcangeli in 1929.
The car is a 1750 Alfa Romeo

Pietro Ghersi/Franco Cortese (Alfa Romeo); fifth, Aldo Bassi/Carlo Gazzabini (OM); and sixth, Caracciola in the Mercedes-Benz.

Down in Sicily the *Giro* was again held a week before the *Targa*, and was again won by Archimede Rosa (OM), this time with the formidable Giuseppe Morandi as co-driver. In this race, the last *Giro* until 1948, and one of the last wins for OM, they spent 11 hrs 40 min. 40.4 sec. on the road, averaging 51.3 mph (82.8 km/hr). In the eighteen years since Cecil Snipe had won the first *Giro* in 1912 the time had been cut by more than half. In the twenty-six years from 1931 until the last *Giro* in 1957 there was only about one-sixth of this rate of improvement.

There was a chance that Albert Divo might win the *Targa Florio* for the third successive time in 1931. Certainly he got under the lap record on race day—but so, unfortunately for him, did Louis Chiron (Bugatti), Count Conelli (Bugatti), Achille Varzi (Alfa Romeo), Tazio Nuvolari (Alfa Romeo), and Giuseppe Campari (Alfa Romeo).

29. Louis Chiron's frantic tyre-change during the 1930 *Targa Florio*

The first two laps looked like an Alfa Romeo benefit: Varzi led from Campari and Nuvolari. But on the third lap Chiron, the laughing lad from the Riviera, began to take life very seriously. He took Nuvolari and Campari and came past the pits thirty-one seconds behind Varzi. And since Chiron had already refuelled, and Varzi hadn't, Chiron was effectively in the lead. Varzi stopped on lap four, and Chiron gained a thirty-second lead. To make Chiron's drive even more impressive, his riding mechanic was ill and semi-conscious, rolling against him dangerously on left-hand corners.

But on the fifth and last lap Chiron crashed and broke two of the alloy wheels on his Bugatti. With feverish haste he and his groggy mechanic—it was the poor mechanic's first race—changed the wheels and set off again, leaving jacks and tools lying by the roadside. Varzi also had his problems: his Alfa Romeo's fuel tank was leaking, and he set off on the last lap with his mechanic leaning out over the back of the car pouring petrol into the tank. When the inevitable fire started the mechanic abandoned the petrol can and began beating at the flames with his seat cushion, while Varzi crouched forward and continued to drive as fast as possible.

Eventually the flames went out, and Varzi won by just under two minutes, after almost seven hours on the road, averaging 48.4 mph (78 km/hr). Conelli (Bugatti) was third; Campari, his Alfa Romeo jumping out of gear, was fourth; and Nuvolari, his Alfa Romeo delayed by a broken spring mounting, was fifth. Albert Divo had retired his Bugatti after breaking a wheel, but then taken over the Bugatti of William Grover-Williams (the French-resident Englishman who had won the first Monaco Grand Prix in 1927), who was suffering from exhaustion in his first Madonie race, and finished seventh. The adventures of Varzi and Chiron pale beside those of Luigi Arcangeli: he rolled his Maserati three times and con-

30. Achille Varzi (Alfa Romeo) winning the 1930 *Targa Florio*

tinued. This feat was almost equalled—two rolls instead of three—by Pedro Rodriguez in the 1960 *Targa*.

Arcangeli had two big wins that year to make up for his problems in the *Targa*. He won the *Tre Province*, after switching from Maserati to Alfa Romeo, beating Mario Tadini in another Alfa Romeo; and he won the *Circuito Automobilistico del Sud*.

This race, organised by the Benevento auto club, was one of several attempts to create a race that could stand comparison with the *Mille Miglia* and the *Targa Florio*. The start and finish were at Benevento, the ancient town about thirty miles north-east of Naples. The circuit, 558.6 miles (901 km) long, headed across the Apennines to the plains of Puglia and the Adriatic, went as far south as Bari and Taranto, and re-crossed the Apennines to Salerno before heading back into the hills to Benevento (see Map 6).

It took Luigi Arcangeli and his Alfa Romeo 10 hrs 14 min. 11 sec. to cover those 901 km, at an average of 54.8 mph (88.4 km/hr), to beat Archimede Rosa (OM) and Guido d'Ippolito (Alfa Romeo).

Arcangeli, again on Alfa Romeo, won another southern race that year, the Cosenza club's *Coppa Michele Bianchi*, with d'Ippolito second, and Rosa third. D'Ippolito had had a southern win earlier in the year, over four laps of a 28.5-mile (46-km) circuit starting and finishing at Taurianova, north of Reggio Calabria (see Map 6).

The Rome club, not to be outdone by the provincials, also organised a road race in 1930, over a single 167.4-mile (270-km) circuit based on Frascati, just south of Rome, and going as far south as Terracina, on the Gulf of Gaeta. The circuit was mainly fast, and Luigi Fagioli (Maserati) won at 62 mph (100 km/hr), from Luigi Castelbarco (OM) and Count Giovanni 'Johnny' Lurani (Alfa Romeo).

ITALY: THE 1930s

1931

The *Mille Miglia* course was altered this year for the first time. Leaving Brescia the cars now headed more westerly, to Cremona, then followed the Po River to join the old route at Casalmaggiore. The critical mountain sections, Bologna to Rome, Rome to the Adriatic, were unchanged.

Rudolf Caracciola was back with a big Mercedes-Benz, with Wilhelm Sebastian, a works mechanic, as crew, but the Italians still did not see him as a likely winner.

The powerful Mercedes-Benz led across the plains to Bologna, followed by Giuseppe Morandi/Archimede Rosa, who were proving that the side-valve O Ms still had some life left. The Alfa Romeos were next, Nuvolari and Borzacchini dead-heating into Bologna, with Campari next. Luigi Arcangeli, the terror of the plains the years before, had thrown two tyre treads before reaching Bologna. Over the Futa he was to burst another tyre. (Arcangeli did not have long to live: he was killed in practice at Monza six weeks later.)

In Florence the Italians began to worry: Caracciola was still in front, leading Nuvolari, Morandi, Campari, Borzacchini, and Arcangeli. Tyre wear was becoming a problem for the Alfa Romeo team. In Rome, where Caracciola had slipped to second behind Nuvolari after stopping to fix a loose exhaust pipe, all the Alfa Romeos changed to Dunlop tyres, as used by Mercedes-Benz.

Soon after Rome Nuvolari retired, but Caracciola could not stop the Alfa Romeo onslaught. By Perugia he was fourth, behind Borzacchini, Campari, and Arcangeli. In Ancona he was still fourth, but Campari now led, from Arcangeli and a slowing Borzacchini.

Once back on the plains Caracciola could use the power of the Mercedes-Benz. By Bologna he was third, and soon he led, and he held his lead to Brescia, despite a puncture twenty minutes before the finish. Borzacchini retired, Arcangeli thumped a wall in Verona. Second at the finish was Campari; third, the Morandi/Rosa O M. Sadly, 1931 was the last fling for O M. Morandi/Rosa won the *Giro di Sicilia* again a few weeks later, but the next year only four O Ms started in the *Mille Miglia*, and none finished. In 1933 only one started, and it finished thirty-eighth.

An innovation in the 1931 *Mille Miglia* was a class for closed cars. Alfa Romeo, not leaving anything to chance, built three special racing coupes with fabric-

31. The Nuvolari/Guidotti 2.3-litre Alfa Romeo before retiring from the 1932 *Mille Miglia*

32. Rudolf Caracciola (Mercedes-Benz SSK) crosses the Raticosa
Pass on his way to winning the 1931 *Mille Miglia*, the first non-
Italian to do so

covered bodies. They finished first, second, and third in class, Franco Cortese/
Renato Balestrero first in eighth place overall.

In 1929 Varzi on works Alfa Romeos had been much more successful than his
team-mate Nuvolari, but after his win in the 1930 *Targa Florio* he was fired by Alfa
Romeo. They said he was becoming too demanding, always wanting the best car.
But why not? He was their best driver, and to prove it he won three major races
for Maserati late in 1930. In the 1931 *Mille Miglia* he drove a Bugatti, retiring
early, and for the *Targa Florio* he again drove a Bugatti.

Alfa Romeo took the 1931 *Targa* very seriously. They had five drivers—Nuvolari,
Campari, Borzacchini, Arcangeli, and d'Ippolito—eleven cars, and twenty-five
mechanics. They had a radio link between the main pits and their service points in
the mountains: their drivers would not have to do a complete lap to find out
their position on the lap before.

A storm before race day had washed away sections of road, forcing the
organisers to revert to the pre-war long Madonie circuit. The Alfa Romeo team
arrived fifteen days before the race to allow their drivers plenty of practice.

The race was over four laps, 370.2 miles (595.3 km), and for the first three the
leader was the lone Bugatti of Achille Varzi. Everything went smoothly for Alfa

33. Tazio Nuvolari (1750 Alfa Romeo) winning the 1931 *Tre Province* race

Romeo—five cars started, five cars finished—but not even Nuvolari could make any impression on Varzi.

But on the third lap it had begun to rain. Within minutes the ninety miles of road were mud. It was then that Alfa Romeo found they had a trump card: their cars had mudguards; the Bugatti did not.

Even with mudguards it was an unpleasant race. Arcangeli stopped with an eye full of mud: it later became infected. Goffredo Zehender took over the car and slithered around to finish sixth—outside the official time limit. René Dreyfus (Maserati) just gave up. Varzi, blinded and freezing, struggled on as the Alfa Romeos caught him. At the finish it was: Nuvolari at 40.2 mph (64.8 km/hr), Borzzachini, Varzi, Campari, and d'Ippolito.

Nuvolari also won the third and last *Tre Province* that year, beating Enzo Ferrari (Alfa Romeo).

The 900-km *Circuito del Sud* of 1930 was not repeated in 1931, but the Bari club, which had seen that race pass through their town, decided to organise a similar event. The course selected was shorter, 421.6 miles (680 km), lacked the long mountain sections of the race of the year before, and did not attract such a good entry. The start and finish were at Foggio. The most interesting part of the course

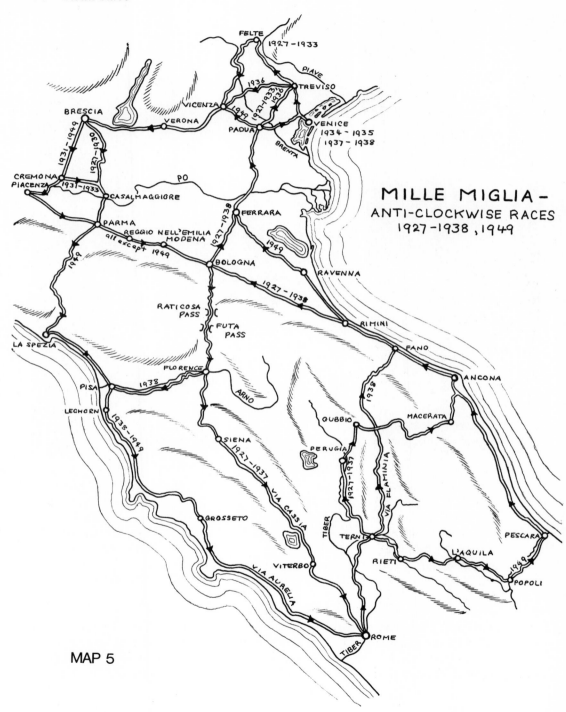

MAP 5

34. Caracciola and Bonini in their 2.3-litre Alfa Romeo before the start of the 1932 *Mille Miglia*. They retired after leading in Rome

was the circuit of the white limestone mass of the Gargano Peninsula (see Map 6). This race, the first and only *Targa Puglia*, was won by Guglielmo Carraroli/ Francesco Severi (1750 Alfa Romeo) at 63 mph (101.6 km/hr), from Guido d'Ippo-lito in a similar car.

1932

The Depression had now hit motor racing hard. Mercedes-Benz were forced out of racing, and it would be two years before cash grants from the Nazi government would bring them back. Caracciola joined Alfa Romeo, despite the efforts of Campari to keep him out. The 40-year-old veteran disliked younger drivers who

35. Nuvolari's car is a 2.3-litre Alfa Romeo

might come between him and any prize money. Caracciola got a rough deal: he slowed to let Nuvolari win the Monaco Grand Prix; and Nuvolari showed his gratitude by disobeying team orders and beating Caracciola in the French Grand Prix. Labour relations were seldom good in the big works teams.

In the *Mille Miglia* Caracciola, Nuvolari, Campari, and Borzacchini were all given identical 2.3-litre, 150 bhp cars. And it was Caracciola who led in Rome by six minutes from Eugenio Siena/Piero Taruffi (Scuderia Ferrari Alfa Romeo), who were followed by Campari, and Borzacchini (who had thrown two tyre treads before Bologna). Nuvolari and Varzi (3-litre Bugatti) had already retired.

Siena, the man running with Taruffi, was a cousin of Campari's and a former riding mechanic for Enzo Ferrari. He rose to be head of the Alfa Romeo tuning shop before he was killed in the 1938 Tripoli Grand Prix. Siena and Taruffi shared the driving of their Alfa Romeo, each doing the section they knew best, a common practice in the early years of the race, but one that became less common as the race became of shorter and shorter duration with rising speeds. It was a valuable practice for a young driver, such as Taruffi, who wanted experience both of driving

36. Umberto Borzacchini (2.3-litre Alfa Romeo) before winning the
1932 *Mille Miglia*. The riding mechanic is Amedo Bignami,
who later worked for Achille Varzi and Juan Manuel Fangio

and of watching a veteran drive. The experiences of Siena and Taruffi are typical of
the period, and are worth looking at in more detail.

Siena lived in Modena, and he was more familiar with northern Italy than
Taruffi, a Roman, so he drove first. They reached Bologna in fourth place behind
Nuvolari, Varzi, and Caracciola after one incident—a spin in the streets of
Modena from which Siena quickly recovered.

At Bologna Taruffi took over for the climb over the Apennines. Near Florence
Varzi retired. Pietro Ghersi crashed his Alfa Romeo in the streets of the city itself,
and Nuvolari, looking over his shoulder at the wreck, also crashed. This put
Caracciola in the lead from Siena/Taruffi, the positions that were maintained to
Rome.

Now Taruffi was on home ground, and, despite a spin soon after Rome, he and
Siena were in the lead by Perugia. But in the run back over the Apennines to the
Adriatic, where Caracciola retired with gearbox trouble, an electrical fault had to
be repaired. When they reached Bologna again they found themselves third.
Campari, too, was now out: he had handed over to his co-driver, Sozzi, who had

crashed the car. Taruffi had now driven all the mountain sections, so Siena took over for the fast run back to Brescia.

But the full-throttle miles began to tell on the engine: the oil-pressure gauge began to flicker. At Padua they stopped, hoping it was the gauge at fault, not the engine. But it was the engine, and they retired.

There remained the problem of getting to Brescia. They accepted a lift with two enthusiasts, who, presumably hoping for an invitation to join the Scuderia Ferrari, drove like madmen and finally collected a roadside post, doing damage to the local trolley-bus service. Siena and Taruffi were uninjured, and hitched another lift home.

The winner, at 68 mph (109.9 km/hr), was Umberto Borzacchini, from a Scuderia Ferrari Alfa Romeo driven by the aristocratic team of Marquess Antonio Brivio/Count Felice Trossi. For the remarkable Trossi, president of Scuderia Ferrari, it was the very first motor race in which he had ever competed. He was soon to become a very good driver. After the Second World War he won two Grands Prix before dying of cancer in 1949. Third and fourth were two 1750 Alfa Romeos driven by Luigi Scarfiotti/Guido d'Ippolito and Nando Minoia/Renato Balestrero.

After the 1931 race on the long Madonie circuit the *Targa Florio* did not revert to the medium circuit, but, for the first time, was held on the short circuit: 44.74 miles (72 km). In 1932 there was also a change in the weather: the storm of the year before gave way to tropical heat.

It was not a good race. Alfa Romeo were again out in force; and Nuvolari led from start to finish to win at 49.2 mph (79.3 km/hr) from his team-mate Borzacchini. The potentially strong Bugatti team had little luck: Varzi retired his car with gearbox trouble and took over from Chiron, who was suffering from heat exhaustion, to finish third.

With that the *Targa Florio* began to go into a decline that was to last for twenty years. Nuvolari, now established as a great driver, was never to compete in it again. Campari and Borzacchini would soon be dead, killed, like Arcangeli, Materassi, and Sivocci, at the grim autodrome of Monza. Minoia and Conelli had retired. It would be 1951 before anyone would beat Nuvolari's 1932 lap record of 52 min. 56.6 sec., 50.6 mph (81.6 km/hr). And it would not be until 1955 that a classic international battle would again take place on the Madonie circuit. The stars of that race would be mainly men who were still very young children in 1932: Stirling Moss, Peter Collins, Eugenio Castellotti.

Now, for the third year in succession, an attempt was made, unsuccessfully, to create another major road race in Italy. This time it was the turn of the L'Aquila auto club, in the Abruzzi north-east of Rome. Their event, the *Coppa Gran Sasso*, had first been run as a rally in 1931, but was now a straight race. The course, of 154.7 miles (248.5 km), was to be covered twice (see Map 4).

The entry was poor, and probably would have contained no leading drivers at all had not Piero Taruffi wrecked an Alfa Romeo in the *Coppa Acerbo* at Pescara

37. The coming of the *Gran Turismo* coupé: the Nando Minoia/
Renato Balestrero 1750 Alfa Romeo crossing the Futa Pass on
its way to fourth in the 1932 *Mille Miglia*

a month before. Enzo Ferrari entered him for the *Coppa Gran Sasso* to help him
regain his confidence. He won easily, at 55.7 mph (89.8 km/hr), beating Carlo
Gazzabini (Alfa Romeo).

Part of the *Gran Sasso* course, the fast coastal run followed by the section up to
L'Aquila, was to be included in the *Mille Miglia* course from 1948 on.

1933

In the 1933 *Mille Miglia* we meet another driver who was to become a star: Luigi
Villoresi. Sharing a Fiat with his elder brother Emilio, who was to be killed racing
in 1939, he finished a lowly thirty-third. In 1951 he was to win the race outright.

Taruffi, Nuvolari, Varzi, Caracciola, Trossi, Fagioli, and Cortese were other drivers whose careers were to span the Second World War, and who were to disprove the thoughtless old saying that motor racing is a young man's sport. Perhaps it is, but only if we adopt a very liberal definition of a 'young man'. Certainly there seems to be no reason for a driver under forty-five to show weakening powers.

The year 1933 was not a vintage one. Caracciola could not race: a seemingly trivial accident at Monaco had smashed his thigh badly enough for him to have to fight to avoid having the leg amputated. He would not return to the *Mille Miglia* until 1952; he was never to race in the *Targa*. On 10 September Campari and Borzacchini were killed at Monza.

In the *Mille Miglia* Alfa Romeo took the first ten places. Borzacchini set the pace from the start and led in Rome, but his engine failed when crossing the Apennines. Nuvolari inherited the lead and won by almost half an hour from Franco Cortese/Carlo Castelbarco. Taruffi was third.

The pattern in the *Targa Florio* was similar: Borzacchini set the fastest lap but did not finish. Antonio Brivio won from Renato Balestrero, Guglielmo Carraroli (winner of the 1931 *Targa Puglia*), and Carlo Gazzabini (second in the 1932 *Coppa Gran Sasso*). All, of course, were on Alfa Romeo. Bugatti and Maserati made little impression in road racing that year.

Brivio also won the Parma–Poggio di Berceto, revived for the first time since 1924, beating Campari (Maserati) and Pietro Ghersi (Bugatti). The course had been shortened very slightly, to 31.7 miles (51 km).

Road racing also returned to Sardinia, for the first time since the Cagliari race won by Ernesto Ceirano in 1922. This time a 24.9-mile (40.2-km) circuit north of Sassari was covered five times. The Alfa Romeos of Pietro Ghersi and Luigi Castelbarco were first and second. Ghersi's speed was 72.4 mph (116.7 km/hr).

In Calabria the Cosenza club's *Coppa Michele Bianchi* was revived—it had last been held in 1930—and was won by Guido d'Ippolito (2.6-litre Alfa Romeo) from Renato Balestrero (2.3-litre Alfa Romeo). The circuit had been shortened slightly, to 78.1 miles (126 km), but it retained its character.

Farther north, on 8 October, the Naples club organised a road race on the grand scale. Theirs, at 487.9 miles (787 km), was longer than the Bari club's 1931 race, but shorter than the Benevento club's 1930 event. Like the Benevento race, and like the *Mille Miglia*, it crossed the Apennines twice (see Map 6).

As usual it was an Alfa Romeo benefit. The 2.6-litre model of Giafranco Comotti/Nando Barbieri won in under nine hours at 55.7 mph (89.9 km/hr), beating the similar car of Felice Bonetto, a sub-Nuvolari wildman with motorcycling experience, and the 2.3-litre Alfa Romeo of Nino Farina, the nephew of the car stylist, who became World Drivers' Champion in 1950. Farina was crewed by Domenico Jovanella.

This race, the *Circuito Province Meridionali*, was, sadly, never held again, and, even more sadly, it caused the death of Guido d'Ippolito, who crashed near Potenza after clipping the edge of a cart. This was a typical hazard of open-road

38. *Targa Florio*, 1933. Winner Antonio Brivio with his riding mechanic, Giulio Ramponi (looking at him), and Vincenzo Florio (in hat)

racing. After the Second World War trucks became an even greater hazard. But it was not until 1956 that the *Mille Miglia* was held on roads that were officially closed, although the police, and, before the war, the Fascist militia, had controlled traffic to some extent.

1934

This was a vintage year in Grand Prix racing: Mercedes-Benz were back; Dr Porsche's extraordinary Auto Union made its first appearance; Alfa Romeo were still competitive. But the German firms showed no interest in racing sports cars. Bugatti and Maserati were fading. Lancia still showed no interest in building competition cars—they would not do so until the 'fifties—although in 1934 the remarkable Ermenegildo Strazza won the Brescia club's Edolo–Pontedilegno hillclimb for the fourth time in his old Lancia Lambda, beating Johnny Lurani (Maserati) and Emilio Romano (Bugatti).

In the *Mille Miglia* that year more than half the fifty-seven starters—the smallest field the race was ever to have—were Alfa Romeo, and most of the rest were small Fiats. But at least a new hero appeared: hillclimb specialist Mario Tadini, sharing an Alfa Romeo with the experienced Nando Barbieri, was first to Rome, driving brilliantly in pouring rain—beating Nuvolari/Siena by five minutes. Achille Varzi, on a Scuderia Ferrari Alfa Romeo, was third, still trying for his first win.

Out of Rome Tadini's gearbox began to fail: first one gear went; then another. Pietro Ghersi and the Swiss Hans Ruesch (who later wrote the novel *The Racers*, filmed with Kirk Douglas), running close together, both crashed on the same corner. Varzi moved ahead of Nuvolari, leading him by two minutes at Perugia. But the weather was beginning to improve, and Nuvolari with it: by Ancona he was only thirty seconds behind.

Varzi's lucky break came at Imola, on the approach to Bologna. Enzo Ferrari was at the refuelling depot, and he had the latest weather reports from the north; they forecast heavy rain. He persuaded Varzi to fit micro-tread tyres—the fine tread of modern tyres was then an innovation—and with them Varzi won, beating Nuvolari by almost nine minutes, at 67.3 mph (108.6 km/hr).

In third place was Louis Chiron, sharing an Alfa Romeo with Archimede Rosa for his *Mille Miglia* début. Other débutants were Nino Farina and Felice Bonetto. Neither distinguished himself—Bonetto was twelfth; Farina retired—but one man who did distinguish himself was Piero Taruffi. Driving a little 1.1-litre Maserati he finished fifth overall, one and a half hours ahead of the next car in that class. The wet conditions, of course, minimised the power advantage of the faster cars, but it was still a remarkable drive.

Class wins were always important in the *Mille Miglia*, just as they once were in the Le Mans Twenty-four Hours. Many of the *Mille Miglia* classes varied from year to year; confusing everyone except the officials who take such delight in dreaming up ever more complex formulae and regulations. But some classes survived relatively unscathed: 1.1-litre sports cars competed in all but one *Mille*

39. Swiss driver Hans Ruesch (2.3-litre Alfa Romeo Monza) in the 1934 *Mille Miglia*. Ruesch later wrote the novel *The Racers*, which was filmed with Kirk Douglas

Miglia, in 1954. At first Fiats dominated, but the more sophisticated Maserati won in 1931 and 1932. Giuseppe Tufanelli/Guerrino Bertocchi driving. In 1933 they retired, letting George Eyston/Johnny Lurani win for M G. Eyston, after years as a small-car specialist, gained his greatest fame with his giant aero-engined *Thunderbolt*, with which he held the land speed record.

Achille Varzi also won the *Targa Florio*; he was the only star present. Second was Nando Barbieri; third, Costantino Magistri; and fourth, Renato Balestrero—all on Alfa Romeo.

Few hillclimbs were held that year, apart from the Parma–Poggio di Berceto, which Nando Barbieri won from Pietro Ghersi—Alfa Romeo again dominating.

But it was not in the style of Mussolini's Italy to let a recession inhibit it. Instead, the Auto Club d'Italia organised a race that was virtually three *Mille Miglia* laid end to end: the *Giro d'Italia*. It was a race, of 3,535 miles (5,687 km), circling the whole of Italy. The route was clockwise, completed in three stages, starting and finishing in Rome. Stage One was from Rome to Sicily, where a circuit of the island was completed before the first night's rest at Messina. Stage Two took the cars all the way up to Milan. Stage Three, the most complex, took the cars as far east as Trieste, back to Milan, and then south to the finish at Rome.

It was a bold experiment, and, had it been held at a time of prosperity, expansion, and international goodwill, might have been a success. But it was a predictable failure. The hoped-for international field did not enter. A hotel in Rome with English-speaking staff that had been reserved for British entries lay empty. The race was limited to production sports cars, giving the amateur a good chance, but this did no apparent good.

The winner, after 65 hrs 57 min. 6 sec., was a Lancia Astura driven by Carlo Pintacuda/Mario Nadilli, averaging 53.5 mph (86.23 km/hr). Second, remarkably close, in 66 hrs 1 min. 46 sec., was the 2.3-litre Alfa Romeo of Archimede Rosa/ Giafranco Comotti. Third was another Lancia Astura, driven by Nino Farina/ Oneto.

1935

By the mid-'thirties Carlo Pintacuda had been around the Italian racing scene a long time. He had first competed in the *Mille Miglia* in 1929. Earlier, in 1927, he had won a minor short-circuit road race in Pisa. It was the *Giro d'Italia* that made his name. For the 1935 *Mille Miglia* Ferrari gave him the 2.6-litre Alfa Romeo he needed to have a chance of winning—and win he did.

It was not a good race. Varzi, driving a Maserati, retired early. In Rome Pintacuda led from Mario Tadini, and at the finish at Brescia the order was the same—the gap between them was forty-two minutes, the biggest in the nine-year history of the race. Pintacuda's speed, 70.8 mph (114.3 km/hr), although quicker than Varzi's in the wet the year before, was slower than Nuvolari's record speed in 1933.

A pleasant surprise in the increasingly insular world of Italian road racing was the return of Louis Chiron to the *Targa Florio*. Driving an Alfa Romeo he finished second behind Antonio Brivio, who was scoring his second win. Third was Nando Barbieri (1.5-litre Maserati), followed by the Alfa Romeos of Costantino Magistri and Renato Balestrero.

That was also the year that Nuvolari in an underpowered Grand Prix Alfa Romeo P3 beat the German teams at the Nürburgring, but for the Italians it was otherwise a barren year.

1936

The 1936 *Targa Florio* shrank to being a two-lap race—it had never before been

VIESTE

– CIRCUITO AUTOMOBILISTICO del SUD:
  START, BENEVENTO; FINISH, AVELLINO; 1930
– TARGA PUGLIA: START, FOGGIA; FINISH, BARI; 1931
– CIRCUITO PROVINCE MERIDIONALLI:
  START/FINISH, NAPLES; 1933

SAN SEVERO

CAMPOBASSO   *1933*   FOGGIA   1931 →   BARLETTA

1930   *1930 →*   *← 1933*   BARI

OFANTO

BENEVENTO   1933   *VIA ADRIATICA*   1931   BRINDISI

← 1933   AVELLINO   BRADANO   MATERA   1930   *1931*

NAPLES   POTENZA   *VIA APPIA*   *1930*   TARANTO   *← 1931*   LECCE

1933   SALERNO   1933   *← 1930*

GRATI

– COPPA della SILA / COPPA MICHELE BIANCHI:
  START/FINISH, COSENZA;
          1924–1930, 1933

BIVIO GARGA

COSENZA   *SILA*   *GIRO →*   CROTONE

GIRO   PARENTI

GIRO   CATANZARO

SOUTHERN ITALY
1924–1956

– GIRO della CALABRIA:
  START/FINISH, CATANZARO;
  1949–1956

MAP 6

REGGIO
di CALABRIA   *GIRO*

less than six laps over the short Madonie circuit—and it was restricted to touring cars. It was a Lancia benefit, with the Turin cars taking the first four places, Magistri being the winning driver. There were only eleven starters and nine finishers; the smallest field since 1910, although there had only been twelve starters in 1934. By the opulent standards of today these are small fields, but it is worth remembering that standards were then very different. Only on six occasions before the Second World War did a Madonie *Targa Florio* attract more than 20 starters: 45 in 1907; 34 in 1921; 42 in 1922; 37 in 1924; 26 in 1926; and 27 in 1928. The biggest field in the 1930s was the 19 who started in 1935.

In most respects 1936 was a bleak year—war in Abyssinia, war in Spain, League of Nations sanctions against Italy—and Italy suffered. But, by a happy coincidence, 1936 saw the closest finish in the whole history of the *Mille Miglia*.

This was the year that saw the début of Clemente Biondetti, born in Sardinia in 1898, a former racing motorcyclist who had turned to cars in 1923. He had little money, and it was not until the late-'twenties that he began to be noticed. In the 1930 Tripoli Grand Prix—the race in which Gastone Brilli-Peri was killed—he was third in a Talbot, and later the same year he beat Nuvolari to win the *Coppa della Consuma* hillclimb—he was now a local boy, living in Florence.

Biondetti's first placing in a classic event came in 1931: third in the French Grand Prix, sharing a works-supported Maserati in this ten-hour race with Nicola Parenti. But this was an isolated success, not to be repeated for many years. So this quiet, plump Florence-resident Sardinian was no more than a competent Grand Prix driver when he entered his first *Mille Miglia* at the age of thirty-eight.

The roads were wet at the start, and Biondetti took the lead on the altered first section of the course (see Map 5). He held his lead over the Apennines and was first to Florence, in front of Pintacuda. After Florence Pintacuda dropped back, and in Rome the order was: first, Biondetti, 5 hrs 23 min. 7 sec.; second, Farina, 5 hrs 24 min. 23 sec.; and third, Brivio, 5 hrs 25 min. 50 sec. Only 2 min. 43 sec. covered the first three cars.

But Biondetti's luck did not hold. He began to drop back, leaving Farina and Brivio to fight for the lead. Brivio began to pull away, until beyond Rovigo, when electrical problems began to slow his Alfa Romeo. Farina closed, but Brivio just made it, winning by thirty-two seconds after more than thirteen hours of racing. Pintacuda was third, over half an hour behind, and Biondetti was fourth, another quarter-hour behind.

1937

The *Mille Miglia* was run in wet, miserable conditions, and was won easily by Carlo Pintacuda in the inevitable Alfa Romeo. Biondetti had nothing but trouble, and arrived in Rome two hours behind Pintacuda.

What was interesting about the race was the performance of the French Delahaye cars: the first indication since Caracciola's 1931 victory that a foreign car might have a chance of winning.

40. *Mille Miglia*, 1937. Franco Cortese/Angelo Guatto (2.3-litre
Alfa Romeo) in the rain

41. The veteran Alfa Romeo works driver/mechanic Giovanni Battista Guidotti (left) with Ercole Boratto, racing driver, and chauffeur to Benito Mussolini. Photo taken 1937. The car is a 2.3-litre Alfa Romeo

A Delahaye driven by René Dreyfus/Pietro Ghersi was second in Florence, second in Rome, and was still second in Perugia. Behind them another Delahaye driven by René Carrière and Laury Schell—father of the future Grand Prix driver Harry Schell—was leading Farina in an Alfa Romeo. At Macerata, approaching the Adriatic, Schell took Dreyfus, and Dreyfus went off the road shortly after. Before the end Farina took Schell, and finished second for the second year in succession. Schell/Carrière were third, and fourth was Ercole Boratto, Mussolini's personal chauffeur, in an Alfa Romeo.

Later that year, in December, Boratto won a road race in North Africa, a 638.6-mile (1,030-km) event from Benghazi to Tripoli in Italian-occupied Libya. He drove a 2.3-litre Alfa Romeo, and completed the course in less than eight hours, at a brisk 82.9 mph (133.8 km/hr). Second, over an hour behind, was the similar car of Rudi Haller/Alfonso Vella. There were twenty-two starters and seventeen finishers: they must have looked very lost on the long roads around the shores of the Gulf of Sidra.

There was no racing on the Madonie circuit in 1937; nor would there be any until 1951. From 1937 to 1940, races for the *Targa Florio* were held in the Favorita Park in Palermo. Vincenzo Florio himself had now left the Sicilian automobile club, and without his drive and enthusiasm there was little incentive to face the problems of racing on the Madonie circuit—especially with the general decline in Italian motor racing.

There was some revival that year on the hillclimb front. The Parma–Poggio di Berceto popped up again for the first time since 1934, and was won by Mario Tadini from Eugenio Siena. Tadini also won the Susa–Moncenisio, not held since 1933, from Piero Dusio and Clemente Biondetti. Everybody, everywhere, on Alfa Romeo.

1938

Major changes were made to the *Mille Miglia* route: Siena and the Chianti were abandoned for Pisa and the Mediterranean; after Rome, Perugia was bypassed, the cars following the Via Flaminia all the way to the Adriatic; Venice was visited, as it had been in 1934, 1935, and 1937 (see Map 5).

In the twelfth *Mille Miglia* Carlo Pintacuda and Clemente Biondetti had identical Alfa Romeos, and the cars stayed healthy throughout—it was a straight

42. Franco Cortese (2.3-litre Alfa Romeo) on the coast road between Leghorn and Grosseto during the 1938 *Mille Miglia*. He finished ninth

race. It was Pintacuda who led initially, and he had four minutes on Biondetti at Rome. There was a dead-heat for third between Piero Dusio (Alfa Romeo) and René Dreyfus (Delahaye).

After Rome Biondetti took the lead, and by Bologna he was a full eight minutes in front. Pintacuda was not finished: by Treviso the deficit was down to three minutes. By Varese they were almost level. But, finally, it was Biondetti who had the edge: he won by two minutes to score the first of his four straight victories in the *Mille Miglia*. Pintacuda was second; Dusio, third; Dreyfus, fourth; and René Carrière (Talbot), fifth.

The Parma–Poggio di Berceto fell to Emilio Villoresi, with Biondetti second, both on Alfa Romeos.

1939

In 1939 there was not even a *Mille Miglia*. For years it had been a favourite of the Italian government: the Fascist militia had policed it; and unfavourable publicity had been suppressed when possible. But the increasing death toll, culminating in several spectators being killed in the 1938 race, led to its banning.

Instead, another road race was held in Libya. The course was fifty per cent longer than in 1937, and ran from Tobruk, through Benghazi, to Tripoli—a total of 930 miles (1,500 km): not quite the magic *Mille Miglia*. The field was not up to standard, either, with only thirty starters.

There was a team of B M Ws entered from Germany—they had raced in the 1938 *Mille Miglia*, winning the 2-litre class—but Alfa Romeo again dominated. Ercole Boratto, the 1937 Benghazi–Tripoli winner, won again, but was only twenty seconds ahead of Clemente Biondetti after over ten and a half hours on the road—an average of 87.86 mph (141.42 km/hr). Third was Pintacuda in another 2.5-litre Alfa Romeo; fourth was Willi Briem on B M W.

Boratto's co-driver was a young Alfa Romeo mechanic named Consalvo Sanesi, who, after the war, would become a very fast driver in his own right.

1940

War; and a planned Berlin–Rome race never took place. But Italy did not enter the war until 10 June 1940, and before that date a last road race was held, subtitled the *13th Mille Miglia*, but more properly known as the *Coppa Brescia*. The circuit was a throwback to the one used in the early years of the century—a triangle: Brescia–Cremona–Piadena–Mantua–Brescia. The distance was 102.3 miles (165 km), to be lapped nine times—921.3 miles (1,486 km). Minus any mountains, it was a poor excuse for a *Mille Miglia*, but it did attract eighty-eight entries, including cars and drivers from Germany and cars from France.

Germany was represented by a large team from B M W; France had two Delages driven by Italians Taruffi and Comotti. There were also two Fiat-based specials built in the workshops of Enzo Ferrari. They were powered by two Fiat 4-cylinder engines mounted in line astern to form a straight-eight. One was driven

43. *Coppa Brescia*, 1940. The third-place BMW of Brudes/Roese.
Adolf Brudes von Breslau, a former motorcyclist, raced for
Borgward after the Second World War, competing in the
Carrera Panamericana as late as 1954, when he was aged
fifty-five.

by Lotario Rangoni, the other by a young racing motorcyclist named Alberto
Ascari, the son of the late Antonio Ascari.

But the Ferrari specials and Delages retired. B M W won: Huschke von Hanstein,
later famous as the Porsche team manager, shared the winning car with Walter
Baumer. They averaged 103.46 mph (166.7 km/hr). Second was Nino Farina
(Alfa Romeo); third, Adolf Brudes/Ralph Roese (B M W); and, fourth, Clemente
Biondetti (Alfa Romeo).

And that, until 1947, was that.

ITALY: 1947–57

1947

The first post-war motor race was held in the Bois de Boulogne in Paris on 9 September 1945. Grand Prix racing proper started in 1946. The first *Mille Miglia* was run—after two postponements—on 27 June 1947.

The rebirth was not easy: the government had to be persuaded to allocate 20,000 gallons of petrol for the race; Pirelli were given the job of supplying tyres for the 163 starters, the vast majority of which were small Fiat and Lancia touring cars, many of them pre-war. Of the new cars the most notable was the 2-litre Maserati of Luigi Villoresi—white-haired after a long spell as a prisoner of war—and the 2-litre V12 Ferrari, the first true Ferrari, of Franco Cortese. And there were the cheap little Fiat-based Cisitalias, built in the factory of Piero Dusio to the design of two engineers: Giacosa, who later became technical director of Fiat; and Savonuzzi, who became director of engineering research for Chrysler. At first thirty single-seaters were built for one-make racing; for the *Mille Miglia* there were both stark two-seaters with cycle fenders, and sleek coupés. The coupés, incidentally, sold for about three times the price of an MG TC. Nuvolari was among those who chose a cycle-fender car. He did no practice, first sitting in the car half an hour before the start.

Clemente Biondetti, the winner of the last *Mille Miglia*, in 1938, wanted to race a Talbot, but his plans fell through, and he accepted a drive with Emilio Romano in an Alfa Romeo coupé that had been exhibited in the 1938 Paris Motor Show. Superchargers were banned from the race, so Romano had replaced the blowers on the 2.9-litre engine with four Solex carburettors. No works Alfa Romeos were entered: the factory was too busy with Grand Prix racing.

The circuit was radically changed: it was clockwise for the first time; it visited Bologna only once; it left Rome by the Via Aurelia, not the Via Cassia; for the first time it went to Alessandria and Turin; and from Turin to Milan and Brescia by the Autostrada, which was closed to all normal traffic—a wise decision which, in a way, marked the beginning of the end for Italian road racing (see Map 7). They were starting to get soft.

The faster cars were soon in trouble: Cortese retired the Ferrari at Fano with leaking head gaskets; the Villoresi/Bertocchi Maserati went out with bearing failure. Taruffi and Dusio, both on Cisitalia—Taruffi was Dusio's test driver—both

44. *Mille Miglia*, 1957

MILLE MIGLIA –
CLOCKWISE RACES
1947-1948, 1950-1957

MAP 7

retired, Dusio with damp ignition: the shape of things to come. By Rome it was raining heavily, and the leader was Nuvolari, by seven minutes from Biondetti, whose big Alfa Romeo was having fuel feed problems. Behind Biondetti the little 1.1-litre cars were solid.

In Florence Nuvolari still led, but he was ill and exhausted. His co-driver, Giuseppe Carena, had to take the wheel for the crossing of the Futa and Raticosa Passes. They had little hope: on the straight roads of the north the little Cisitalia was much slower than the big Alfa Romeo.

But Biondetti had lost top and third gears, and it was not until Asti that he took the lead, snug in his coupé while the ageing Nuvolari battled on soaked to the skin. The final blow came on the Autostrada after Turin: a cloudburst turned it into a skating rink. The veteran Balestrero, who had survived the world's toughest races for over twenty years, was so blinded by rain that he stopped under a bridge for the worst to pass. Nuvolari stopped with flooded ignition, and it took fifteen desperate minutes to get the system sparking again.

Fifteen minutes lost—and Biondetti won by just sixteen minutes. The winning speed was 69.9 mph (112.2 km/hr).

The race is remembered mainly for Nuvolari's drive—Carena's active role as co-driver and mechanic is too often ignored—but Biondetti's drive was equally brilliant: he was minus two gears; he stopped five times to adjust the fuel feed; and he drove a car that was much more difficult to handle in the wet than the Cisitalia. Biondetti was forty-nine years of age; Nuvolari was fifty-four.

Less than a month later, on 20 July, the Venice automobile club organised the first *Coppa d'Oro delle Dolomiti*, the Dolomite Gold Cup, a mountain race over a single 188.3-mile (303.8-km) circuit starting and finishing at Cortina d'Ampezza (see Map 1), a circuit that later became a regular part of the Alpine Rally course.

The winner of the first Dolomite Cup, at 47.4 mph (76.5 km/hr), was Salvatore Ammendola (2.5-litre Alfa Romeo), who beat Piero Dusio (Cisitalia).

Dusio was also second in the revived Aosta–Gran San Bernardo hillclimb, being beaten over the 21.1 miles (34 km) by Giovanni Bracco (Maserati).

1948

The last *Giro di Sicilia* had been held in 1931, when it had attracted only thirty-three starters, and had been won, for the third successive time, by Archimede Rosa. On 4 April 1948 it was revived, now running clockwise around the island. There were eighty-six starters. Clemente Biondetti (2-litre Ferrari) won at 55.2 mph (88.9 km/hr), beating Piero Taruffi (Cisitalia) by over a quarter of an hour.

The entry for the *Mille Miglia* was much improved over 1947. Ferrari entered four of his little V12s for Nuvolari, Biondetti, Cortese, and Ferdinando Righetti, a Florentine amateur. Maserati entered Alberto Ascari—still a long way from being the masterly world champion of 1952 and 1953—Ovidio Capelli, and Salvatore Ammendola. These post-war cars were challenged by old 3-litre Alfa Romeos, one driven by Consalvo Sanesi, aged thirty-seven, Alfa Romeo's chief tester. Mixed

45. Clemente Biondetti (1949), the master of the *Mille Miglia*,
after his fourth successive victory

in among the big cars was a special superstreamlined 1.3-litre Cisitalia coupé for Taruffi.

Ascari led initially, from the Ferraris of Nuvolari and Cortese, and Taruffi. Ascari's Maserati was soon slowed by engine trouble, and it was Cortese who led along the Adriatic, from Nuvolari, Ascari, and the big Alfa Romeo of Sanesi. But by the time the Apennines had been crossed it was Nuvolari who led, over twelve minutes ahead of Sanesi. Next was Cortese, whose Ferrari had lost third gear from its five-speed box, and the two Maseratis of Ascari and Capelli. Biondetti was behind them, sixth.

Then the leaders started to crash: Sanesi ended up in the sea at Santa Marinella, north of Rome, seriously injured; Ammendola crashed his works Maserati, killing Bai, his co-driver; Nuvolari hit a wall near Leghorn, damaging the rear suspension of the Ferrari. He staggered on: at Florence he led; at Bologna—where team-mate Cortese retired—he still led, but soon the Ferrari subsided by the road-side.

Of the new Ferrari and Maserati cars which started the race, only one was nursed to the finish: the Ferrari of Clemente Biondetti. He won, finishing one and a half hours ahead of the second car, the 1.1-litre Fiat of Alberto Comirato/Lia Comirato. Biondetti's speed was 75.2 mph (121.2 km/hr).

Of the 186 starters in that race four were brothers: Giannino, Paolo, Umberto, and Vittorio Marzotto; from a wealthy family of textile manufacturers. They had two Lancia Aprilia touring cars: Giannino sharing with Umberto; Vittorio with Paolo. Giannino, a cool, calculating driver, was to win the *Mille Miglia* outright in 1950 and 1953. The more exuberant Paolo was less brilliant, but won the *Giro di Calabria* in 1952 and the *Coppa Dolomiti* in 1954. Vittorio was a reliable driver who won the *Giro di Sicilia* in 1951 and was second in the 1954 *Mille Miglia*. Umberto was the only black sheep: he chopped his Ferrari in half in the 1950 *Mille Miglia* and wisely retired from racing.

A new event was held in 1948, the *Giro dell'Umbria*, with start and finish at Perugia (see Map 4). The winner, at 86.75 mph (110.9 km/hr) over two 116.25-mile (187.5-km) laps, was Inico Bernabei (1.1-litre Cisitalia). The second Dolomite Cup attracted a much better entry: Giovanni Bracco won at 51.2 mph (82.6 km/hr) from Luigi Villoresi, both on Maserati.

1949

The *Giro di Sicilia* of 1949 again opened the road racing season, and again Biondetti (Ferrari) won. It rained, and speeds were low. Motorcycle racer Dorino Serafini (Frazer Nash) led early on, but retired after hitting a kerb at Ragusa. Roberto Vallone (Ferrari) then led to Catania, where rear-axle trouble put him out. This left Franco Rol, a wealthy private owner, in a special short-chassis 2.5-litre Alfa Romeo coupé, duelling with Biondetti, but Rol got stuck at a level crossing for five minutes and could only manage second.

In the *Mille Miglia* Ferrari were the favourite again, and it was four of their

46. *Mille Miglia*, 1950. Winner Giannino Marzotto (right) with
Dorino Serafini, who finished second

cars that snarled into the lead: Felice Bonetto leading Taruffi, Cortese, and
Biondetti. The only possible challenge came from Franco Rol in his Alfa Romeo.
At Rome Bonetto still led, with Taruffi still second. The ever-unlucky Cortese had
retired, leaving Biondetti third and Rol fourth. The route this year was very
different: it was anti-clockwise; both Bologna and Florence were avoided for the
Parma–Poggio di Berceto route over the Apennines; and after Rome the route met
the Adriatic farther south than usual, at Pescara (see Map 5).

Bonetto was not known as an intelligent driver: on the southern crossing of the
Apennines he was forced to stop for twelve long minutes to try to adjust some
stopping power back into his brakes.

Taruffi now led from Biondetti, and on the fast straights of the Adriatic coast
there seemed to be no stopping the silver-haired Roman. At Roseto he was timed
at 130 mph (210 km/hr) through a timing trap—and that, perhaps, was his
problem. At Ravenna he retired with engine trouble, leaving Biondetti to win by
over half an hour from Bonetto, averaging 81.5 mph (131.5 km/hr). Franco Rol

did well to finish third after hitting a house. The touring car class was won by a 105 mph (170 km/hr) 2.4-litre Healey, at that time the fastest series production car in the world—an early sign of the post-war revival in British motor sport.

The second *Giro dell'Umbria* fell to Roberto Vallone (2-litre Ferrari), from the Argentine Adolfo Schwelm (2.6-litre Alfa Romeo). Vallone also won the Dolomite Cup, this time beating Franco Cornacchia (Ferrari) and Franco Rol (Alfa Romeo).

Later in the year two new road races appeared. The first *Coppa della Toscano*, over a single 374.5-mile (604-km) circuit (see Map 4), was won by Ugo Bormioli, averaging 69.3 mph (111.8 km/hr) in a little Fiat-based Ermini. The first *Giro di Calabria* also was won by a 1.1-litre, Dorino Serafini's Osca, at 50.6 mph (81.6 km/hr). The veteran Luigi Fagioli, also on Osca, was second. The circuit (see Map 6), starting and finishing at Catanzaro, was of 448.3 miles (723 km)—making it the third longest circuit, after those of the *Mille Miglia* and *Giro di Sicilia*, then in use in Italy.

1950

In the 1948 London Motor Show the Jaguar XK120 had been first shown to the world; in 1950 it began to have an impact on international racing.

Clemente Biondetti himself drove one in the *Giro di Sicilia*, and initially ran second behind Alberto Ascari (2.4-litre Ferrari). The Ferrari went out with engine trouble, leaving Biondetti heading towards his third successive win. But then the Jaguar, too, failed, leaving Franco Rol (Alfa Romeo) in the lead from Franco Cortese (Frazer Nash). But—a final but—both the Alfa Romeo and the Frazer Nash retired with split fuel tanks. The Bornigia Brothers, motor dealers from Rome, Giancarlo and Mario (2.5-litre Alfa Romeo), won from Inico Bernabei (2-litre Ferrari), at 53.9 mph (86.9 km/hr).

Sadly, the 1950 *Giro* was the last race for Tazio Nuvolari, at the age of fifty-seven: he crashed his 1.1-litre Abarth Fiat harmlessly early on.

Five Jaguars were entered for the *Mille Miglia*. Biondetti paid particular attention to lightening his car, although he added some weight in the form of a radio to listen to race reports: one of the major problems for a *Mille Miglia* competitor, particularly a private entrant as Biondetti now was, was knowing where your rivals were.

Biondetti was looking for his fifth straight win, but his rivals were better equipped than ever. Ascari and Villoresi, both lured away from Maserati, drove big 3.3-litre Ferraris. Bonetto, the pace-setter of the year before, had a special works Alfa Romeo: a 4.5-litre V12 which had started life as a Grand Prix car in 1937. New cars, coupés, were entered for Consalvo Sanesi (3-litre) and Franco Rol and Juan Manuel Fangio (both 2.5 litre).

Fangio, the middle-aged Argentinian with the diffident manner and the squeaky voice, had arrived in Europe in 1949 and immediately started to win races. Now he was a member of the Alfa Romeo Grand Prix team. He was not the first non-European to make an impact on Grand Prix racing—David Bruce-Brown and

Jimmy Murphy from the USA and Guy Moll from Algeria had done so in the past—but Fangio was the first outsider to conquer Europe, and lay the foundations of the cosmopolitan sport that motor racing is today.

The *Mille Miglia* route was again clockwise, as it would remain until the end; and Bologna and Florence had been reinstated (see Map 7).

The race began with carnage. Aldo Bassi, who had led the 1947 race briefly, crashed on wet roads a few miles from the start. He was killed, but his co-driver survived—a rare occurrence: it was usually the man in the suicide seat who died. Others crashed. Robin Richards, the British rally driver who became better known later on as a BBC race commentator, racing his Healey Silverstone while still under treatment for two broken legs, crashed—and broke one again. Sanesi went off at the same spot. Another British Healey driver, Philip Wood, crashed, and his co-driver, Peter Monkhouse, was thrown out and killed against a hoarding on which was written, in English, the words 'Good Luck'.

By Ravenna the leader was Giannino Marzotto (2.4-litre Ferrari), from Villoresi (3.3-litre Ferrari), Dorino Serafini (2.4-litre Ferrari), and Bonetto in the big 4.5-litre Alfa Romeo, a far from ideal car in the wet. Biondetti in the Jaguar was seventh.

On the fast run along the Adriatic the roads were dry: Villoresi used his power to take the lead; although team-mate Ascari was finding the power too much—tyre treads began to fly off. The works Ferraris both stopped in the Apennines with broken transmissions. Franco Rol also went out in the mountains: his Alfa Romeo suffered brake fade, and he went harmlessly over a twenty-feet bank. Englishman Leslie Johnson, making his *Mille Miglia* début in a Jaguar XK 120, lost his windscreen wipers, and spent the next 600-odd miles propped up to look over the screen.

In Rome Giannino Marzotto led by only twenty-one seconds from Dorino Serafini. About ten minutes behind was the remarkable Fangio, who had driven only one practice lap before the race, and was finding the narrow Italian roads, littered with non-competing cars and trucks and foolhardy spectators, a trial after the better-organised conditions of Argentine road racing. Beside him was Alfa Romeo test driver Augusto Zanardi, shouting instructions into his ear from a notebook description of the course.

There is a persistent myth, at least in the English-speaking world, that the use of pace-notes such as these was invented by Stirling Moss and Denis Jenkinson, and first used by them in the 1955 *Mille Miglia*. Another version says that Louis Klemantaski, another bearded British co-driver, was the true pioneer. What Moss and Jenkinson probably did invent was the practice of writing pace-notes on a long roll of paper and winding it through a specially-constructed viewing box. A water-tight box, with the instructions viewed through perspex, is obviously essential in an open car, but today in rallying in closed cars pace-notes are almost always just written in a notebook, a simpler and more flexible method.

The first four to Rome—Giannino Marzotto, Serafini, Fangio, and Giovanni

Bracco/Umberto Maglioli (2-litre Ferrari)—stayed that way to the end. Biondetti lost all chance of another crafty win when his Jaguar suffered a broken spring. The forty minutes needed to repair it saw him finish in eighth place. A most remarkable drive was put up by Leslie Johnson: still peering over his windscreen into blinding rain, driving on a road he hardly knew, he finished fifth—ahead of Cortese, Fagioli, Biondetti, Vittorio Marzotto, and many other Italian veterans. Johnson, an amateur in both the best and worst senses of the word, was the owner of the E R A racing car firm during its last few dismal years. He is in danger of being remembered, when he is remembered at all, for his bad points—his health was so bad he raced with a little case of life-restoring drugs in the car beside him; he failed to recognise the ability of Stirling Moss—but he was a genius at handling a car. His performances that are in the record books, like that fifth in the *Mille Miglia*, were only the tip of an iceberg of enormous talent that never came anywhere near being fully realised.

That little fifty-kilometre road race, the Parma–Poggio di Berceto, was revived on 14 May for the first time since the war, and was won by Giovanni Bracco (2-litre Ferrari), who beat Sergio Sighinolfi (Fiat) and Biondetti (Jaguar). The *Coppa della Toscana*, on a circuit lengthened to 421.6 miles (680 km), fell to Dorino Serafini (2-litre Ferrari) at 79.2 mph (127.7 km/hr), who beat Franco Cornacchia (2-litre Ferrari) and Piero Scotti (1.1-litre Ermini). The *Giro dell'Umbria*, in its third year, attracted a poor entry, and was won by Mario Giogetti (1.1-litre Stanguellini). But the Dolomite Cup saw a good field: Giannino Marzotto (2.3-litre Ferrari) won at 52.7 mph (85 km/hr), only fourteen seconds in front of Giovanni Bracco, who this time drove a 2-litre Maserati. Third was Cornacchia (2.3-litre Ferrari, not content with the 3.3-litre cars that had smashed their transmissions hillclimb in the north, but Serafini (2.3-litre Ferrari) was there to win for the second successive year, at 53 mph (85.5 km/hr). The consistent Franco Cornacchia, also on a 2.3-litre Ferrari, was second.

1951

By now, with Alfa Romeo fading and Lancia yet to make a full-scale assault on motor racing, Italian sports car racing was becoming more and more a Ferrari benefit. In the *Giro di Sicilia* Ferrari were first and second, Vittorio Marzotto leading home Piero Taruffi by just over a minute, at 62.3 mph (100.5 km/hr)—the first time 100 km/hr had been exceeded in the *Giro*.

The *Mille Miglia* course was altered again: the most radical change was the abandonment of the Mediterranean coast roads. The route now went over the hills through Viterbo and Siena.

Ferrari, not content with the 3.3-litre cars that had smashed their transmissions the year before, now had 4.1-litre engines. These brutish cars were driven by Villoresi, Ascari, Serafini, and Vittorio Marzotto. Villoresi, commenting on the delicacy needed to handle these cars, said: 'I hope it doesn't rain—for us it's raining all the time.'

It did rain, and sixteen miles from the start Ascari skidded into a parked car and bounced into the crowd, seriously injuring two spectators. About fifteen minutes later the Jaguars of Leslie Johnson and Stirling Moss, making his *Mille Miglia* début, went off at the same spot. Moss was the only one to restart, but his transmission failed soon afterwards.

Another early retirement was the once invincible Clemente Biondetti. He was driving a Jaguar special: an X K 120 engine, transmission, and suspension hung on a lightweight Italian-built frame—a concept that anticipated the very successful Lister-Jaguar by six years. But the frame proved too light: on a level crossing it flexed and the fan chopped through the radiator hose.

At Ravenna two Ferrari coupés led: Giannino Marzotto's 2.6-litre from Villoresi's 4.1-litre. Serafini was third on another 2.6-litre, but he soon crashed, breaking an arm and a leg. Marzotto went out with a broken axle, so it was Villoresi who led in Rome, ten minutes ahead of the Lancia Aurelia coupé of Bracco and Maglioli. This order, as happened in similar conditions the year before, was maintained to the finish, although Villoresi doubled his winning margin, averaging 75.5 mph (121.8 km/hr).

Third in Rome had been the Bornigia brothers, but on the Futa Pass they lived every driver's nightmare and went over the edge. They were very lucky to land, injured but alive, sixty feet below the road and on their Alfa Romeo coupé's wheels.

Third at the finish was Piero Scotti (3-litre Ferrari), the burly Tuscan; fourth was Paolo Marzotto (2-litre Ferrari).

What was this Lancia Aurelia which could take second place ahead of two Ferraris? Simply an 80-bhp touring car, which had never been designed for racing.

It is probably an exaggeration to claim, as the Lancia company do, that with the Aurelia they invented the Grand Touring car of today. Fast tourers existed well before it: Lancia's own Lambda took fourth in the 1927 *Mille Miglia* and third in the 1928 race. The Lambda was an open car, as tourers were by definition in the 'twenties, but high-speed closed cars did exist. Back in 1916 Barney Oldfield, the pioneer American 'Speed King', had Harry Miller build him a sleek racing coupé, the *Golden Submarine*. Body panels were of arc-welded aluminium over a light steel frame; a form of construction that Italian coachbuilders made their own twenty years and more later. Oldfield's car even had a built-in roll-over bar for crash protection.

Closed-car racing started in Europe in 1922, with the French Touring Car Grand Prix, and in 1931 a closed-car class was introduced into the *Mille Miglia*. But the special Alfa Romeos that dominated this class were not civilised touring cars, but racers with roofs on—much like racing coupés that became popular after the war. In fact, of the five post-war *Mille Miglia* we have looked at, only one, in 1949, had been won by an open car.

The Lancia Aurelia was no racer-with-a-roof-on-top, but an ordinary modern touring car with a pressed-steel body/chassis unit. There were no mysteries about it: its designers, Gianni Lancia, son of Vincenzo, and the great Vittorio Jano, late of Alfa Romeo, had just come up with a near-perfect car. Bracco and Maglioli could not, of course, have challenged the 250-bhp Ferrari with their 80 bhp had it not been for the wet and slippery roads of the 1951 *Mille Miglia*. The primitive tyres of the period were also not helpful to powerful cars. Today, with tyres capable of transmitting a thrust greater than the force of gravity—once thought impossible —giant-killing acts are far less likely.

There was no *Giro dell'Umbria* in 1951, but a new race was held in Sardinia, the *Trofeo Sardo*—the Sardinian Trophy—over the 260.4 miles (420 km) from Cagliari to Sassari and back. That this resulted in racing cars going in opposite directions on the same stretch of road did not seem to bother anyone. That first year it was very much a local event, won by Franco di Suni/Francesco Madau (Lancia Aurelia) at 74.8 mph (120.6 km/hr), but in later years it attracted good drivers from the mainland.

In the mountainous Dolomite Cup the good-handling Lancia Aurelias finished first and second, Enrico Anselmi beating 'Ippocampo'. Third was the 1.1-litre Osca of Giulio Cabianca. Cabianca was also third in the *Giro della Calabria*, behind Paolo Marzotto (2.7-litre Ferrari) and Sergio Mantovani (Lancia Aurelia).

Farther south still, on 9 September, another race took place—the first *Targa Florio* on the Madonie circuit since 1936. The race was over eight laps, 358.2 miles (576 km): the longest since 1932, when Nuvolari had won and set a lap record which still stood in 1951.

The early leader was Giovanni Bracco (4.1-litre Ferrari), but at the end of the second lap he retired, handing the lead to Antonio Stagnoli (2.6-litre Ferrari). Bracco took over Franco Cornacchia's 2.6-litre Ferrari and began to climb back through the field. It was a bad day for Ferrari: everywhere their cars suffered from suspension or clutch problems. By the end of the third lap it was the Frazer Nash of Franco Cortese that led, and it stayed there to the finish, winning at 47.5 mph (76.6 km/hr). Bracco broke Nuvolari's lap record on lap six, averaging 51.1 mph (82.4 km/hr), and the Bracco/Cornacchia car finished second, but over four minutes behind Cortese. Third was the 2-litre Maserati of Inico Bernabei/ O. Pacini; fourth, the 1.1-litre Abarth of Emilio Romano, owner and co-driver of Biondetti's Alfa Romeo in the 1947 *Mille Miglia*.

1952

The *Giro di Sicilia* of 1952 saw another Marzotto win, this time by Paolo in a 2-litre Ferrari, who beat, on a wet road, the Lancia Aurelias of Felice Bonetto, Gino Valenzano (co-driven by Emilio Giletti, a driver in his own right), and Salvatore Ammendola.

In the *Mille Miglia* it was the year of the German invasion: Mercedes-Benz, rising from the ashes of 1945, entered three sleek 300 SL coupés with light multi-tubular frames and 215-bhp, 6-cylinder engines. The most striking feature of the

47. Vicenza, during the 1952 *Mille Miglia*. Stirling Moss (Jaguar
C-Type), competing for the second time, about to overtake the
Bartecchi/Case Alfa Romeo

cars was the upward-opening gull-wing door, which was not, however, a Mercedes-
Benz invention. It had been used in the late 'forties on a Volkswagen special built
by an aircraft engineer, Herbert Gomolzig.

The Mercedes-Benz drivers, too, appeared to have risen from the ashes. There
was Rudolf Caracciola, winner of the *Mille Miglia* twenty-one years before;
Hermann Lang, who had been the fastest Grand Prix driver in the world in 1939;
and Karl Kling, who was a rally driver before the war, but whose racing career had
not started until after the war, when he was thirty-seven years old.

Ferrari were weakened that year: Ascari was away at Indianapolis; Villoresi
was recovering from a road accident. Their most formidable combination seemed
to be Piero Taruffi in a car powered by a 4.5-litre Grand Prix engine. Certainly,
with over 350 bhp, it was the most powerful car on the road, and Taruffi had vast

experience of the *Mille Miglia*; although Mercedes-Benz were doing their best to offset the Italians' advantage by giving all their drivers at least ten practice laps.

At Ravenna the leader was Bracco (2.7-litre Ferrari), five and a half minutes ahead of Kling, who was driving on pace-notes from co-driver Hans Klenk. Then came Vittorio Marzotto (Ferrari), the Aurelias of Enrico Anselmi and Luigi Fagioli, and the Ferraris of Biondetti, Taruffi, and young Eugenio Castellotti. Kling was fighting the Italians single-handed: Lang had crashed near Ferrara; Caracciola could not stay with the leaders.

Bracco's rapid driving proved hard on tyres: frequent changes began to drop him down the field. By L'Aquila, the Abruzzi crossed, Kling was in front, thirteen and a half minutes ahead of Castellotti, with Taruffi in the powerhouse third. But Castellotti's fine drive, in his second *Mille Miglia,* ended when he crashed near Rieti. In Rome Kling still led, the first foreigner ever to lead in Rome in his first *Mille Miglia.* Taruffi was second, twelve minutes behind.

By Siena Taruffi had cut Kling's lead to 2 min. 22 sec., but the Ferrari's transmission then broke near Poggibonsi. A few miles on, near Florence, Biondetti, too, was out when his Ferrari caught fire.

In the Apennines mist shrouded the road and its unprotected drops. Bracco, coming from behind, excelled in these conditions: by Bologna he was 1 min. 20 sec. in front of Kling. Bologna was also the retirement point for Stirling Moss (Jaguar): he might have finished third had he lasted.

By Brescia Bracco had extended his lead to four and a half minutes, to win at 79.7 mph (128.6 km/hr). Third was the durable Luigi Fagioli (Lancia Aurelia), followed by Caracciola (Mercedes-Benz) and Enrico Anselmi (Lancia Aurelia).

So Bracco was the winner, the hero, leaving Kling a bitter loser. Bitter, because he had lost by only four and a half minutes, and he could remember a pit stop when a wheel had bound to the hub. Time lost: 6 min. 38 sec.

The most persistent story about the 1952 *Mille Miglia* is that Giovanni Bracco spent the whole race chain smoking and drinking brandy. He was driving a closed car, so there was nothing very eccentric about smoking, and even the brandy is not too strange. Louis Chiron used to carry a flask of champagne when he raced. Nuvolari, on occasions, carried whisky. None was a drunkard. Drinking and driving is not a sensible practice; but then driving a sports car for more than twelve hours, virtually non-stop, is not sensible either.

The *Targa Florio* was brought forward to mid-season, 29 June, but before then the two well-established road races in the middle of Italy were held: the *Coppa della Toscana* was won by Bruno Sterzi (2.6-litre Ferrari); and the *Giro dell'Umbria* by Giulio Cabianca (1.1-litre Osca).

In the *Targa Florio* Franco Cortese was back again with his Frazer Nash, and again had to contend with Giovanni Bracco in a 4.1-litre Ferrari. Bracco led initially, and again his car failed him. This time it was Giulio Cabianca (1.3-litre Osca) who took the lead, followed by Cortese, and a string of Lancia Aurelias. On lap five Felice Bonetto in the leading Aurelia had taken Cortese, but Cabianca still

48. Giovanni Bracco after winning the 1952 *Mille Miglia*. On the
right is Renzo Castagneto, clerk of the course and one of the
founders of the *Mille Miglia*

looked safe—until lap seven, when his rear axle broke. A lap later, the final round,
Cortese lost a wheel—a great relief to Bonetto, who ran out of fuel 200 yards from
the finish line and had to grind home on his starter motor, but still averaged a new
race record of 49.6 mph (80 km/hr) to win.

Lancia took the first three places, Bonetto, Luigi Valenzano, Enrico Anselmi,
followed by Aldo Terigi (1.1-litre Ermini). Fifth was one of the new 2-litre Fiat 8V
coupés driven by Ovidio Cappelli; sixth, a 2-litre Ferrari driven by British driver
T. A. S. O. Mathieson, better known today as a motor sport historian.

The *Coppa Dolomiti* was a Marzotto benefit: Paolo (2.7-litre Ferrari) won from Giannino (4.1-litre Ferrari), with Cabianca (1.1-litre Osca) third. The *Giro della Calabria* was another win for Paolo Marzotto: he beat Sergio Mantovani (Aurelia) —and Cabianca was again third, this time using a 1.3-litre engine.

In September the Sardinian Trophy was held for the second time, and was won by Emilio Giletti (2-litre 8V Ferrari) from Diego Capelli (Fiat 8V). The sleek 8V, one of the very few limited-production sports cars ever made by Fiat, was beginning to challenge the Aurelia for the title of Italy's best Grand Touring car.

1953

This was the year that Lancia, for the first time in their history, built a competition car. Piero Taruffi drove an early 2.5-litre version in the *Giro di Sicilia*, and proved its worth by duelling with Luigi Villoresi (4.1-litre Ferrari) until half distance, when the Lancia failed. Villoresi went on to win, at 60.9 mph (98.25 km/hr), from Gino Valenzano (Aurelia)—improving on his third of the year before—and Pietro Carini (1.9-litre Alfa Romeo).

Mercedes-Benz did not contest the *Mille Miglia*: they had withdrawn from all racing to prepare for their assault on Grand Prix racing in 1954. Their road racing star, Karl Kling, moved to Alfa Romeo, who entered two of their new 3.6-litre, 270 bhp *Disco Volante* (Flying Saucer) coupés for Kling, Juan Manuel Fangio, and Consalvo Sanesi. Lancia entered sports racers, now with full 3-litre engines, for Taruffi, Biondetti, Bonetto, and young Umberto Maglioli, who had learnt his craft as Giovanni Bracco's co-driver. Ferrari had their 4.1-litre V 12s.

The weather was fine. Sanesi in the Alfa Romeo set a blistering pace, averaging 113 mph (182 km/hr) to Verona, leading Taruffi's Lancia and Farina's Ferrari. The Lancia soon blew its engine. The other Alfa Romeo drivers began to move up. By Ravenna the order was Sanesi, Farina, Kling, Franco Bordino (in a French Gordini), Fangio, and the Ferraris of Giannino Marzotto and Giovanni Bracco. Bordino was soon out with engine failure, moving Fangio up to fourth. Into the mountains after Pescara the first two went out: Sanesi with engine failure; Farina when he hit a wall.

For the second year in succession Karl Kling, aided by Hans Klenk, led in Rome. But soon he crashed. Bracco, too, was out, with a broken differential. By Florence the leader was Juan Manuel Fangio in his Alfa Romeo, from the Marzotto brothers, Giannino and Paolo, in their Ferraris. But shortly after Florence Fangio noticed the steering of the Alfa Romeo was strange, particularly on right-hand bends—he had lost all steering on his left-front wheel.

The crossing of the Apennines was slow and frustrating in the crippled Alfa Romeo, and Giannino Marzotto had no trouble taking the lead. Beyond Bologna, on the final stretch across the plains, Fangio opened up to average more than 100 mph to Brescia. He finished second, twelve minutes behind Marzotto, who averaged 88.25 mph (142.35 km/hr) over the whole course. He was the first winner to complete the course in less than twelve hours: 10 hrs 37 min. 19 sec.

49. Juan Manuel Fangio's Alfa Romeo *Disco Volante* (Flying Saucer) comes to the start-line for the 1953 *Mille Miglia*, in which he finished second

Brother Paolo had his car catch fire and burn out only fifty miles from the finish — third was finally taken by Felice Bonetto (Lancia). Fourth was the American amateur Tom Cole (Ferrari), making a very impressive *Mille Miglia* début. He was to be killed a month later at Le Mans. Fifth was the English veteran Reg Parnell, a bluff and kindly Derbyshire man. A competent rather than a brilliant driver, Parnell showed his brilliance later when he was a team-manager. He introduced John Surtees, Jim Clark, and Chris Amon into Formula One.

For the *Targa Florio* Lancia entered four racing coupés for Bracco, Taruffi, Bonetto, and Maglioli. They scored a walk-over win against largely second-grade opposition from Ferrari and Maserati. Entering the last lap Taruffi led from Maglioli, but he got two pit signals: one, from his wife, saying 'O K', the other, from the Lancia pits, saying 'Faster'. He believed the pits, went faster, unnecessarily, and crashed. So Umberto Maglioli scored his first major international win, his first of three in the *Targa Florio*, averaging 50 mph (80.6 km/hr). Second was the 2-litre Maserati of Emilio Giletti; third, the similar car shared by Sergio Mantovani and Juan Manuel Fangio. The first Ferrari, Giulio Cabianca's 3-litre, was back in sixth.

Lancia's success did not end there. They filled the first three places in the *Coppa della Toscana*, Clemente Biondetti leading home Gino Valenzano and Roberto Piodi. In the *Giro della Calabria* it was the same, Pietro Palmieri winning from Piodi and Enrico Anselmi. In the *Coppa Dolomiti* Taruffi on Lancia was second, sandwiched between the 3-litre Ferraris of winner Paolo Marzotto and Umberto Maglioli. And Biondetti managed third in the *Trofeo Sardo*, which for the first time attracted works entries. Eugenio Castellotti (2.7-litre Ferrari) won from Gerino Gerini (2.7-litre Ferrari) and Biondetti.

One of Castellotti's main rivals as Italy's most promising young driver, Luigi Musso, won the *Giro dell'Umbria* on a 2-litre Maserati, beating the Lancia Aurelias of Roberto Piodi and Gino Valenzano.

The season ended in November with the first running of a unique little event: a 44.7-mile (72-km) race from Florence to Siena (see Map 4). The winner, Bruno Venezian (1.1-litre Osca).

In terms of the number of races Italian road racing was now at its peak—in 1953 there were eight long races in the *Targa Florio*/*Mille Miglia* tradition. The *Mille Miglia* itself attracted 502 starters; an increase of 200 over 1952, and a number that was only to be exceeded once, in 1955, when there were 521 starters. As always, they ranged from tiny Fiats to the world's fastest sports cars, all going faster and faster on increasingly crowded roads. To keep all drivers happy there was an enormous proliferation of classes. In 1952, when this proliferation reached its height, the keen spectator had to sort out the following classes: military vehicles; 750 cc touring cars (national); 750 cc production sports; 750 cc Grand Touring (international); 750 cc sports; 1.1-litre touring (national); 1.1-litre production sports; 1.5-litre touring (national); 1.5-litre production sports; over 1.5-litre touring (national); 1.5-litre Grand Touring (international); 1.1-litre sports; 2-litre Grand Touring (international); 2-litre sports; over 2-litre Grand Touring; over 2-litre sports. The *Mille Miglia*, despite being one of the most dangerous motor races in the world, was given all those national classes to cater for inexperienced amateur drivers—it was regarded as a suitable training ground. Even in the austere year of 1949 Italy had no less than 3,000 drivers with national competition licences, and 1,200 with international licences.

1954

The Lancia D24 racer now had the 3.3-litre engine that was to take it to its greatest successes. In the *Giro di Sicilia* Piero Taruffi, on Lancia, got into a duel with Umberto Maglioli (Ferrari)—it ended when Maglioli crashed and overturned,

50. Alberto Ascari storms up the Apennines from Florence on his way to winning the 1954 *Mille Miglia*. The car about to be overtaken is the Brandoli/Claes 750 cc Fiat, which had started 6 hours 21 minutes before Ascari's Lancia

injuring himself slightly. Taruffi won from Pietro Carini (1.9-litre Alfa Romeo), Gerino Gerini (3-litre Ferrari), and Luigi Musso (2-litre Maserati). Taruffi beat Carini by almost an hour—road racing can be very dull.

In the *Mille Miglia* it was the Lancias of Taruffi and Ascari, the current world champion, that led from the start. Ferrari's number one, Nino Farina, crashed early on, breaking an arm. By Ravenna the order was: Taruffi, Ascari, Castellotti (Lancia), Maglioli (Ferrari), Paolo Marzotto (Ferrari), and Giannino Marzotto (Ferrari). Giannino Marzotto's chance of a third win ended before Pescara, when his car failed.

In Rome Taruffi still led, chasing his elusive victory, by four and a half minutes from Ascari. Castellotti had retired in the Apennines, so Maglioli was third, followed by Paolo Marzotto, the young Englishman Peter Collins (Aston Martin), and the first of the 2-litre cars, Luigi Musso's Maserati. Clemente Biondetti was back at tenth in his 3-litre Ferrari.

51. Alberto Ascari after winning the 1954 *Mille Miglia*

52. Hans Herrmann

53. Pietro Carini (Alfa Romeo 1900 T I) on his way to a class win
in the 1954 *Giro di Sicilia*

North of Rome Taruffi's customary bad luck intervened. Overtaking a much
slower car he was forced off the road, breaking an oil pipe to a cooler in the nose of
his Lancia. After losing over an hour trying to get it repaired in a local workshop
he retired for good.

Ascari won, in a year of heavy retirements, averaging 86.6 mph (139.6 km/hr) to
beat the 2-litre cars of Vittorio Marzotto (Ferrari) and Luigi Musso (Maserati),
and the 3-litre Ferrari of Clemente Biondetti. Fifth was another 2-litre car, Bruno
Venezian's Maserati, and sixth was the first 1.5 litre, the Porsche of a young
German named Hans Herrmann, who, a year later, was to be in the Mercedes-Benz
Grand Prix team.

Another young German, a far-from-rich Count named Wolfgang von Trips,
finished thirty-third in another Porsche, the first 1.3-litre Grand Touring car to
finish. Herrmann had made his *Mille Miglia* début the year before, but for Trips
it was not only his first *Mille Miglia*, but also his first-ever motor race—he had done
two rallies—and the first time he had driven a car at more than 135 km/hr (about
85 mph).

54. A cheerful Umberto Maglioli after retiring his Ferrari from the 1954 *Mille Miglia*

In the *Targa Florio* it was the young drivers who set the pace: Castellotti (Lancia) leading from Musso (Maserati), with Taruffi (Lancia) third. At half-distance, lap four, Castellotti retired. On the last lap the inexperienced Musso, completely exhausted, had stopped for a drink, leaving Taruffi to win. The Roman veteran had known it was impossible to drive flat-out for more than four or five of the eight laps, and had paced himself accordingly.

Third, behind Musso, was Roberto Piodi (Lancia), Luigi Belluci (Maserati), and Clemente Biondetti (Ferrari). Biondetti had little success on the Madonie circuit, but no doubt if races had been held on it when he was at his peak in the late-'thirties and late-'forties he would have done much better. This fifth was his best placing.

Lancia were now concentrating their resources on preparing for Grand Prix racing, so they took little interest in the more minor road races, which gave Ferrari a chance to score some wins.

Gerino Gerini (3-litre Ferrari) won the *Trofeo Sardo* from the identical car of Vittorio Colocci. Piero Scotti (4.5-litre Ferrari) won his local *Coppa della Toscano* from Franco Bordino (Gordini) and Roberto Piodi in a Lancia Aurelia. Gerini had another win, in the *Giro dell'Umbria*, this time beating Luigi Musso (2-litre Maserati). In the mountainous *Coppa Dolomiti* a 2-litre Maserati won outright, driven by Sergio Mantovani. Giulio Cabianca (1.5-litre Osca) was second; Gerini (3-litre Ferrari) was third. The *Giro della Calabria* saw another giant-killing: Francesco Giardini (1.1-litre Osca) beat Biondetti (3-litre Ferrari) and Musso (2-litre Maserati). Finally, Lancia had one winner: Castellotti in the Siena–Florence from Giardini in his little Osca.

This second Siena–Florence race was to be the last held. Already a decline was starting in Italian road racing: there were to be no more circuits of Tuscany, nor of Umbria. Soon others, too, would go.

1955

But the *Giro di Sicila* was still very much alive, and it proved it by another duel between Taruffi and Maglioli—both were now on Ferrari; Taruffi's a 3.7 litre, Maglioli's a 3.3 litre. It was the younger driver, Maglioli, who led at first, but between Gela and Catania Taruffi got by, and eventually won by almost ten minutes. Musso (3-litre Maserati) was third.

Lancia's withdrawal from sports car racing was well compensated for by the return of Mercedes-Benz, who had re-entered Grand Prix racing in 1954 for the first time since the war, and were now back in sports car racing: not with the 300 S L, which had been refined into a production car, but with their W 196 R (sometimes known as the 300 S L R), a sports version of their straight-eight Grand Prix car. Their team for the *Mille Miglia* was Juan Manuel Fangio, Stirling Moss, Hans Herrmann, and Karl Kling.

55. Mercedes-Benz team, 1955 *Mille Miglia*

56. Juan Manuel Fangio (Mercedes-Benz W 196 R) at the start of the 1955 *Mille Miglia*. He finished second to Stirling Moss, slowed by a down-on-power engine

The Italians were not at their strongest. Ascari, Villoresi, and Farina did not race. The only Marzotto present was the hard-driving Paolo. Maserati started only one big car, a 3-litre for young Cesare Perdisa. But Ferrari had a good team: Taruffi, Maglioli, Marzotto, and works test driver Sergio Sighinolfi all drove 3.7-litre, 6-cylinder cars. Castellotti was entrusted with a similar car powered by a 4.4-litre Indianapolis engine.

The weather, for once, was good: the best it had been since 1936, the year that Clemente Biondetti made his début. Now, for the first time since then, Biondetti was not at the start at Brescia. He had died of throat cancer, aged fifty-six, in a Florence hospital on 24 February 1955.

Paolo Marzotto led from the start, but, just past Verona, barely fifty miles from the start, a tyre threw a tread and he braked gently to a standstill with damaged dampers. Castellotti inherited the lead, and by Ravenna he was in front of Moss,

57. Number One. The Anselmo/Peluso Iso buzzes down the ramp to
start the 1955 *Mille Miglia*. It averaged around 45 mph to
finish last, soundly beaten by 276 other competitors

Taruffi, Herrmann, Kling, Maglioli, Perdisa, and Fangio—who had a flat engine.
So the Ferrari and the Mercedes-Benz teams were evenly matched, with Perdisa
in the Maserati keeping up.

But there was something wrong with Ferrari's Pirelli tyres. Castellotti, like
Marzotto, threw a tread and retired. Moss took over the lead—Mercedes-Benz
were using German Continental tyres—and began a long duel with Taruffi. At
Pescara, where the mountain sections began, Taruffi led by fifteen seconds.

In the Apennines Moss, with navigator Denis Jenkinson reading the pace-notes,
moved ahead once more, and by Rome he led by almost two minutes. Third,
behind Taruffi, was Hans Herrmann, crewed by a Mercedes-Benz works mechanic,
followed by a dead-heat between the other two Mercedes-Benz, driven solo by
Fangio and Kling. Kling knew the circuit better than the other Mercedes-Benz
drivers, having completed around fifty laps of the 1,000-mile course. But his

experience failed him soon after Rome, when he crashed, breaking several ribs.

Taruffi was not finished yet: in the hills north of Rome, on the road on which he had competed in his first motoring event, in 1923, he retook Moss, and by Viterbo he led by more than a minute. Twenty miles farther on his transmission broke.

Mercedes-Benz now held the first three places: Moss, Herrmann, Fangio. Beyond Florence, on the Futa Pass, Herrmann had the bad luck to have a stone puncture his fuel tank; so it was Fangio, his engine still short of power despite efforts to adjust the fuel injection during pit stops, who came home second to Moss. Third, the first Ferrari, was Maglioli; fourth was the 2-litre Maserati of Francesco Giardini; fifth, the first Grand Touring car, was the Mercedes-Benz 300 SL of the American amateur John Fitch. Fitch, a remarkably good driver considering how seldom he raced, had fought off a strong challenge from the up-and-coming young Belgian Olivier Gendebien, also on Mercedes-Benz, who had led him by forty-four seconds in Rome.

Gendebien's break came two months later. Again driving a 300 SL, he won the *Coppa Dolomiti* outright, beating Castellotti (2-litre Ferrari) and Giulio Cabianca (1.5-litre Osca). This obscure win was in its way even more remarkable than Moss's *Mille Miglia* victory—the Belgian not only beat the Italians on their home ground, but he did it in a privately entered car against works entries, and in a car much less suitable than theirs for the conditions. He was given an immediate Ferrari contract, and repaid their confidence many times over. Among his numerous victories were three in the *Targa Florio*, three at Sebring, and four at Le Mans.

The *Trofeo Sardo* was run for the last time in 1955. Winner was Gaetano Starabba (2-litre Maserati) from Mario Bornigia (Ferrari). Third was a British entry, a Jaguar C-Type driven by Dan Margulies. His riding mechanic was a 26-year-old Londoner named Graham Norman Hill—seven years later he would be World Champion.

On the mainland the seventh *Giro della Calabria* was won by the Sicilian veteran Luigi Belluci (2-litre Maserati), beating Pietro Carini (2-litre Ferrari).

The *Targa Florio* that year was the first truly international race of the post-war series, and counted towards the World Championship of Makes. To meet international regulations the race had to be at least 1,000 kilometres long, so the number of laps was increased from eight to thirteen.

Mercedes-Benz arrived three weeks before race day to give their drivers plenty of practice. A fleet of touring cars was supplied for initial practice, with eight W 196 Rs, three of which were to be raced, attended by forty-five mechanics, available for full-speed practice. Stirling Moss, for example, did forty-eight practice laps, learning the circuit totally—he knew not only which way the road went, but all bumps and changes in road surface. Two drivers per car were now obligatory, so Mercedes-Benz teamed Moss with Peter Collins, Fangio with Kling, and John Fitch with Desmond Titterington, a very talented Irishman whose career faded away only a year later.

Ferrari, without Mercedes-Benz's resources, had only three cars in Sicily, two

58. Mercedes-Benz team, 1955 *Targa Florio:* John Fitch, Desmond Titterington, Peter Collins, Stirling Moss, Juan Manuel Fangio, Karl Kling

for racing. Their drivers were Eugenio Castellotti/Robert Manzon, and Umberto Maglioli/Sergio Sighinolfi.

As had happened before, the circuit was damaged by the weather, but by race day it had been repaired, and the weather was clear and hot. It was Moss who led from the start, pulling out over a minute on Castellotti on the first lap. By lap three the settled order was Moss, Castellotti, Titterington, the 3-litre Maserati of Villoresi/Musso, and the Ferrari of Gino Munaron and the American Carrol Shelby. Then the drama started: Moss went off, ending up 800 feet from the road in a field. The car was virtually undamaged, but eight minutes were lost as spectators manhandled it back to the road. Back at the pits Moss handed over to Collins.

Castellotti now led, but once he handed over to Robert Manzon it was obvious that Ferrari lacked strength-in-depth. The Frenchman was no quicker than the slowest of the Mercedes-Benz drivers, Fitch. By lap five the Fangio/Kling

Mercedes-Benz led the Ferrari, with Collins chasing them hard. Collins spun once, but quickly recovered. For the final spell Moss took over, and there was no stopping the English pair, who won, averaging 59.7 mph (96.3 km/hr). Second was Fangio/Kling; third, Castellotti/Manzon; fourth, Titterington/Fitch; and fifth the 2-litre Maserati of Francesco Giardini/Azzuro Manzini.

1956

Castellotti's brilliant form—and wretched luck—continued in the 1956 *Giro di Sicilia*. Driving a 3.5-litre Ferrari he led at Syracuse, just after half-distance, by six minutes from Taruffi (3-litre Maserati), who was five minutes in front of Peter Collins (3.5-litre Ferrari). But Castellotti's rear axle then broke, leaving Taruffi and Collins to duel to the finish. Collins finally won by less than a minute, averaging 67 mph (108 km/hr), the first Englishman to win the *Giro* since Cecil Snipe in 1912. Third was Villoresi (1.5-litre Osca), followed by Gendebien (2-litre Ferrari), and Maglioli (1.5-litre Osca).

The Mercedes-Benz works team had withdrawn from all motor racing. Stirling Moss had joined Maserati, and with Taruffi and Perdisa also in their *Mille Miglia* team they at last had a real chance of beating Ferrari.

Only fifteen miles from the start of the *Mille Miglia*, near Lake Garda, an Alfa Romeo touring car crashed into the crowd, killing one and injuring four. The day ended with seven dead—five drivers and crew; two spectators—and sixteen injured, making it the bloodiest *Mille Miglia* since 1938. One of the dead was 42-year-old John Heath, driving a Jaguar-engined car made by his own company, HWM.

Eugenio Castellotti was the early leader, forty-seven seconds ahead of Taruffi at Verona, followed by Luigi Musso (3.5-litre Ferrari—he had left Maserati at last), Perdisa, Moss (finding his car difficult to handle), and the Ferraris of Fangio and Collins. By Padua Castellotti had stretched his lead to over a minute, and Moss had moved up to third behind his team-mate Taruffi. After Padua the rain came.

By Ravenna Taruffi, driving brilliantly, had closed to within twenty seconds of Castellotti, while Moss, wrestling with his car, had slipped back down the field. Third now was Wolfgang von Trips, driving a Mercedes-Benz 300 S L. Behind him was another German, rally specialist Gunther Reiss, in another snug 300 S L coupé. Fifth, his lack of power no disadvantage on the wet road, was Giulio Cabianca in a 1.5-litre Osca, followed by Collins, Maglioli (1.5-litre Osca), and Musso.

Taruffi's challenge ended a few yards short of the Rubicon, when his waterlogged brakes caused him to crash. By Pesaro, where the long straights of the Adriatic began, Trips actually led Castellotti, with Reiss third. But the power of the Ferrari soon told, and by Pescara Castellotti had two minutes on Trips, who was followed

59. *Targa Florio*, 1955. Peter Collins in the winning Mercedes-Benz W 196 R he shared with Stirling Moss

by Reiss, Collins, Fangio, and Moss.

In the Abruzzi the struggle between Moss and his Maserati ended in victory for the car—only a solitary tree stopped them going over a cliff. Trips, with only a year of racing experience, also crashed, but Reiss still hung on. In Rome the order was Castellotti, Collins, Reiss, Fangio, Musso, Gendebien (Ferrari GT), and Prince Paul Metternich, driving another 300 SL.

The order stayed that way to the finish, except that Reiss slid down the field. In Florence he was sixth, behind his main Grand Touring rival, Gendebien. In Brescia he was tenth.

Castellotti scored a brilliant win in the most terrible conditions, a win that will be remembered long after his Grand Prix drives are forgotten. Peter Collins, second, came out with almost as much glory. With Collins, as with Moss, there was nothing in his background to suggest he would make a great road racer. The Italian drivers had grown up with road races and long Alpine hillclimbs, but Moss and Collins were both products of the 500 cc movement, driving tiny motorcycle-engined cars on circuits laid out on deserted military aerodromes—about as far from the Futa or the Abruzzi as it is possible to get. Moss admits today that he never liked the prospect of the *Mille Miglia*, although he enjoyed it once he got started. He never learned the circuit, which worried him. He was dependent on his navigator, Denis Jenkinson, a former sidecar racing passenger, and while he trusted him as far as he trusted any man, it was not the same thing as having a map of the course in his own mind.

Looking through the list of also-rans in the 1956 *Mille Miglia* we see a new generation of Italian drivers—Ludovico Scarfiotti, Carlo Facetti, and Corrado Manfredini among them—but they would have little chance in the years to come to develop their road racing skill.

Another name with a future was Giorgio Scarlatti, who that year won the *Trofeo Sardo* in a 2-litre Maserati, beating Luigi Olivari, in a similar car, and Camillo Luglio (Ferrari GT). And Giulio Cabianca was still as fast and consistent as ever, winning both the *Coppa Dolomiti* and the *Giro della Calabria* for Osca. In the north he beat Gendebien (3.5-litre Ferrari) and Maglioli (1.5-litre Osca); in the south he beat Villoresi (1.5-litre Osca) and Camillo Luglio (Ferrari GT).

Ferrari's defeat by Mercedes-Benz in the 1955 *Targa Florio* had been largely a defeat by money. Mercedes-Benz could afford more cars and more and better drivers. Ferrari's defeat in 1956 was more annoying.

Peter Collins and Eugenio Castellotti shared a 3.5-litre Ferrari, and built up a commanding lead before its transmission broke. This handed the lead to a German car, a little 1.5-litre Porsche RS driven by Umberto Maglioli—in the first year of his long association with Porsche—and Huschke von Hanstein, the German veteran who had started racing motorcycles in 1929 and cars in 1933. They won, at 56.4 mph (91 km/hr), beating Taruffi (3-litre Maserati), Gendebien (3.5-litre Ferrari), and Scarlatti (2-litre Maserati). For the Italians it was a traumatic experience.

60. The Aosta–Gran San Bernardo hillclimb during the 'fifties.
The car is a Fiat 8V with Zagato body

1957

In 1957 foreign wins continued. Olivier Gendebien (Ferrari GT) won the *Giro di Sicilia* from a very annoyed Piero Taruffi, who had slid his Maserati into a wall less than a hundred miles from the finish. Third was Giorgio Scarlatti (Maserati).

But in 1957 foreign wins proved to be the least of Italy's problems: Eugenio Castellotti, the best Italian driver, was killed at Modena autodrome on 14 March while testing a Formula One Ferrari.

The *Mille Miglia* entry was the strongest and most international ever. Stirling Moss had a 4.5-litre V8 Maserati. Hans Herrmann had a Maserati with 3.5-litre V12 engine—basically the same engine that powered the Cooper-Maserati Formula One cars ten years later. The third Maserati driver, Frenchman Jean Behra, broke a wrist in a practice crash.

Another who crashed in practice, hitting a bridge parapet without hurting himself, was the Spanish amateur Alfonso 'Fon' de Portago, the 17th Marquis de Portago and Count of Mejorada. Apart from being a driver, de Portago was three times French amateur champion jockey, an Olympic-class swimmer and bobsleigher, a polo player, a marksman, and the sort of man who, unshaven and wearing a greasy leather jacket, was surrounded by beautiful women. He drove a 3.8-litre Ferrari, as did Wolfgang von Trips. More powerful, 4.1-litre cars were driven by Taruffi and Collins.

The most unusual entry was the first American sports-racing car ever entered

61. *Mille Miglia*, 1957. British journalist Gregor Grant (Lotus 11)
about to mount the starting ramp

in the *Mille Miglia*, Ak Miller's *Caballo II*. Miller, a Californian, was a pioneer of hot-rodding from the 'thirties, and one of the founders of the Hot Rod Association of America. In 1954 he had finished fifth in the *Carrera Panamericana de Mexico* driving a crude sports rod built in his own workshop.

Caballo II was more sophisticated. The frame was by Kurtis, strengthened to stand the pounding of Italian roads. The engine was a 6.4-litre Chrysler V8 with hemispherical combustion chambers—the same engine that has won numerous NASCAR (the National Association for Stock Car Auto Racing) stock car races in the USA. Gearbox was by Jaguar, rear axle by Lincoln, as were the twelve-inch diameter disc brakes, which had Chrysler internals. The body was rolled from aluminium by expatriate English craftsman Jack Sutton.

Unfortunately, after all his efforts, Miller retired early in the race: *Caballo II* proved too fragile for the conditions. Another early retirement was Stirling Moss: just seven miles and three minutes from the start the Maserati's brake pedal snapped off. He drove slowly back to Brescia—the hand-brake was useless—where his anger evaporated at the sight of the Maserati mechanics in tears.

In Verona it was Peter Collins who led, by ten seconds from Trips, with Taruffi and Portago—in his first *Mille Miglia*—close behind. By Padua Trips had taken Collins and pulled out thirty seconds.

Near Forli, on the fast straight on the Adriatic, Collins in his 4.1-litre car passed

62. Veteran Californian hot-rodder Ak Miller built his Chrysler-powered *Caballo II* especially for the 1957 *Mille Miglia*, but retired early in the race with multiple mechanical problems. Co-driver is Doug Harrison

Trips's 3.8, and soon Taruffi, in the other 4.1-litre, also got by. By Pesaro the order was: Collins, Taruffi, Trips, Portago, Gendebien (Ferrari GT), Scarlatti (Maserati), and the Scotsman Ron Flockhart, who was finding his Le Mans-winning Jaguar D-Type ideal on the faster sections of the course.

Taruffi pushed Collins hard until they turned into the mountains after Pescara, when the young Englishman began to pull away decisively. By Aquila he was three minutes in front; by Rome, more than five minutes in front, with Trips another four minutes behind Taruffi. On the Rome–Viterbo section, Taruffi's home ground, Collins pulled out another ninety seconds. Siena, Florence, the Futa Pass (rain and light snow), then Bologna, where Collins was eleven minutes in the lead. This was a feat that not even Moss had managed: to outdrive completely Taruffi and the rest of the Italians.

But approaching Bologna, in the last valley of the Apennines, both Collins and Taruffi began to hear a growl from their rear axles. Taruffi was prepared to retire: he had memories of a terrifying crash at the Nürburgring in 1935, when the transmission of his Bugatti had locked. Enzo Ferrari, at the Bologna control, changed his mind by telling him that Collins had the same trouble. Taruffi drove on, changing gear gently, using only half throttle, giving him a top speed of around 130 mph (210 km/hr).

Collins retired at Parma, while Taruffi nursed his car on. Wolfgang von Trips,

63. Peter Collins overtakes Wolfgang von Trips during the 1957
Mille Miglia

behind in his healthy Ferrari, seemed a certain winner—except that Enzo Ferrari had had a quiet word with him at Bologna. Ferrari knew that it was Taruffi's last race; that he had promised his wife he would retire; and Ferrari asked Trips to let Taruffi win. Which he did. The two Ferraris crossed the line in convoy, Taruffi three minutes ahead on corrected time and averaging 94.6 mph (152.6 km/hr).

It was not until an hour later that the news came through. Fon de Portago had crashed—with a burst tyre, or a mechanical failure, nobody will ever know for sure—killing himself, his American friend and co-driver, Ed Nelson, eleven spectators—and the *Mille Miglia*.

64. Piero Taruffi

CARRERA PANAMERICANA DE MEXICO: 1950–54

Road races have been held on every type of road. They began on the Napoleonic highways of France, which had had their surfaces improved to meet the demands of the cyclist lobby. In backward parts of the world—Sicily, Argentina—it was the mule, not the bicycle, that dictated the style of road-building. In the speed sections of modern rallies there is a strong tendency to use roads that are much rougher than the modern norm, unlike the classic Italian road races, which accepted and used whatever roads existed in any place and period. The forest rallies of Britain and Scandinavia are often closer to autocross or the off-the-road desert races of the Western USA and Mexico than to the classical road race.

Very few races have been held on modern motor roads, but one that was, and which gained international fame, was the *Carrera Panamericana de Mexico*—generally just called the Pan-American road race, or the Mexican road race.

The Pan-American Highway was planned in 1924. Its original inspiration, as with most highways throughout history, was military: to give the USA swift land access to the Panama Canal. For this reason there has been a marked reluctance to complete the Darien section of the highway south of the Canal, which would give the South American republics access to it, but much of the rest of the highway, from Alaska to Patagonia, is now complete. The Mexican section, connecting the USA with Guatemala, was completed in the late-'forties. To celebrate this event the first Pan-American road race was held in May 1950 (see Map 8).

Apart from its length and ruggedness—the equivalent of a journey from Stockholm to Istanbul, with the road climbing as high as 10,000 feet—the first *Panamerican* was not the major event it was to become. It was limited to touring cars only, those complying with the American AAA stock car regulations, which naturally were of little interest to European manufacturers. The only European works entry was from Alfa Romeo, who hoped to start an assembly plant in Mexico. Most of the 126 starters were American, and few of them had any idea of the servicing problems of a six-day motor race. It soon became obvious that the *Panamericana* was the most difficult race for the service crews there had ever been or was ever likely to be. With the enormous distances and primitive conditions it was very difficult to set up service depots in advance. Aircraft, with all the complexity and expense involved, were the best answer.

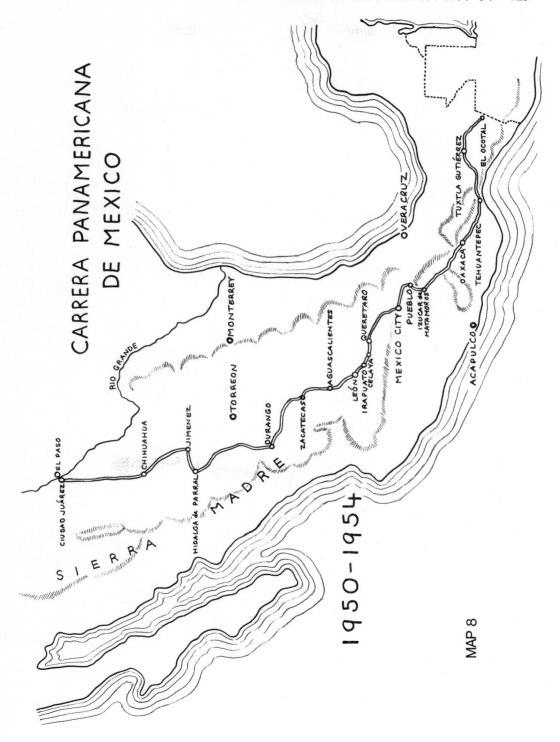

CARRERA PANAMERICANA
DE MEXICO

1950-1954

MAP 8

65. *Carrera Panamericana de Mexico*

66. Felice Bonetto's Alfa Romeo during the first *Panamericana*, in 1950

1950

The first *Carrera*, with all the starters almost equally poorly prepared, was a race of attrition. It started in the north, at Ciudad Juárez on the Rio Grande, and went south through Chihuahua, the former headquarters of Pancho Villa, through the silver-mining town of Hidalgo de Parral, then Durango, then León, to Mexico City. This section proved fast and easy, favouring the big American cars rather than the smaller, 2.5-litre Alfa Romeos of Piero Taruffi and Felice Bonetto. The leader in Mexico City was Johnny Mantz from California in a Lincoln. By fast and intelligent driving—he was never out of the first four in each of the six stages to Mexico City—he had built up a twelve-minute overall lead.

But on the next stage, in the mountains south of Pueblo, the Lincoln suffered rear-brake failure, and, to slow him still further, Mantz was suffering badly from dysentery. He arrived in Oaxaca sixty-ninth out of the seventy-five cars still running. Felice Bonetto, his Alfa Romeo at home on the mountain roads, won the stage, and his team-mate, Taruffi, was second, despite a stop to change tyres and another to siphon petrol from a parked car to refuel his dry tank—Taruffi, never missing a trick, had saved twenty pounds in weight by taking the bare minimum of petrol, but had run short.

On the next stage, the last but one, from Oaxaca to Tuxtla Gutiérrez, Johnny Mantz won and pulled back up to fourth on overall placings. On the final stage, to El Ocotal, he started well and looked like being fastest—until the last ninety miles.

In the north the Pan-American Highway had been a motorist's dream: smooth, straight, fast, with gently banked corners; but on the journey south it became less good. The final ninety miles were not even tarred, and had not even been properly graded—it was just the broken, lumpy rock that the bulldozers had left as they broke the trail through the hills. Mantz blew seven tyres. The low-slung Alfa Romeos were in even worse trouble, their sumps bumping along the road and shedding oil.

The winner, through sheer consistency, was Hershel McGriff from Oregon, whose Oldsmobile suffered both a broken sump and a ruptured fuel tank on the final stage—but only half a mile from the finish, so he could limp home to 17,381 dollars. Second, only 1 min. 16 sec. behind, was Tom Deal, a Cadillac dealer from El Paso, the Texan town just across the river from Ciudad Juárez, the starting-point of the *Carrera*.

When the news agencies wired the results out to the world they said that third place had gone to Ray Pat Connor from El Paso, driving a Nash. But this car was disqualified when it was discovered that the driver was no longer Connor, but a very large young man, a lumberman by trade, named Curtis Turner.

In 1950 Turner was well on his way to becoming a legend on the stock car ovals of the southern states. Like most southern drivers he claimed to have learnt his driving (from the age of nine) by outracing Federal revenue agents in a car loaded with moonshine whisky. He began racing on small dirt tracks in 1946 and was an almost immediate success, developing a broadsiding cornering technique that was very similar to the one used by Scandinavians on ice and introduced by them into international rallying in the early 'sixties.

Curtis Turner started the 1950 *Panamericana* in a Nash shared with Bill France, a stock car ace of the 'thirties, the creator of N A S C A R, and, much later, Presidential campaign manager for Governor George Wallace of Alabama. The Nash was fourth in the first stage of the race, but was later slowed by tyre and wheel trouble. With only that last, bumpy stage to go they were twentieth—and it was then that Turner took over the sixth-place Nash of Ray Pat Connor, who was ill. Turner drove as though he had Federal agents on his tail, and, despite a stop to change a flat tyre, won the stage and beat Taruffi, the mountain king, by 3 min. 25 sec., hoisting the car up to an overall third place—until the inevitable disqualification.

So, with the Connor/Turner car out, third fell to Pikes Peak hillclimb specialists Al and Roy Rogers (Cadillac), and fourth to Taruffi. Bonetto in the other Alfa Romeo was eighth, and Johnny Mantz, the early leader, was ninth.

1951

The 1950 race had been held in May, a month when many of the leading American and European drivers were bound to be busy elsewhere—the race ended

67. *Panamericana*, 1950. Felice Bonetto (in the 2.5-litre Alfa
Romeo) with works mechanic

only three days before the start of qualifying at Indianapolis—so in 1951 it was
sensibly changed to November.

The race was again confined to production cars, but the regulations were liberal-
ised, allowing Ferrari to enter two 2.6-litre coupés for Piero Taruffi/Luigi Chinetti
and Alberto Ascari/Luigi Villoresi—one of the rare cases where top-line drivers
were teamed in the same car. Alfa Romeo stayed away, but Lancia entered two
Aurelia GTs for Felice Bonetto and Giovanni Bracco. Louis Chiron brought a
Delahaye from France.

The race direction was reversed: now it ran from south to north, and the bumpy
stage at the extreme south was left out. The start was at Tuxtla Gutiérrez, the tiny
capital of Chiapas, Mexico's most southerly state. The journey north to the Rio
Grande was to be done in eight stages in five days, with a rest day at Durango, a
format that was to survive until the race was banned. In detail, it looked like this:

Day One, Tuxtla Gutiérrez to Oaxaca: Twisty at first, from the start at 1,800 ft
(548 m) the road climbed 1,000 ft (308 m), then dropped 1,500 ft (457 m) to the
Isthmus of Tehuantepec at 328 ft (102 m), the lowest point on the entire course.

A 25-mile (40-km) straight, scarcely broken by two gentle bends, took the cars back into the mountains, where there were almost a thousand corners before they reached Portillo San Dinonisio at 6,500 ft (2,002 m). Descent to Oaxaca (4,600 ft/ 1,417 m). Distance: 330 miles (531.3 km).

Day Two, Oaxaca to Mexico City, in two stages: The most mountainous section, climbing to the peak of Tamazulapan (7,400 ft/2,280 m) in 100 miles (161 km), then dropping to El Marques (2,700 ft/823 m) and climbing again to the control at Pueblo (7,000 ft/2,156 m). Forty miles (64.4 km) of hairpins took the cars to the peak of the Llano Grande (10,382 ft/3,198 m). Mexico City is at 7,400 ft (2,280 m). Distance: 328 miles (528 km).

Day Three, Mexico City to Durango, in two stages: Again, mountainous with bad roads, until the start of the prairie at Querétaro, from where there were fast straights into the control at Durango. Distance: 590 miles (950 km).

Day Four, Durango to Chihuahua, in two stages: The fastest section of the course, with straights of between twenty and forty miles. Control at Hidalgo de Parral. Distance: 437.5 miles (704.4 km).

Day Five, Chihuahua to Ciudad Juárez: Almost a straight line. Distance: 222.5 miles (362.2 km).

From the start of the 1951 race the Ferraris were in trouble. After only a few miles both cars had stopped with stripped tyre treads, and, with only two spares on board and none available from road-side depots, they had to be nursed to the finish of the first stage at Oaxaca. The winner of this stage was Frenchman Jean Trévoux, a four-times winner of the Monte Carlo Rally. Trévoux had gone to the USA early in the war to try to qualify at Indianapolis—he failed—and had later settled in Mexico City. In 1950 he raced a Delahaye in the *Carrera*, unsuccessfully, and now, in a Packard, he was leading. Second, in a second-hand 1948 Mercury, was Troy Ruttmann, who, a year later, was to become the youngest driver ever to win the Indianapolis 500. Ruttmann was a brilliant natural driver, whose later career was marred by alcoholism. Third was Mexican Douglas Ehlinger (Packard). The crew of one car, Jose Menocal/Miguel Gonzales, were killed when they drove over a cliff.

On the second stage, to Pueblo, another crew were killed—the Alfa Romeo driven by Carlos Panini crashed, killing his daughter Teresa, who was acting as co-driver. Panini himself died a few hours later. This tragedy brought the first outcry against the race, but three more years were to pass and many more were to be killed before it was finally banned.

The Ferrari team were now sorting out their tyre problems: Ascari/Villoresi won the second stage, although they were still well down the field on overall placings. It was Ehlinger who had moved to the front, from Bill Sterling (Chrysler), and Taruffi/Chinetti, who were steadier than their faster team-mates. Louis

68. Troy Ruttmann

Chiron in his Delahaye arrived very late at Pueblo, suffering from tyre trouble, and was disqualified.

By the end of the third stage, Mexico City, Troy Ruttmann led in his old Mercury, despite suffering from dysentery. Ehlinger was second, and Taruffi/ Chinetti, who had won the stage, third.

North of Mexico City Taruffi/Chinetti stormed through into an overall lead— and only just in time, for the fast straights of the northern prairies were to favour the more powerful American cars. But the Italians' lead proved sufficient, and they cruised home at the head of the field, Taruffi/Chinetti first and Ascari/Villoresi second. The end of the race was enlivened by the Indianapolis ace Tony Bettenhausen, who, having lost time with brake trouble on the early stages, won the final two stages in his Chrysler Saratoga. But he was too far behind to challenge the leaders.

The winning Ferrari averaged 88.2 mph (142 km/hr) in almost twenty-two hours on the road. Behind the winning Italian cars came Bill Sterling (Chrysler), Troy Ruttmann (Mercury), and Jean Trévoux (Packard).

1952

The introduction of a sports car class meant that the American sedans no longer had any chance against European sports cars. The *Panamericana* became, in effect, two separate races, one American, one European.

The prize entries of the 1952 race were the three works Mercedes-Benz 300 S Ls— the lightweight coupés that had already won that year at Le Mans and finished second in the *Mille Miglia*. Drivers were Karl Kling, their best road racer, Hermann Lang, the pre-war Grand Prix ace, and the American amateur John Fitch. The organisation, under team-manager Alfred Neubauer, was up to the usual Mercedes-Benz standard.

But the Ferrari team was, on paper, even stronger. There were 4.1-litre coupés for Alberto Ascari, Luigi Villoresi, and Carlo Chinetti, who shared with Frenchman Jean Lucas. Giovanni Bracco, who had beaten Kling to win the *Mille Miglia* that year, had a 3-litre Ferrari. There were also works Lancia Aurelias for Felice Bonetto, Umberto Maglioli, and Giulio Cabianca, works Gordinis from France for Jean Behra and Robert Manzon, and various private C-Type Jaguars.

In the stock car class the only works team was from Lincoln. Among the private opposition was an Oldsmobile lent by a Mexico City dealer to Piero Taruffi. *El Zorro Plateado*—the Silver Fox—as the Mexicans called the grey-haired Taruffi, had arrived in Mexico expecting a Ferrari to be waiting for him, but had been told that if he wanted to race the car he would have to buy it. He would not race a Ferrari again for two years.

The first stage proved disastrous for many drivers: Ascari crashed his Ferrari; Bonetto and Manzon both retired with mechanical problems; Villoresi was delayed by gearbox trouble. To a lot of people's surprise, it was the frail Gordini of Jean Behra that led at Oaxaca, in front of Bracco (Ferrari), Kling (Mercedes-

69. *Carrera Panamericana de Mexico*, 1952. Karl Kling and Hans
Klenk in their winning Mercedes-Benz 300 SL

Benz), Maglioli (Lancia Aurelia), and the American amateur Jack McAfee
(Ferrari).

Behra continued to lead on the second stage, until, almost within sight of
Pueblo, he crashed off the road and down a bank, suffering skull and chest injuries.
Ten other drivers crashed on this same corner, and near by a Mexican crashed his
Jaguar, killing himself and seriously injuring his co-driver.

With Behra out, Bracco took over a comfortable lead, and coolly held on to it,
sparing his car, as the Mercedes-Benz team and Villoresi's Ferrari stalked him.
Bracco led at Pueblo, at Mexico City, at León, at Durango—by now Villoresi
had retired—at Hidalgo de Parral—until, finally, on the fast prairie straights, the
Ferrari's transmission failed, ending Bracco's masterful drive.

Kling inherited the lead from Bracco, and held it to the finish, winning at an

70. Alfred Neubauer congratulates American John Fitch for winning the final stage of the 1952 *Panamericana*. But Fitch was later disqualified

average speed of 102.6 mph (165.2 km/hr). Second, over half an hour behind, was the second Mercedes-Benz of Lang, followed by the Chinetti/Lucas Ferrari, which had only top gear left, Maglioli's Lancia Aurelia, and McAfee's big Ferrari.

The only disappointment for Mercedes-Benz was Fitch's disqualification for allowing a mechanic other than his co-driver to work on the car during the Parral–Chihuahua stage. Had it not happened he would have been fourth. After early delays with suspension and steering problems he made up time rapidly and won the final stage.

The stock car class was dominated by Lincoln: Chuck Stevenson leading home Johnny Mantz by just forty-seven seconds; Walt Faulkner in another works Lincoln being third. Fourth was a private Lincoln driven by Bob Korf and entered by Carl Kirkhaefer, the manufacturer of Mercury marine outboard motors. Fifth was another Kirkhaefer entry, Bob McFee's Chrysler. For some reason Kirkhaefer wanted the Chrysler to win, so he protested that the works Lincolns were non-standard, even though his own Lincoln was in the same trim and would have been excluded as well, had the protest been upheld, which it wasn't.

71. Chuck Stevenson

1953

Lincoln were again out in force this year: twenty-two of their cars started; four of them works entries for Chuck Stevenson, Johnny Mantz, Walt Faulkner, and great Bill Vukovich, better known for his drives at Indianapolis. Other Indy drivers were competing: young Roger Ward, who was to win at Indianapolis in 1959 and 1962, drove a Lincoln; as did the veteran Duane Carter, who had already been racing for twenty-one years. Another Lincoln driver was Argentina's Oscar Galvez, one of eighty specially invited drivers from the home of Latin American road racing.

There were no works Ferraris, but Franco Cornacchia's Scuderia Guastalla entered five 4.5-litre cars for Umberto Maglioli, Antonio Stagnoli, Guido Mancini, Luigi Chinetti, and Mario Ricci. The strongest sports car team was that of Lancia: their 3.3- or 2.9-litre cars were driven by Juan Manuel Fangio, Piero Taruffi, Felice Bonetto, Giovanni Bracco, and Eugenio Castellotti.

Servicing regulations had been tightened: at the end of each stage mechanics were given three hours to work on the cars before they were impounded for the night—overnight rebuilds were out.

Of all the Pan-American road races, this was the bloodiest. On the first stage, at the end of the long Tehuantepee straight, Bob Christie crashed his Lincoln. Spectators crossed the road to view the wreckage just as Mickey Thompson (Ford) arrived on the scene. He swerved to avoid the crowd and crashed off the road to end beside Christie's car—unaware at first that there were six bodies under his own car. Thompson, who later became famous for his world land speed record attempts in his four-engined *Challenger I*, had a nightmare journey back to the USA, hitching lifts where he could, wondering if relatives of the dead spectators would catch him, and, in the accepted Mexican way, murder him.

On the same stage Antonio Stagnoli crashed his Ferrari coupé—a tyre may have burst—and his co-driver Scotuzzi was killed instantly. Stagnoli died later in Oaxaca hospital.

Lancia dominated the first stage, Bonetto leading home Taruffi, Fangio, Castellotti, Maglioli (Ferrari)—who had lost ten minutes on roadside repairs—and Jean Behra (Gordini). Bracco came next, delayed, like his friend Maglioli, by repairs *en route*.

It remained Lancia's race from start to finish. Bonetto led the first three stages to Mexico City. Lincoln had no trouble dominating the stock car class. The small, 1.6-litre sports car class saw an interesting duel between Porsche and Borgward. The favourite in this class, Porsche-mounted Karl Kling, retired on the third stage, from Pueblo to Mexico City.

On the fourth stage, Mexico City–León, Taruffi caught up with Bonetto on the road and took the lead on corrected time. He followed closely for many miles until, approaching the ancient town of Silao, Bonetto pushed Taruffi off the road—deliberately, on Taruffi's own account. While Taruffi struggled to repair his car, poetic justice took place in a very harsh form: Bonetto crashed and was killed. He had hit a *vado*, a shallow drainage ditch across the road, without slowing down. Ironically, before the race Bonetto, Taruffi, and Fangio had reconnoitred the course together in a Chevrolet, and had marked the approach to every *vado* with a painted sign on the road—and the sign to mark the *vado* that had killed Bonetto had been painted by Bonetto himself.

Fangio now inherited the lead, and held it steadily to the finish—his only road race win outside Argentina. The only challenge came from Umberto Maglioli in the big Ferrari, but on the fifth stage, León–Durango, the car lost a wheel and crashed. After the rest day at Durango Maglioli took over the Ferrari of Mario Ricci—driver replacement was now allowed—and went on to win the final three stages. But it was far too late to catch the leaders on corrected time.

First was Fangio, at 105.7 mph (170.2 km/hr); second, Taruffi, about eight minutes behind; third, Castellotti; and fourth, Guido Mancini in the first of the Scuderia Guastalla Ferraris. Louis Rosier was fifth in a 4.5-litre Talbot, followed by the Ricci/Maglioli Ferrari, over two hours behind Fangio, the Mexican-entered Ferrari of Efrain Ruiz Echeverria, and the Californian-built special of Ak Miller. Miller had fitted a 250 bhp Oldsmobile engine into a 1927 Ford Model T chassis, covered it with a crude body, named it the *Caballo de Hierro*—Iron Horse—and collected this remarkable eighth place, the first American to finish in the sports car class.

Other Americans in the sports car class had a less happy time: Phil Hill drove a Ferrari, crewed by another future Grand Prix driver, then only a mechanic, Richie Ginther, but they crashed; an all-American effort, a Chrysler-engined Kurtis, was driven first by Tony Bettenhausen, then taken over by Duane Carter, but it was a complete flop.

The 1.6-litre sports car class was won by the Porsche driven by Jose Herrarte of Guatemala, the only finisher in the class. Among the retirements was a Borgward driven by 18-year-old Hans Herrmann.

Chuck Stevenson in a Lincoln was seventh, ahead of Ak Miller, winning the stock car class for the second successive year, leading home his team-mates Walt Faulkner, Jack McGrath, and Johnny Mantz. Indianapolis driver Jim Rathman was originally placed fifth in an Oldsmobile, but was disqualified for having a non-standard engine. With him out, the first non-Lincoln to be classified was the Chrysler of Tommy Disdale. Oscar Galvez was eighth; Roger Ward crashed. A class for small stock cars was won by 60-year-old C. D. Evans (Chevrolet) from El Paso.

1954

Only one European works team competed that year: Alfa Romeo, who entered the 2-litre touring car class. All the nineteen entries in the big sports car class, from which the overall winner inevitably came, were private. The firm favourite was Umberto Maglioli (4.9-litre Ferrari).

But it was the 4.5-litre Ferrari of Phil Hill/Richie Ginther that jumped into an

72. Jack McGrath

73. Jack McGrath (Lincoln) leads Consalvo Sanesi (Alfa Romeo)
early in the 1954 *Panamericana*

early lead, winning the first stage from Maglioli and three 1.5-litre cars, the
Borgward of Gunther Bechem, the Porsche of Jaroslav Juhan, a Czech living in
Guatemala, and the Porsche of Hans Hammernick. There was tragedy already:
Jack McAfee had crashed his 4.5-litre Ferrari, killing his co-driver, Ford Robinson.
Retirements were heavy: among them was a Ferrari shared by Ernie McAfee and
the Dominican playboy Porfirio Rubirosa, and the Austin Healey of Lance
Macklin and Donald Healey—although another works Healey, driven by Texan
Carrol Shelby, was sixth in the big sports car class. The works Lincolns of Chuck
Stevenson and Johnny Mantz were out with burnt pistons—the official petrol
supplied at Tuxtla Gutiérrez had been sub-standard.

For the seemingly invincible Lincoln team it was a worrying race: on the first

74. Walt Faulkner

day Jack McGrath crashed; and on the second day, a few miles south of Petlal-cingo, Bill Vukovich did the same, rolling five times down a ravine, finally stopping on a narrow ledge. With several hundred more feet of daylight beneath them, Vukovich and co-driver Vern Houle unfastened their safety belts and crawled gingerly from the wreckage, afraid it might start rolling again. Back on the road, Houle hitched a ride to Mexico City with Giovanni Bracco, who had been delayed in his Ferrari coupé. Houle was alarmed at being asked to steer one-handed while Bracco, his foot hard on the throttle, lit one of his frequent cigarettes.

Maglioli had also been delayed, first by a flapping boot lid, then by a burst tyre, but by Mexico City he was only thirty-nine seconds behind Phil Hill, with no other challengers for the lead. Gunther Bechem had lost the lead in the 1.5-litre sports class when his Borgward collided with the Spanish Pegaso driven by works test driver Joaquin Palacio, and entered by the Dominican dictator, Trujillo. Bechem went off the road, and Palacio did the same shortly afterwards, the expensive Pegaso being burnt out. Carrol Shelby hit a kilometre stone head-on, almost slicing his Healey in two, being lucky to escape himself with a broken arm. The most unpleasant crash came north of Panuelas, on the third stage, when Hector Palacios crashed his Dodge. Palacios lost both legs, and his co-driver, Vicente Solar, died later in hospital.

75. The outskirts of Ciudad Juárez, the finish-line of the *Pan-americana*. Assorted sedans cross the line in 1954

Beyond Mexico City Maglioli soon took control of the race, while Hill settled down to a steady drive into second place. For Maglioli, averaging 107.9 mph (173.7 km/hr), it was a resounding win, the best he was to have in his career spanning more than twenty years. He won five of the eight stages, and finished second to Hill in the other three. In contrast, Fangio the year before had driven a tactician's race, winning overall without winning a single stage, and getting only two seconds, four thirds, and two fourths.

Behind Maglioli and Hill came Hans Herrmann (Porsche), winner of the 1.5-litre class, Jaroslav Juhan (Porsche), Franco Cornicchia (4.5-litre Ferrari), Luigi Chinetti (4.5-litre Ferrari), Ak Miller (*Caballo*), French veteran Louis Chiron (1.1-litre Osca), and the Lincolns of Ray Crawford and Walt Faulkner.

The works Alfa Romeos won the 2-litre touring car class, Consalvo Sanesi leading home Sergio Mantovani; in the class for smaller American stock cars Tommy Drisdale beat C. D. Evans, who was now sixty-one; both drove Dodges. Oscar Cabalen (Ford) from Argentina had led this class earlier, but dropped back to finish seventh. Ninth at the finish was Piero Taruffi, driving a Ford Six entered by US publisher Floyd Clymer. Taruffi was very fast in the early mountain stages, but on the prairie he was easily outpaced by his V8-powered rivals.

The death toll in 1954 was eight—four drivers, two crew, and two spectators. It was decided that the toll was too high, and so ended the *Carrera Panamericana de Mexico*.

MADONIE AND MUGELLO: 1958–73

1958

After the final *Mille Miglia* all road races in Italy were cancelled. The *Targa Florio* was run in 1957 as a sedate rally. But a year later, thanks to the remarkable safety record of the Madonie circuit—only two deaths since 1907—it became a full-blooded race again, the only survivor of the Italian road racing tradition.

With the retirement of Maserati from both Grand Prix and sports car racing at the end of 1957, Ferrari were left to represent Italy alone, increasingly challenged by British cars: Vanwall and Cooper in Grand Prix; Aston Martin in sports cars—Jaguar were by now fading. Apart from Franco Cortese's win in 1951, British cars, though, had never done well in the *Targa*; in fact, they were seldom entered, but in 1958 a 3-litre Aston Martin DBR2 did appear driven by Stirling Moss and Tony Brooks. Brooks, although often overshadowed by his team-mate Moss, had had a big following in Sicily since his sensational win in the 1955 Syracuse Grand Prix, when he had beaten the Italian works team with a Connaught, a generally unsuccessful car.

From the start it was the Ferraris that led: 3-litre V12 cars driven by Luigi Musso/Olivier Gendebien, Mike Hawthorn/Wolfgang von Trips, and Peter Collins/Phil Hill. For Hill it was his first *Targa*, although his road-racing ability had been well-proven in the *Carrera Panamericana*. The only challenge to the Ferraris did not come from the Aston Martin—Moss had damaged a wheel on the first lap, losing half an hour—but from the little 1.5-litre Porsche RSK driven by Jean Behra/Giorgio Scarlatti. Behra moved up among the Ferraris into second, although Scarlatti slipped back a place when he took over on lap six. Moss retired on lap five after breaking his own 1955 lap record twice, leaving it at 42 min. 17.5 sec.

The Italians had a scare at the end of lap eleven, when Musso in the leading car stopped with no brake fluid, but the system was topped up and Gendebien got away without losing the lead. They won, almost six minutes ahead of the Behra/Scarlatti Porsche, averaging 56.7 mph (91.3 km/hr), with the Ferraris of Hawthorn/von Trips and Collins/Hill behind. Fifth was the consistent Cabianca, sharing his Osca with ex-Gordini driver Bordoni.

76. *Targa Florio*, 1973

1959

The speed of the Behra/Scarlatti Porsche in 1958 was, in fact, the beginning of the most enduring challenge to Italian supremacy in the *Targa Florio* since the Bugatti wins of 1925–9. The Mercedes-Benz win of 1955 was a one-off effort, and the Porsche win of 1956 could be explained away to bad luck, but the German onslaught to come, coupled with the British rise to supremacy in Formula One, was the biggest setback for the Italians since the German domination of Grand Prix racing in the 'thirties.

Aston Martin, who won the world sports car championship in 1959, did not enter the *Targa*, so Ferrari's chances could not have been better. Their Number One driver that year was Tony Brooks; he was teamed with Jean Behra. Olivier Gendebien, co-winner the year before, was teamed with Phil Hill. All the cars were 3-litre V12s, and the most powerful one, with a Le Mans engine, was shared by Dan Gurney, the American who had taught himself to race by driving sports cars around deserted country roads near Los Angeles, and Cliff Allison, the very competent and experienced British driver whose career was virtually finished by a bad crash at Monaco in 1960. It is hard now to judge just how good a driver

77. Huschke von Hanstein, Paul Freré, Olivier Gendebien

Allison was, or might have become, but there is no doubt that Gurney was one of the best and most versatile drivers America ever produced—and one of the most precocious.

The 1959 *Targa* was only his fifteenth motor race, and for the first two laps he led, from team-mate Behra and a pack of five Porsches. But on lap three it was the Swede Jo Bonnier who came through in the lead in his Porsche, and a lap later Edgar Barth, the German veteran who had started racing on motorcycles in 1934, had also moved ahead of the Ferraris, which were beginning to crumble. Gurney's rear axle broke. Behra, approaching Campofelice, struck oil, slid sideways down the narrow road for a hundred yards, and rolled his car. The tough little Frenchman—in 1955 he had lost an ear in a crash—crawled out from under the car, righted it with the help of two locals, and drove back to the pits. Tony Brooks took over, but finding steering affected, and the rear axle about to go, retired.

By lap seven—half distance—the Ferraris were beaten. The Bonnier/Wolfgang von Trips Porsche led from the Umberto Maglioli/Hans Herrmann Porsche, which, however, went out with a broken gearbox, allowing the Barth/Seidel car

78. Jo Bonnier and Wolfgang von Trips

back into second. This broken gearbox now gave Porsche something to sweat about —and on the last lap, twenty-five miles from home, the leading car did indeed stop with a broken gearbox. But the Barth/Seidel car survived, to come home twenty minutes ahead of a private Porsche RSK driven by Strahle/Mahle/Linge. Third was a Porsche Carrera coupé driven by Sicilian Antonio Pucci and Huschke von Hanstein, the 1956 co-winner. Fourth was another Carrera, driven by Strahle/Mahle/Linge, who had spent an enjoyable race playing musical chairs with their two cars.

1960

By the following year musical chairs had been played between Ferrari and Porsche. Trips, who had been in the Ferrari Formula One team since 1956, now rejoined their sports car team, while Gendebien, who had been racing Ferrari sports and GT cars since late-1955, without getting the single-seater drives he wanted, had gone to Porsche (and to the British Yeoman Credit team for a Cooper Formula One drive).

Gendebien did not begin the 1960 *Targa* very well: he wrecked an RSK in prac-

79. Graham Hill with Porsche and friends, 1960 *Targa Florio*

tice, weakening the Porsche team seriously. On race day they had Edgar Barth and Graham Hill sharing one 1585 cc car (Hill was just starting to establish himself as a really fast Formula One driver; his first World Championship was to come in 1962), with Jo Bonnier, Olivier Gendebien, and Hans Herrmann sharing two 1630 cc cars.

Bonnier took an immediate lead, but at the end of the first lap he was only twenty-three seconds in front of Umberto Maglioli in one of the new 2.8-litre Maserati Type 61 cars—the model called the Birdcage after its complex frame of slim steel tubes. Theoretically this construction was stronger and lighter than the simpler space-frames used by such manufacturers as Porsche and Lotus, but in practice there was no advantage. Entrant of this car in the *Targa* was the American Camoradi Racing Team. Co-driver was Nino Vaccarella, a Sicilian teacher of law who had been racing since 1957.

Third, behind the Maserati, was Gendebien; fourth, Cliff Allison in the first 3-litre V12 Ferrari; and fifth, the British Italian-resident Colin Davis, son of the 1927 Le Mans winner S. C. H. 'Sammy' Davis, who drove a Maserati-engined Cooper.

An oil leak soon put this Anglo–Italian hybrid into the pits, but the Birdcage Maserati continued to run well in second place—until Herrmann replaced Bonnier in the leading Porsche and Maglioli moved into the lead. And the third-place Porsche had slipped as well, Gendebien being overtaken by the Trips/Phil Hill Ferrari, which had already disposed of the Allison Ferrari.

At the end of lap five Maglioli handed over to Vaccarella—and there was instant panic when the big Maserati, covered with mud from the rain in the mountains, would not start on the button. But it was push-started, and a lap later the order was still Vaccarella, Herrmann, Phil Hill, Gendebien, and the Willy Mairesse/Ludovico Scarfiotti Ferrari. The Allison/Richie Ginther Ferrari, running next, was promptly eliminated when Ginther hit a tree.

By lap seven Vaccarella had stretched his lead to over three minutes. Herrmann handed over to Bonnier, who now had three laps to try to regain the lead.

But for the gallant Maserati pair it was soon all over: a stone punctured the fuel tank. Vaccarella drove on, trying to reach the pits to make a temporary repair. To conserve fuel he coasted where he could, and it was while travelling fast downhill with the engine switched off that he hit a bank and put the car out of the race.

So it was the Bonnier/Herrmann Porsche that won, averaging 59.24 mph (95.334 km/hr), by six minutes from the Trips/Phil Hill Ferrari. Third was the Gendebien/Herrmann Porsche—Herrmann doing the donkey work in both Porsches, making up in reliability what he lacked in speed—fourth, the Mairesse/Scarfiotti/Cabianca Ferrari, fifth, the consistent Barth/Graham Hill Porsche, sixth, the Strahle/Linge/Kainz Porsche Abarth coupé, and seventh, the young Rodriguez brothers, Pedro and Ricardo, from Mexico City, who had spent the race bouncing their Ferrari Dino—a front-engined version—off banks and walls. Pedro topped it all by rolling the car—and continuing.

1961

Porsche, after two straight wins, were back the next year with an even stronger team: two 2-litre cars were entered for Jo Bonnier/Dan Gurney—Porsche's Formula One drivers—and for Stirling Moss/Graham Hill; while a 1.7-litre car was driven by Herrmann/Barth. Maserati, encouraged by their showing the year before, had two new rear-engined Type 63s, entered by the Italian Scuderia Serenissima and driven by Nino Vaccarella/Maurice Trintignant and Umberto Maglioli/Ludovico Scarfiotti. Trintignant, the 43-year-old Frenchman who had been racing since 1938, was a slightly strange choice. He had never raced over the Madonie circuit, and was the sort of plodding, competent driver who was not likely to adapt to it quickly. But at least he was not likely to do anything silly.

Ferrari got off to an unhappy start: their original driver pairing was Olivier Gendebien/Phil Hill and Wolfgang von Trips/Richie Ginther in 2.4-litre cars with rear-mounted Dino V6 engines, backed up by Willy Mairesse/Pedro Rodriguez in a conventional V12 front-engined car. But before the start Hill was switched to the Ginther car, while Trips went in with Gendebien. Ginther was the least experi-

80. Phil Hill

enced of the four, and Hill was furious at this apparent demotion, which was generally blamed on Gendebien.

Hill started after Trips, but quickly caught him and tried to get by, wanting to prove he was the better driver. Hill spun, recovered, and again caught Trips and began to press him. But again he lost control, and this time went off the road for good.

The race developed into the now traditional battle between Porsche and Ferrari, with Moss and Bonnier getting the better of Trips early in the race. The big, ugly Maseratis were outpaced. But Graham Hill was not as quick as Moss, and the Ferrari did its share of leading when Moss was resting. However, on the last lap Moss led in the Porsche by fifteen minutes—until the transmission broke four miles from the finish.

The Trips/Gendebien Ferrari won, at 64.12 mph (103.43 km/hr—the first time the 100 km/hr mark had been broken), from the Bonnier/Gurney Porsche, the Herrmann/Barth Porsche, and the two Maseratis, the Vaccarella/Trintignant car in front.

1962

Before the 1962 *Targa* Porsche's trump card, Stirling Moss, had ended his racing career in a high-speed crash at Goodwood in the south of England. But Porsche now had a new engine: a horizontally-opposed 8-cylinder developed for Grand Prix racing. In enlarged 2-litre form it was installed in two cars entered by Scuderia Serenissima, one, a coupé, driven by the very strong team of Bonnier and Vaccarella, the other, an open version, by Dan Gurney/Graham Hill.

Ferrari also had a new engine: a 2.5-litre V8. Phil Hill set fastest practice lap in the one car with this engine, before the throttle jammed and he screeched off the road with locked brakes. Hill blamed the standard of preparation of the car, and in the ensuing argument he found himself without a drive. His co-driver, Gendebien, was transferred to the 2.4 V6 already assigned to Willy Mairesse and Ricardo Rodriguez.

A 2-litre V6 was entered for two young Milanese drivers: Lorenzo Bandini, twenty-five, was a garage owner who had started out as a mechanic; Giancarlo Baghetti, twenty-seven, was the son of a wealthy industrialist. Baghetti had already made a tremendous impact in international racing, winning both the Syracuse and French Grands Prix in a Formula One Ferrari entered by a federation of Italian racing teams, who were out to foster new talent. But despite Baghetti's brilliant beginnings there were many who felt that Bandini was the better driver, and eventually it was Bandini, a tougher and more persistent character, who established himself as Italy's Number One driver. Baghetti's career fizzled, and he retired in 1968—after Bandini, the success, was dead.

Unfortunately the new Porsches were not really raceworthy. The Stuttgart factory, after many years of using drum brakes, had started to make their own discs—and on the second lap Dan Gurney, troubled by brake fade, hit a bridge

81. Herbert Müller and Willy Mairesse after winning the 1966
Targa Florio for Porsche

parapet. He changed a wheel at the mountain depot, but had to retire when he reached the main pits. His co-driver, Graham Hill, was transferred to the other Porsche.

The start-to-finish leader was the Ferrari of Mairesse/Ricardo Rodriguez/ Gendebien, with Mairesse, then the Ferrari test driver and at the peak of his career, very impressive. But even more impressive was the performance of Ludovico Scarfiotti in an Osca, who got up to second before his engine blew up. Baghetti hit a wall in the 2-litre Dino, but, despite a long delay in the pits, still finished second. The Porsche of Bonnier/Vaccarella/Graham Hill, slowed by brake fade, was third. Fourth and fifth in this poor year were the Ferrari GTs of Ferraro/ Scarlatti and the brilliant rally pair of Lageneste/Rolland. Adding a light touch to the race was a BMC Mini Cooper driven by Prince Paul Metternich, the veteran German road racer, and Bernard Cahier, the French photojournalist.

The Ferrari's winning average was 63.32 mph (102.14 km/hr)—slower than the year before, although Mairesse set up a new lap record, of 40 min. 6 sec., 66.94 mph (107.97 km/hr), which was to stand for three years.

1963

Porsche again entered two 2-litre, 8-cylinder cars this year, but against them there was now the new Ferrari 250 P, a 3-litre rear-engined V12. And the Porsche team of drivers was less strong: Jo Bonnier had to share a car with Carlo Abate, an Italian veteran better known for steadiness than for speed; the other car was driven by Maglioli/Baghetti. Vaccarella had gone to Ferrari.

But before the race even started things began to go wrong for the Italians: Vaccarella lost his driving licence for a traffic offence. Early in the race they led, with the English driver/engineer Mike Parkes at the wheel, but after he handed over to John Surtees, the man who was to win them the World Drivers' Championship a year later, Surtees went off the road and broke the fuel tank. The Mairesse/Scarfiotti 250 P flattened a fuel line over a bad bump, and it, too, was out. Mairesse and Scarfiotti transferred to a 2-litre Dino, and, with Abate not able to match Bonnier's speed in the fastest Porsche, Mairesse found himself on the last lap with an enormous fifty-minute lead—until he spun and staggered to the finish with bodywork trailing. Bonnier was running behind on uncorrected time, so the Ferrari team had to wait and watch the clock to see if the Porsche could make up the deficit. It did, and Bonnier had driven one of the best races of his career to win by twelve seconds, averaging 64.42 mph (103.91 km/hr). The Maglioli/Baghetti Porsche had retired, as had all but one of the sports Ferraris, so after these two survivors came a string of GT cars, led by the Linge/Barth Porsche. Interestingly, the sixth place Ferrari GTO was co-driven by Fangio's Argentinian protégé, Juan Manuel Bordeu, making a rare appearance in Europe, sharing the car with Giorgio Scarlatti.

There were various curiosities farther down the field. In twenty-seventh place at the finish was a twin-engined Mini—the second engine was in the back seat—

82. Incident in the *Targa Florio*, during the 'sixties

driven by Paul Frère and Sir John Whitmore, which had proved its ability to tear up a set of tyres in a single 45-mile lap. And among the drivers who did not finish were young Nanni Galli and Ignazio Giunti, both in Alfa Romeo GTs, and Bernard Fiorentino in a Fiat.

1964

In 1964 Porsche had an easy win: there were no works Ferraris racing. The most interesting entries were four of the big Anglo–American AC Shelby Cobras, two of them driven by the formidable combinations of Phil Hill/Bob Bondurant and Masten Gregory/Innes Ireland. Another was driven by Tommy Hitchcock/Prince Tckotoua, two wealthy young men who had bought a Ferrari GTO a year before and taught themselves to drive by tearing in an erratic and spectacular fashion around Modena autodrome. Hitchcock was later to turn himself into a competent racing driver, but at this stage they were both dangerous. Tckotoua was, among other things, a chronic sufferer from car sickness, even when he was driving, which made things very unpleasant for both him and his co-driver.

In the *Targa* Bonnier was the customary leader in a works Porsche, but a broken transmission on the second lap put him out; his co-driver, Graham Hill, not getting a drive. Other Porsches retired, as did the Cobras, unsuitable and frail on the bumpy roads, leaving Colin Davis and Antonio Pucci to win in their Porsche 904 GT, at the slowest race average for four years.

In 1964 the lonely *Targa Florio* at last got a companion: the Mugello circuit near Florence was revived. A Mugello race had been held in 1955, but only over a shortish 12-mile (19.3-km) circuit—now the length was 41.15 miles (66.2 km). The race attracted sixty-seven entries: four more than in the *Targa* itself that year, but not of the same quality. Winner was Gianni Bulgai (Porsche 904 GT).

1965

Ferrari, after two successive defeats in the *Targa*, entered a strong team of three Type 275 P2 cars with rear-mounted V12s of 3.3-litres. Drivers were Vaccarella/ Bandini, Scarfiotti/Parkes, and Baghetti/Jean Guichet. Guichet, a Marseilles industrialist with a distinguished war record in the French resistance, had put up an excellent performance the year before in a Ferrari GTO.

Porsche's Number One team of Jo Bonnier/Graham Hill were entered in a new lightweight car, a *Bergspyder* designed for hillclimbs. But Bonnier and Hill thought it too fragile to last, so instead raced a heavier 904—a decision they were to regret. There was a sad absence from the Porsche team: Edgar Barth was near death from stomach cancer.

In the event, Ferrari's strength-in-depth team proved superfluous. Nino Vaccarella set a blistering pace from the start, and he and Bandini kept the 275 P2 in front right until the end, with Vaccarella breaking Mairesse's three-year-old lap record. Scarfiotti held second for two laps until he crashed the car, so the Baghetti/Guichet car took over second until it, too, went out on lap seven, with ignition trouble. The Porsches were outpaced, but by the end it was the unwanted *Bergspyder* that was second, driven by Colin Davis and the German ex-motor-cyclist Gerhard Mitter. Third was a 6-cylinder Porsche 904 driven by Maglioli/ Linge; fourth, the similar 8-cylinder car of Bonnier/Hill.

In 1965 Ford, for the first and only time, entered a works car in the *Targa*: an open version of their Lola-based GT40 driven by Bob Bondurant and Sir John Whitmore. It got up to third at one stage, but a wheel came off when Whitmore was driving, and later Bondurant went off the road for good.

Mugello did not attract any works entries. It was dominated by privately entered Ferrari 250LM models, with the winning car driven by Mario Casoni, who did most of the driving, and Antonio Nicodemi.

1966

Ferrari returned to the *Targa* in 1966 with exactly the same team as the year before: three cars, a 4-litre 330 P3 for Vaccarella/Bandini, and V6 Dino models for Scarfiotti/Parkes and Baghetti/Guichet. Porsche were relying upon their new 906 Carrera Six, successor to the 904 GTs, with about half the horsepower of the Ferraris. The latest fuel-injected versions were given to Bonnier/Mitter and Herrmann/Dieter Glemser, the latter a saloon specialist. And there was a special Carrera with a 2.2-litre, 8-cylinder engine installed at the rear, driven by Colin Davis and Gunther Klass, a young rally specialist who had finished fifth in the

Targa the year before, sharing a Porsche GT with Antonio Pucci, the 1964 winner. And to most people's amazement it was Klass who was quickest in practice.

Vaccarella stormed into the lead at the start, and at the end of the first lap was three minutes in front of Mitter, who was followed by Scarfiotti, Mairesse (in a Porsche Carrera Six entered by the Geneva-based Scuderia Fillipinetti and co-driven by Herbert Müller), Klass, and Guichet. So the order was Ferrari, Porsche, Ferrari, Porsche, Porsche, Ferrari.

On lap two Mitter managed to catch Vaccarella and come through twenty-one seconds ahead, but even more spectacular progress was being made by Gunther Klass, who was up to third. On lap four, with rain falling, he took the lead. On lap six, past half-distance, the order was Klass/Davis, Vaccarella/Bandini, who had got past Mitter/Bonnier, and Mairesse/Müller.

But lap seven was a farce. Bandini, coming up to pass a slower car, thought that a hand signal from the driver in front meant 'Pass' when it really meant 'Hold'. Bandini crawled out from under his wrecked Ferrari in a very bad mood. Meanwhile Mitter was moving up on Klass on the road and made a move to pass. Klass didn't see him and pushed him off the road. Klass's now very secure lead did not last long: a weld broke in the Porsche's suspension and he was out.

Willy Mairesse, with Herbert Müller, cruised home to his second win, at 61.35 mph (98.96 km/hr), from the Baghetti/Guichet Ferrari Dino. All the Dinos had had trouble with their windscreen wipers.

The 1966 Mugello race was unique in one respect: it was the only time in recent years that single-seater cars have been allowed to race on a really long road circuit. A Formula Three race was organised to run concurrently with the sports car race for the first two of the full eight laps. It was not a great success—spins and crashes were numerous—but the winner was the then current star of Italian Formula Three, the expatriate Englishman Jonathan Williams (De Santis-Ford). Many of the Formula Three drivers then co-drove sports cars in the main event.

For the first time Mugello attracted a strong foreign entry, and, despite the early lead held by Giampiero Biscaldi (Abarth), it was a foreign entry that won: the Porsche 906 of Gerhard Koch and Jochen Neerpasch. Second and third were Alfa Romeo GTAs driven by Enrico Pinto/Rinaldo Parmigiani and Ignazio Giunti/ Nanni Galli.

1967

After the speed shown by their 2.2-litre, 8-cylinder engine in 1966, Porsche made this unit their mainstay in 1967, now fitted in their Type 910 coupé. Jo Bonnier was not in the Porsche team for the first time in nine years—an era had passed. Of the 'fifties drivers, only Hans Herrmann and Umberto Maglioli were left. Among the new drivers, apart from Gerd Mitter, were Jo Siffert from Switzerland, already well established in Formula One, Udo Schutz, Jochen Neerpasch, and Rolf Stommelen, all from Germany, Paul Hawkins from Australia, and an English rally driver in his very first international race: Vic Elford.

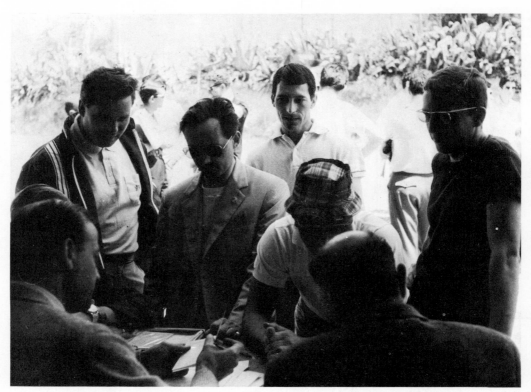

83. Some of the Porsche team at the 1967 *Targa Florio*: Udo Schutz
(1969 *Targa* winner), Colin Davis (1964 winner), Vic Elford
(1968 winner), Gerhard Mitter (1969 winner, with Schutz), and
Rolf Stommelen (1967 winner)

In all there were six works Porsches, challenged by two works Ferraris (a big
4-litre for Vaccarella/Scarfiotti—Bandini was dead—and a rapid Dino for Gunther Klass/Mario Casoni), a Filipinetti Ferrari 4-litre (Müller/Guichet), four of
the new Alfa Romeo Type 33 2-litre cars (Nanni Galli/Ignazio Giunti, Andrea de
Adamich/Jean Rolland, and Giancarlo Baghetti teamed with our old friend Jo
Bonnier), plus a strange vehicle from Texas called a Chapparral.

The Chaparral had three notable features: the monocoque hull was made
largely of fibreglass; the transmission was automatic; and it was fitted with an
inverted wing, mounted on the rear suspension, to keep the drive wheels firmly
planted on the road. Although wings were first used on a motor vehicle back in
1927—on a rocket-powered Opel—it was the Chaparral, designed and financed by
Texan Jim Hall, that led to that almost universal use of wings on competition cars.

For the third year running it was the local hero Nino Vaccarella who set the pace from the start, and it was again Mitter who held second, leading the Porsches, followed by Siffert, Müller in the Swiss Ferrari, and Phil Hill in the Chaparral, which was proving clumsy on the mountain roads.

The Ferrari team crumbled rapidly: Klass went off on the first lap, and on the second Vaccarella hit a wall. The carnage continued as Mitter went off as well, and it was little Herbert Müller who led at the end of the second lap, a full eight minutes in front of Jo Siffert. Andrea de Adamich was third in the leading Alfa Romeo, in front of Italian rallyman Leo Cella in a Porsche Carrera Six, and Paul Hawkins in a Porsche 910.

Siffert immediately dropped back with loss of gears, and Cella took de Adamich for second, before handing over to his co-driver, Giampiero Biscaldi, who slid from second to fifth in one lap. Rolf Stommelen, taking over from Hawkins, did just the opposite, climbing from fifth to second. This proved to be the critical move of the race.

On lap six Guichet in the leading Ferrari got into trouble: suffering from heat exhaustion he spun once, and had to be lifted from the car at the end of the lap. The Stommelen/Hawkins Porsche took the lead. Müller screamed back into the race to catch them—and the transmission promptly broke. The Alfa Romeo team also disintegrated, leaving Porsche to run one-two-three at the end, Stommelen/ Hawkins winning at 67.61 mph (108.85 km/hr) from Cella/Biscaldi and the steady Elford/Neerpasch. Two laps from the end the Chaparral had been holding fourth with Hap Sharp at the wheel when it stopped with a flat tyre. A spare was on board, as demanded by the regulations, but it, too, was flat, and there was nothing to pump it up with. Fourth at the finishing line were Jonathan Williams/Vittorio Venturi (Ferrari Dino). Fifth was a Ford GT40 entered by Ford France and driven by Henri Greder/Giorgi.

At last, in the fourth year of the Mugello revival, there were works entries: Porsche entered six cars, Alfa Romeo three, and Ferrari two. Ferrari withdrew before race day when, sadly, Gunther Klass was killed in a crash.

Within a few miles of the start of the race Mario Casoni harmlessly crashed the Filipinetti Ferrari that he was sharing with Herbert Müller, thus eliminating the biggest threat to the Porsche team. Andrea de Adamich in the quickest Alfa Romeo got up to third early in the race, but eventually the whole team retired. Mitter/ Schutz in a Porsche 910 won, from Stommelen/Neerpasch in a similar car, and Vic Elford/Gijs van Lennap were third in a lightweight Porsche 911R, a racing version of the standard Porsche road car. Fourth was a lumbering 7-litre Ford Mark Two entered by Ford France and driven by Jo Schlesser/Guy Ligier.

1968

This year saw Ford win the world sports car championship after a close fight with Porsche. Ford won at Le Mans, Monza, and Brands Hatch; Porsche at Daytona, Nürburgring, and in the *Targa Florio*, where the quickest Fords were not entered, leaving only Alfa Romeo to challenge Porsche. Ferrari, tired of the constant

84. Nino Vaccarella, with the Alfa Romeo team, 1968 *Targa Florio*

changes in international regulations which made cars rapidly obsolete, did not race sports cars all season.

Practice for the *Targa* started badly for Porsche—Scarfiotti hit a tree with one of their cars—but then a highly prophetic incident occurred: Vic Elford, now well-established in the Porsche team, set off on his first practice lap, from a standing start. Out on the circuit he stopped to confirm that Scarfiotti was all right—and still completed the lap in ten seconds under the lap record.

For Porsche the race started even worse than practice. Jo Siffert went off on the first lap, and limped back to the pits. Elford felt a wheel loosen, stopped to tighten it, continued, but went off the road when it loosened again. The car was still mobile, but he had to change a punctured tyre. Time lost: fifteen minutes.

Scarfiotti led for Porsche for the first two laps, ahead of the dreaded Nino Vaccarella in an Alfa Romeo 2.5 litre. Both retired, and as the attrition continued Porsche came out worst. By half-distance, five laps, the Alfa Romeos of Ignazio Giunti/Nanni Galli and Mario Casoni/Lucien Bianchi were first and second. The Porsches, it seemed, were broken.

85. Umberto Maglioli, who still raced in shirt-sleeves in the age of
fire-proof overalls, with Vic Elford after they had won the 1968
Targa Florio for Porsche

But by lap seven the Milanese team began to feel uneasy: Vic Elford and
Umberto Maglioli in their Porsche had pulled back almost a quarter of an hour of
their first-lap deficit, and were only about a minute behind. The Alfa Romeos
fought back, but on lap nine Elford took the lead, and, averaging 69 mph (111.5
km/hr), went on to win by less than three seconds from the Galli/Giunti Alfa
Romeo. Elford also set a new lap record, of 76.4 mph (123 km/hr).

The Porsche team did not contest Mugello, but there were several fast private
Porsches to challenge the works Alfa Romeos. One Porsche 910 was entered for
Siffert/Rico Steinemann; another for Elford/van Lennap—but Elford wrecked
this car in practice.

Siffert was easily the fastest man in the race, building up a big lead, but co-driver
Steinemann, a Swiss, could not maintain the pace, and made matters worse by
spinning twice in trying. Siffert, in a fury, took over to try to regain the lead, but
the Alfa Romeo 33 of Galli, Bianchi, and Vaccarella was two minutes ahead at the
finish.

86. Mugello, 1968. Teodoro Zeccoli in an Alfa Romeo Type 33

1969

The 1969 *Targa* was a victim, like so many other races, of a congested racing calendar: it was held on the same day as the Spanish Grand Prix. Ferrari had returned to sports car racing after a one-year absence, but their first loyalty was to Formula One, so they missed the *Targa*.

Porsche entered six of their 3-litre 908 spyder models against meagre opposition; Alfa Romeo entered only a single 2.5-litre car, the rest being 2-litres; while there was a single 5-litre Lola-Chevrolet T70 entered by Scuderia Filipinetti and driven by Jo Bonnier/Herbert Müller. The Lola, not designed for road racing, had been strengthened by the works.

Elford, paired again with Maglioli, was quickest in practice, before, driving a training hack, he crashed through an Armco barrier above Cerda. Englishman Brian Redman, a new recruit to Porsche, also crashed. A local lad wrecked his Alfa Romeo Giulia S S, but managed to borrow another one for the race. Crashes in the Madonie are a way of life, not a source of shame, and seldom a source of injury, speeds being relatively low.

Predictably, it was the Porsches of Elford and Mitter that came through one-two at the end of the first lap. But the eyebrow-raiser was Müller in the Lola: he had been delayed by ignition trouble at the start and had got away last, with two minutes to make up before he even caught the car in front. Yet at the end of that first lap he had overtaken sixty cars, and was third on corrected time, ahead of Rolf Stommelen in a works Porsche. The first Alfa Romeo was the Giunti/Galli 2-litre car, running sixth; Vaccarella in the 2.5 litre was ninth, with a sick engine.

On the second lap Elford and Müller were delayed seriously: Elford by a broken alternator belt, which took seven minutes to replace; Müller by a puncture, which necessitated a long, slow limp back to the pits. Mitter now led from Stommelen and Giunti.

The real drama started on lap four. Mario Casoni (2-litre Alfa Romeo), running tenth, went off the road and cut the car in half against a tree. Casoni was taken to hospital by helicopter with burns on his hands and face. The third-place Alfa Romeo also went out: Elford, making up time rapidly, pushed Giunti into a barrier. The Alfa Romeo limped in to retire, while Elford set a new lap record on that very lap.

By lap five, half distance, the Mitter/Schutz Porsche was five minutes ahead of the English-driven Porsche of Brian Redman/Dickie Attwood, who were two seconds in front of the Stommelen/Herrmann car. Elford/Maglioli were fourth, and the Vaccarella/de Adamich 2.5-litre Alfa Romeo fifth—but the Alfa retired a lap later. The Müller/Bonnier Lola retired on the fifth lap.

Of the six Porsches, the Redman/Attwood car was the only one to retire, with a broken half-shaft, and Porsches took the first four places: Mitter/Schutz won at 73 mph (117.43 km/hr), from Elford/Maglioli, and the all-German crews of Stommelen/Herrmann and Karl von Wendt/Willy Kausen. Fifth was a 2-litre Alfa Romeo driven by Enrico Pinto/Giovanni Alberti. Of the twenty-five finishers, thirteen were Porsches—Porsche had gained a dominant position in sports car racing stronger than had been seen since Alfa Romeo's peak in the 'thirties.

The only works team at Mugello was from the Abarth factory in Bologna, and, after the privately entered Alfa Romeo of Galli/Giunti crashed on the first lap, it was Arturo Merzario in a 2-litre Abarth who won, driving single-handed in very hot weather for four and a quarter hours. Second was another Abarth driven by Gijs van Lennap/Johannes Ortner, and third a British-entered Lola-Chevrolet T70 driven by Vaccarella and de Adamich. They found the big car, with its wide tyres, very unsuitable for the twisting, pebble-strewn roads—which makes Müller's first lap in the *Targa Florio* in an identical car all the more remarkable.

1970

Porsche's wealth and resources became even more conspicuous in 1970: they even went to the trouble of building a special lightweight 908 solely for use in the *Targa Florio* and at the Nürburgring, while using their big 917 coupés on faster circuits. No official works team was maintained, but full technical support was given to the Gulf–Wyer team in England and Porsche Salzburg in Austria.

Ferrari did not have the money to build a special road racing car, so they were forced to enter a big 5-litre V12 512S in the *Targa*, for Nino Vaccarella/Ignazio

87. 'Nino! Nino! Nino!' Vaccarella (Ferrari 512S) passes through
Campofelice on his way to third place in the 1970 *Targa Florio*

Giunti to drive. An identical car was entered by Scuderia Filipinetti for Herbert
Müller/Mike Parkes, the Englishman having made a comeback after three years
out of racing.

Alfa Romeo entered three cars with full 3-litre engines, but their hopes took a
serious blow only five kilometres from the start when Umberto Maglioli, driving
in his twenty-first *Targa*, hit a wall. But Porsche weren't doing much better: after
seventeen kilometres the suspension of Elford's car collapsed.

At the end of lap one it was Frenchman Gérard Larrousse in an old-model
Porsche 908 who led the lightweights of Jo Siffert and Leo Kinnunen from
Finland, another old Porsche driven by van Lennap, the Alfa Romeos of Piers
Courage and Toine Hezemans, and Vaccarella in the big Ferrari—seven cars
covered by less than a minute.

On the third lap Kinnunen, driving brilliantly on his first visit to the Madonie,
took the lead from Larrousse, and a lap later Siffert was up to second. Larrousse
handed over to Austrian Rudi Lins, who could not maintain the speed needed to
stay near the front, but when Kinnunen handed over to Pedro Rodriguez, and
Siffert to Brian Redman, there was no slowing down, especially now that the
Vaccarella/Giunti Ferrari was starting to move.

By lap five Vaccarella was second, and on lap six he was in the lead, although
tiring himself rapidly as he fought to keep the big car at the limit and on the road.
By lap seven the Ferrari had to give best to the Siffert/Redman Porsche, which
went on to win at 74.66 mph (120.1 km/hr), with the Kinnunen/Rodriguez
Porsche also getting past the Ferrari, leaving the gallant Vaccarella and Giunti with
third place and badly blistered hands. The older Porsche of Gijs van Lennap and
Hans Laine finished a remarkable fourth—two laps from the end a front wheel

88. *Targa Florio*, 1970. The fourth-place Porsche 908 of Hans Laine/
Gijs van Lennap approaching Campofelice and the sea

flew off, but Laine kept going, touching 145 mph on the straight, and reached the pits for a new wheel with little time lost. The Alfa Romeo challenge had crumbled completely.

At Mugello Arturo Merzario (2-litre Abarth) won again, pushed this year by Leo Kinnunen in another works Abarth, the little Finn using his rally experience to master the long circuit very quickly. Third was van Lennap in yet another Abarth. The main challenge to the Italian cars came from local boy Nanni Galli (1.8-litre Lola T210), who set fastest lap before retiring with a broken throttle cable. Vic Elford drove a Spanish-entered Chevron B16 coupé, but an overfilled fuel tank soaked his overalls in petrol, causing irritating burns. A stop to change overalls lost him seven minutes, and later, still squirming, he crashed. Vaccarella also wrecked his car, a works Abarth.

And that, sadly, was the last race on the Mugello circuit. The authorities were turning more than ever against road racing, and even the *Targa* was beginning to feel the pressure.

1971

Porsche had now won their fifth straight *Targa* victory, matching the record of Bugatti during 1925–9. Could they now win one more and match Alfa Romeo's record of 1930–35? The answer turned out to be no, and the people who stopped them were, appropriately, Alfa Romeo.

Alfa Romeo had withdrawn from sports car racing in 1953. In 1964 they had founded a new subsidiary company, Autodelta, to organise their return to racing. Early successes came with the TZ, a very noisy and fast front-engined 1.6-litre coupé. In 1967, as we have seen, the rear-engined V8 Type 33 appeared, first as a

89. The Siffert/Redman lightweight Porsche 908 winning the 1970
Targa Florio

2-litre, then as a 2.5, and finally, in 1970, as a full 3-litre, the maximum capacity
allowed by the world championship regulations.

The Alfa Romeo team was considerably strengthened for 1971. Porsche men
Leo Kinnunen, Rolf Stommelen, and Gijs van Lennap joined the team; Vaccarella,
de Adamich, and Toine Hezemans remained. Against them were Porsche 908
lightweights for Siffert/Redman, Rodriguez/Müller (deserting Filipinetti after four
years), and Elford/Larrousse. There were no Ferraris.

The first lap was hairy. Stommelen's Alfa Romeo broke its transmission and
went off at Cerda. Redman, his Porsche handling badly, crashed in the mountains.
A helicopter flew him out to have burns treated. At Collesano Rodriguez skidded
on paint on the road and hit a kerb, breaking the Porsche's front suspension. The
paint, put there by a local patriot, was to cover the word 'Porsche', presumably
painted by a local radical.

As in 1970, it was Larrousse who led at the end of the first lap, this year in the sole
remaining Porsche. Vaccarella was barely four seconds behind, followed by de
Adamich, and Jo Bonnier in a little 1.8-litre Lola. On the second lap Vaccarella
took the lead, and at the end of the lap Larrousse handed over to Elford. The chase
was on, with the Porsche 1 min. 45 sec. behind.

Lap three: Vaccarella handed over to Hezemans, with the margin over Elford
now sixty-nine seconds. Lap four: Elford in the lead, eighteen seconds in front of
Hezemans. Lap five: Elford hands back to Larrousse—leading margin now twenty-
nine seconds. Lap six: Larrousse has fifty-eight seconds on Hezemans. Lap seven:
the Porsche suffers a puncture. Larrousse starts to change the wheel, using a light-

weight wheel spanner—which breaks. He drives fourteen miles on rim to mountain depot, where new wheel is fitted. But by now more than a lap has been lost. The Porsche is eliminated when Larrousse hits a kerb and breaks the front suspension.

So Alfa Romeo win, Vaccarella/Hezemans averaging 74.6 mph (120 km/hr) to lead home the Alfa Romeo of de Adamich/van Lennap, and the little Lola of Bonnier/Attwood. Elford broke the lap record, recording 79.5 mph (128 km/hr).

It was Alfa Romeo's eighth victory on the Madonie circuit, making them second only to Porsche, who had won ten. Peugeot, Bugatti, and Ferrari had all won five—but Ferrari, at least, were not going to let it rest there.

1972

Porsche, for the first time since 1953, were out of European sports car racing. Instead, they were concentrating on racing in the USA. So, for the first time since 1954, the *Targa Florio* became virtually an Italians-only race—Alfa Romeo versus Ferrari.

Ferrari had dominated sports car racing that year, but, typically, they entered only one car for the *Targa*, a 3-litre flat-12 312P for Arturo Merzario/Sandro Munari. The latter, a Lancia rally star, had won the Monte Carlo Rally a few months earlier. It seems that a *Targa* drive had become a standard prize for Monte winners: Elford had won the Monte in 1968, and Bjorn Waldegard had won it in 1969 and 1970. But Waldegard's *Targa* drives, unlike Elford's, were not particularly distinguished.

Alfa Romeo were out in force, with four cars for Vaccarella/Stommelen, Elford/van Lennap, de Adamich/Hezemans, and Galli/Dr Helmut Marko—the latter an Austrian, and, like Vaccarella, a lawyer.

The race turned into a titanic battle between the lone Ferrari and the horde of Alfa Romeos—a horde, though, that began to dwindle rapidly. On the first lap Elford went out with a blown engine. On the third lap Vaccarella's car, lying second to Merzario's Ferrari, dropped a valve. A lap later Hezemans bounced off a roadside rock and spent five minutes changing a tyre. So now the score was even: one Ferrari versus one Alfa Romeo (Galli/Marko), with, at the end of lap five, the Alfa Romeo a minute and a half in front.

A lap later, however, the Ferrari had got past and was nineteen seconds in front. But after another lap the Ferrari had to change tyres and was almost a minute behind.

A minute behind—but just ahead on the road. On lap eight, going down the hill towards Collesano, Munari in the Ferrari, on entering a corner, overtook a small Lancia. The Lancia driver got such a fright that he spun—right in front of Galli in the Alfa Romeo. Galli deliberately spun himself to avoid a head-on collision, and in so doing stalled his engine. He sat there with the starter motor grinding, like a scene from a cheap film, as the Ferrari sped into the lead.

Arriving back at the pits about two and a half minutes late, Galli was almost thrown out of the car by Marko, who, after tyres had been changed, screamed off in pursuit. A lap later Munari came in to hand over to Merzario for the final two-lap spell. Their lead was 1 min. 50 sec.—a good margin, if Merzario had not been exhausted, with blistered hands and stomach cramp caused by guzzling cold drinks under the burning Sicilian sun.

In one lap Marko pulled back seventy seconds, reducing Merzario's lead to forty seconds. At that rate Marko could win by half a minute. But, somehow, Merzario responded to the 'Avanti!' signals from the pits, and came home with seventeen seconds still in hand. Arturo Merzario, the slim little 29-year-old from Civenna, Northern Italy, was lifted from the car a hero. And Sandro Munari had equalled Vic Elford's remarkable feat of winning the Monte and the *Targa* in the same year. The Ferrari's winning average was 76.14 mph (122.5 km/hr).

1973

Finally, time had run out for the *Targa Florio*. The international motor sport authorities decided that the Madonie circuit could no longer be used for world championship racing. Some races for production cars might be held in the future, but no longer would the Madonie circuit host an event that would mean very much to the outside world. In effect, classical European road racing came to an end with the fifty-seventh *Targa Florio*, held on 13 May 1973.

Sadly, it was a poor race. Only three really fast cars started: two of them works Ferraris for Arturo Merzario/Nino Vaccarella and Brian Redman/Jackie Ickx (the Belgian Grand Prix star making a belated *Targa* début); the other a new, almost untried, Alfa Romeo flat-12 for Rolf Stommelen/Andrea de Adamich.

By half-way round the fourth lap all three of these cars were out, leaving the Porsche 911 Carrera of Herbert Müller/Gijs van Lennap to speed on to an unchallenged victory, averaging 71.1 mph (114.69 km/hr)—the slowest speed for four years, despite perfect weather conditions.

So that was that.

The mountains of Madonie have changed a lot since 1906. They are a little more prosperous, and the peasant may leave his cart at home and take the modern bus service that connects the villages, although the villages themselves are still mean and ugly. The main streets are just respectable, but behind, in the back streets, goats and children play among the piles of manure and broken bottles and old motor tyres. A secondary road in Sicily is still a cart-track, and once away from the villages nothing seems to have changed. Streams must be forded; stone farmhouses are lopsided; shepherds sleep under trees; their dogs bark at you; a tethered horse rolls in the dust in a cloud of flies.

The flies are everywhere, and at times you feel that they are the true owners of the countryside. They are fat and make a lot of noise, and you may mistake them for another noise, a louder noise, far off, a distant snarl from across the hills. A sound you will remember very well. But you will be wrong. Racing engines will never again be heard in the mountains of Madonie.

AUTOMOVILISMO

If a Dark Continent exists in the world today, that continent is South America, not Africa. Much of it, such as the jungle of the Amazon basin, is really dark—just as dark to a resident of Rio de Janeiro as it is to a Londoner. And the rest of South America, the cities, the towns, the farms, remain murky for most Europeans, the Balkans of the modern world.

For the motor sport follower it remains equally mysterious. A great driver emerged from South America, Juan Manuel Fangio, and suddenly we all knew the name of one potato town in Argentina, Balcarce, where Fangio was born and lived. But when Fangio retired the light shining on Argentina promptly went out. Within two years of his retirement Argentina even stopped holding an international Grand Prix. Then, after ten years of darkness, with the rise of Emerson Fittipaldi, the light began to shine on Brazil. Motor racing is held in other isolated parts of the world: in New Zealand, for instance. But almost every national race in New Zealand is reported, however briefly, in the British motor sport press. Similar races in, say, Argentina, are not reported in the Spanish motor sport press, nor in the press of any other European country. Six-hundred-page encyclopedias of motor sport are published in Europe with scarcely a word about the motor sport of many South American countries. They might just as well be racing on the moon.

Not that South Americans are insular or inbred. The original colonisation may have been Spanish or Portuguese, but it didn't stop there. Fangio is of Italian descent. Emerson and Wilson Fittipaldi are of Italian and Latvian descent. The late Jochen Rindt, after being shunted off a track by Argentina's Carlos Reutemann, very waspishly said that Indians should stay in the jungle, but Reutemann, like Rindt himself, is a descendant of the land of Goethe and Schiller. So was an earlier great name of Argentine racing, Arturo Kruuse, whose family had settled in the Lake District of Patagonia. One of Bolivia's tiny *élite* of racing drivers was Dieter Hübner, and in Peru there is Herbert Grimm, his daughter Sabine, a woman rally champion, and Peter Kube, although they are often beaten by John Henry Bradley, of North American descent, called *El Gringo*, not to be confused with *El Zorro*, the Fox, who is an Indian, Teodoro Yangali, and whose Ford Mustang was bought for him with great difficulty by a syndicate of peasants. Fangio, in the same way, was helped by friends to buy his first road racing coupé.

Educated Chileans usually speak English as well as a Dutchman or a Swiss, and their government ministers often seem to have Scottish names, but Chile's greatest racing driver was Emilio Karstulovic, whose parents were Yugoslavian. He spent much of his life in Argentina, where other Eastern Europeans raced. Karel 'Carlos' Zatuszek won numerous Argentine races for Mercedes-Benz in the 'twenties and 'thirties. Today there are such names as Santiago Kovacevich and Domingo Geronimo Novisky, who sounds like a scalp-hunting Cossack. There was a Venezuelan driver, killed in the 1955 Barranquilla–Cartagena road race in Colombia, who had the truly beautiful name of Pancho Pepe Crocker.

In 1891 a 17-year-old Brazilian, Alberto Santos-Dumont, visited Paris for the first time with his father, a wealthy coffee grower. In Paris Alberto bought a Peugeot with Daimler engine, which he took home to Brazil—the first automobile to reach South America. Santos-Dumont, of course, later became a pioneer aviator: the first man to fly a heavier-than-air craft in Europe. In fact, as far as the vast majority of Latin Americans are concerned, little Santos-Dumont was the first man to fly anywhere. The Wright Brothers are considered gringo impostors.

But despite the arrival of Santos-Dumont's Peugeot in Rio de Janeiro in 1891, the beginnings of motor sport in South America came in Argentina, not Brazil. Argentina, with heavy British investment and the largest British community outside the Empire, was the first South American country to develop industrially, and went on being the richest country in South America until well after the Second World War—or the least poor, since in picturing the economic development of South America we must still think of Greece, or Yugoslavia, or Portugal, not of the riches we take for granted in Northern Europe or north of the Rio Grande. Even today, despite the much-publicised renaissance of Brazil, which has shown in motor sport as much as anywhere else, there are still more racing circuits in Argentina than in all the other countries of South America combined. Brazil's wealth is concentrated on the Rio de Janeiro–São Paulo coastal strip, and its motor racing is similarly concentrated—until recently there was only one circuit, Interlagos at São Paulo. Brazil, with Interlagos, was almost as much a one-circuit country as is the Netherlands with Zandvoort, even though Brazil is as big as the USA and the Netherlands is little more than one-quarter of the size of New York State.

But our concern is with road races, not with circuits, and here, too, Argentina, the eighth largest country in the world, has predominated.

90. *Turismo de Carretera* racing, Carlos Paz, Cordoba, 1966

ARGENTINA: 1904–34

The beginnings of motor sport in Argentina are poorly documented. Some persons claim to have seen a race in Buenos Aires city at least as early as 1904, won by Marcelo T. de Alvear, later to be President of Argentina. There are claims, too, of a flying kilometre sprint on a horse track at Belgrano, a favourite British suburb in the north of Buenos Aires, in 1904. The late Juan Cassoulet, one of the undisputed pioneers of Argentine motor sport, claims to have won it on a Rochester, a light steam buggy made in Rochester, New York, at 45.63 mph (73.469 km/hr). But no documentary evidence can be discovered.

We are on firmer ground on 9 December 1906, when a race—or a trial—was held from Buenos Aires to Tigre, about twenty miles north of the capital, now a popular boating resort. Roads were dirt and especially rolled for the event—or events, since there were two, one from Buenos Aires to Tigre and the other both there and back.

The outward run attracted eight entries, all entered in the names of their entrants, and not necessarily their drivers, who in some cases were professional chauffeurs. The Heinemann Rail Company, for instance, has been immortalised as the entrant of a 25/30 hp Opel, but the driver's name has vanished into oblivion. The other seven cars were two Chenard-Walckers, one Darracq, one Mercedes, one Daimler (presumably British; German Daimlers had all been called Mercedes since 1902), and one Spyker. The race—or trial—finished in a dead-heat between the Spyker, entered and driven by Daniel MacKinlay Jr, and the Darracq, driven by chauffeur L. de Santos.

The return event attracted sixteen entries, again mainly French cars, although there was one Oldsmobile and an original Spanish-built Hispano-Suiza. The most popular make was De Dion Bouton, with three cars entered, one driven by Juan Cassoulet. But the winner was the Darracq that had co-won the first event: now it was driven by its owner, Miguel A. Marin. Second and third were two Dietrichs, driven by chauffeur Francisco Rade and by gentleman Emilio Laborde.

After these two events in December 1906 there is no record of any races for more than a year. But in 1908 five events were held—races, sprints, or trials—and in 1909 there were five more, all in or near Buenos Aires, all contested by the wealthy and enthusiastic members of the A C A, the Automovil Club Argentino. As yet no long road races had been held, mainly because of the appallingly rough condition of all

Argentine roads outside the towns, but the ACA did realise that road races would be a logical way of showing that these roads could be negotiated by automobile, and thus encourage motor touring and all forms of road transport.

The breakthrough came in January 1908, when Juan Cassoulet set off in his De Dion Bouton to drive from Buenos Aires to Cordoba, a route of great significance in the development of the Argentine Republic. Cordoba was, and remains, the largest of Argentina's ten original settlements of what the geographers call the Andean region (although Cordoba is some 300 miles from the Andes proper), all of which developed into towns in the late-sixteenth century, when Buenos Aires was little more than a trading post on the banks of the Rio de la Plata, a minor satellite of Asuncion. The Andean towns, all of which will appear later in this story, fall into two groups: those founded from Peru (going from north to south: Jujuy, Salta, Tucuman, Santiago del Estero, La Rioja, and Cordoba); and those founded from Chile (San Juan, Mendoza, and San Luis). Right up until the 1880s, when the roads from Buenos Aires were made safe by the extermination of the *pampas* Indians, these towns had much closer connections with their parent countries than they did with their own nominal capital, Buenos Aires. Argentina was a country divided in two, and when Juan Cassoulet set off on his epic drive he was creating another bond between these halves.

And some idea of the state of the roads can be gained by noting that he took 87 hours for the 465 miles (750 km). The return journey was quicker: 62 hrs 15 min.

Cassoulet's example led to the staging, in March 1910, of the first *Gran Premio Nacional*, a race from the Buenos Aires suburb of Nunez to Cordoba, via Rosario, where there was a break. There were seven starters: Jean Cassoulet (15 hp De Dion Bouton), Benjamin Odell (Ford), Andres Castro (25 hp Panhard), Francisco Almada (Fiat), Victor Laborde (28/40 hp Delaunay-Belleville—the French luxury make widely considered the best in the world up until 1914), Ventura Lopez (Mercedes), and J. Marin (50 hp Panhard-Levassor).

The most amazing thing about this race—with seven cars on 465 miles of road—was that two competitors actually succeeded in colliding. Laborde on the Delaunay-Belleville was the wild man. Having won the first stage, to Rosario, he crashed into a ditch, spent a whole day rounding up horses to pull the car out, continued, crashed again, bending his front axle, straightened it, continued again—and rammed Odell's Ford. Undaunted, Odell had his car towed into Villa Maria and rebuilt it.

The winner, of both the second stage and the race, was Juan Cassoulet. The secret of his success was caution: at times he would even get out of his De Dion and reconnoitre the road ahead on foot, looking out for giant pot-holes and ruts in the road that might steer him straight into a ditch. The only people who liked ditches were the local *gauchos*, who, in later races, realised there was a lot of money to be made hauling stranded drivers back on to the road. If no sufficiently dangerous ditch was handy they would dig their own and happily wait for a competitor to fall into it.

Cassoulet took 30 hrs 42 min. to reach Cordoba, an average speed of 14.15 mph (24.43 km/hr). Castro on Panhard was twelve hours behind, with Laborde another ten hours back. Odell, the fourth and last finisher, was a mere four hours behind Lamborde.

Shortly after the first *Gran Premio* the Argentine government banned all road racing, and it seemed for a time that Argentina might go the way of England, and become a motor racing backwater. Some impromptu races were still held, but they frequently ended at the local police station. Motor sport finally got under way again in 1913—not before an event of great significance to the future had occurred. On 24 June 1911 in Balcarce, Buenos Aires province (then a small town—now a flourishing small city), near Mar del Plata, a child named Juan Manuel Fangio was born.

The next *Gran Premio* was held in March 1914, over a shortened route, from Buenos Aires to Rosario and back, avoiding the bad roads farther on. This route was used five times in all, in 1914, 1916, 1921, 1922, and 1923, before the route was extended to Cordoba again. The 1914 race was won by a Belgian Springuel car, a make already taken over by Imperia, driven by Abel J. Poblet. Second was an American Case, made by an American manufacturer of agricultural machinery, driven by Santiago Turina, and third an Imperia driven by Isidro Pastor. Poblet's winning average, 32.27 mph (52 km/hr), was over twice Cassoulet's speed of four years before.

The 1916 *Gran Premio*—Argentina stayed neutral throughout the First World War—was again won outright by a European car, Manuel Diez's Mors, but the individual stages, from Moron on the outskirts of Buenos Aires to Rosario, and from Rosario to Moron, were both won by American cars: the outward run by Gordon Brown's Ford; the homeward run by William Paul Rhoads's Studebaker. Rhoads, an American who had the backing of the local Studebaker representative, went on to support racing with spectacular success in the 'twenties, winning four successive *Grandes Premios* during 1922–5. Rhoads was second in the 1916 race; third was Juan Cassoulet's brother Eugenio on an Overland, another make that would have a long history in Argentina. The I K A Torino, one of the most successful cars in Argentine racing in recent years, was an offspring of Henry Kaiser's Willys-Overland empire.

By 1918 motor racing was well established in Argentina, with seven events held that year, two of them on a big 25-mile (40-km) circuit at Moron. A race on the Belgrano horse track was won by Mariano de la Fuente (Ford), the man who was to win the next *Gran Premio*, the 1921 event, for Packard. De la Fuente, who later became one of the pillars of the A C A, was one of the pioneers of the professionalism that developed in Argentine racing in the early-'twenties: the race cars, although based on production models, were completely rebuilt for racing, and fitted with lightweight two-seater bodies. De la Fuente even went to the trouble of carrying unditching gear on board, and of strapping spare parts to the under-floor of his cars.

91. Domingo Bucci, 1926. The car is a Hudson, a typical conversion
from an American touring car of the period

Many of the drivers were still wealthy amateurs, who sometimes spent vast sums of money on their hobby. Among them was Martin 'Macoco' de Alzaga Unzué, second in the 1921 *Gran Premio* in a Hudson, who ventured abroad to Europe and to Indianapolis. But the biggest spender of all was John 'Juan' Malcolm, the son of a fabulously rich Anglo–Argentine landowning family, who first appeared in 1922, winning a five-lap race at the Moron circuit at the end of the season. He never won the *Gran Premio*, although he was fourth in 1923 and fifth in 1925, but he had more success in circuit races, often driving the best racing machinery that money could buy. There is no exact record of what cars Juan Malcolm owned, partly because his own collection was destroyed in a warehouse fire in 1946, and partly because of his endearing habit of giving away cars to his riding mechanics. But he did own and race, apart from Hudson and Chandler stock cars, both V 12 and straight-eight Delages, and various Alfa Romeos and Maseratis. He claimed that he once bought three Grand Prix Maseratis at once from the factory, but that may have been an old man's exaggeration. He died in 1972, run over by a passing car as he changed a wheel while on a holiday trip.

Not all drivers were rich: Domingo Bucci was born of Italian parents in San Carlos Centro, Santa Fe province, in 1894. At the age of seven he was helping his father maintain a threshing machine, and in his early teens he was apprenticed to the engineering trade. For boys like him there was no easy road to success, but they had the singlemindedness and determination that the privileged seldom have. There is a legend that 'Mingo' Bucci's co-driver always carried a pistol to shoot at drivers who didn't move over quickly enough. Bucci first got in the record books in 1921, when he won a 200-mile (320-km) road race out of San Francisco in Cordoba province. He drove a Case, but later turned to Hudson, and for them won the 1928 *Gran Premio*. On that memorable day he crossed the finish line at Moron flanked by two other Hudsons: the Hudson importer didn't want the crowd to hear the metallic rumble coming from Bucci's engine—two bearings had gone.

In the 'twenties motor racing began to generate enormous popular enthusiasm in Argentina, an enthusiasm that survives to this day. This brought a keen interest from importers and dealers, who saw it as an ideal way to publicise their cars. Among the many importers to support racing in the 'twenties was Luis Angel Firpo, who had the Stutz concession. Firpo is far better known as a heavyweight boxer, the original Wild Bull of the Pampas, who knocked Jack Dempsey out of the ring in a title fight in New York, although Dempsey got back in to win on points. Among Firpo's drivers was Rufino Luro Cambaceres, who is better remembered as an aviator: he was one of Antoine Saint-Exupéry's colleagues in the early days of the mail flights to Patagonia, which Saint-Exupéry wrote about in *Night Flight*.

Every *Gran Premio* in the 'twenties was won by an American car: Studebaker won four times (Antonio Ovides 1922, William Burke 1923, Mariano de la Fuente 1924, Angel Marelli 1925); Hudson three times (Tomas Roata 1926, Mingo Bucci 1928, Raul Riganti 1929); Packard once (Mariano de la Fuente 1921); Hupmobile once (Juan A. Gaudino 1927); and Chrysler once (Juan A. Gaudino 1930). The only time European cars got among the leaders was in 1925, when Ernesto Zanardi was third in an Alfa Romeo, behind the Studebakers of Angel Marelli and Paris Giannini, and ahead of Cambaceres's Stutz, and in 1928, when Carlos Zatuszek was third in a Mercedes-Benz SS.

Karel Zatuszek was born in Austro–Hungarian Poland in 1897, and emigrated to Argentina after the First World War, soon becoming known as 'Carlos'. He began racing in 1927, when almost thirty, and his very successful racing career lasted for ten years. He always raced 7-litre Mercedes sports cars—he owned probably three of them—and modified them extensively to stand up to the rugged Argentine conditions. One he even converted to front-wheel-drive for a time, but it wasn't a success. He was killed in a crash in 1937.

Most of Zatuszek's successes came in track races, where Mercedes power was an obvious advantage, and it is often said that he wasn't an especially good driver. But almost none of the circuits in use in Argentina at the time could really be called drivers' circuits. Zatuszek excelled on tracks that were generally not even ovals, but just two parallel straights gouged out of the earth, sometimes with farm machinery, with tight corners at each end—similar to the beach tracks that have at times been popular in many parts of the world. The *Gran Premio* itself was run over mainly straight roads across the *pampas*, where cornering was of little

92. One of the very successful racing Plymouths of the early
    'thirties

importance. What was important was dealing with widely varying road conditions.
If it rained there was mud and pools of water, and when this dried it left a bumpy,
rutted road that could destroy a car in a few miles. If long months of the right
weather had left the roads perfect, high speeds were possible, which demanded
exceptional courage: on a dirt road on primitive suspension and narrow tyres
sudden braking is impossible.

The fastest race of the 'twenties was in 1929, when ex-motorcyclist Raul Riganti
(Hudson) cut almost an hour and a half off Mingo Bucci's winning time of the year
before, making the trip from Moran to Cordoba and back in 14 hrs 13 min.
43.4 sec., an average of 65.36 mph (105.42 km/hr). When Juan Antonio Gaudino,
another ex-motorcyclist, won a year later there was rain, and the journey to
Cordoba and back took four hours longer, dropping the winning average to
51.1 mph (82.426 km/hr). That year, 1930, was also the first time that the *Gran
Premio* was run as a two-stage event: before that, in 1927–9, it was a three-stage
race, with a stop at Rosario on the outward journey, and in 1924–6 there were stops
at Rosario on both outward and homeward legs. These overnight stops had a big
influence on the character of Argentine road racing. Extensive rebuilding between
stages became normal—in time even crankshafts and gearboxes were changed
regularly.

In 1931 Carlos Zatuszek scored his one win in the *Gran Premio*, and in 1932
it was the turn of Ernesto H. Blanco, his arch-rival in track events, who drove
a Reo. Blanco, yet another ex-motorcycle racer, was a cool, precise driver, who
on one occasion made the mistake of acting as riding mechanic for his friend
Raul Riganti, who was fiery and impetuous. Blanco knew the road well, and gave
Riganti constant advice on where the bad corners were and where to slow down.

93. Ernesto Blanco with his Reo, 1926

Riganti soon got irritated with this negative advice—pace-notes had not yet been invented—and called Blanco a coward. Blanco responded by keeping his mouth shut as they approached an enormous pot-hole at full speed. The car flew off the road backwards, and when it finally stopped Riganti and Blanco began to scream recriminations at each other.

In 1933 came the first radical change in the history of the *Gran Premio*. Cordoba was forgotten, and the route was run south-west from the Buenos Aires suburb of Florencio Varela to Bahia Blanca in southern Buenos Aires. It was slightly longer than the old route: 1,024 miles (1,650 km). The outward stage was won by Ernesto Blanco (Reo), and twenty of the twenty-eight starters reached Bahia Blanca. But on the homeward stage heavy rain began to fall, and one by one cars began to get bogged down and completely stuck.

At the finishing line in Buenos Aires officials saw the hour set for the last classified finisher to arrive, 10 p.m., pass with no cars in sight. Communications were poor, and nobody knew what could have happened to them. They extended the deadline to midnight, and with only thirteen minutes to spare a mud-covered Ford Model A appeared out of the darkness. The sole finisher and undisputed winner was Roberto Lozano, a relative newcomer to racing. It is sometimes said that he was a complete novice, but in fact he was good enough to finish third in the first stage, and the year

94. The death of Domingo Bucci, Arrecifes, March 1933

before he had won a race at Lincoln, a small town in Buenos Aires province west of the capital.

Overall, 1933 was a bad year. A month after the farcical *Gran Premio*, at the Arrecifes event on 5 March, Mingo Bucci was critically injured in a crash, and died two days later. This led to a ban on racing in Buenos Aires province in 1934, forcing the *Gran Premio* to move north into the Chaco, where it was run over almost dead-straight roads from Santa Fé to Resistencia and back. Power was the critical factor, and it was a big Mercedes-Benz driven by Chilean Emilio Karstulovic that won, at 70.84 mph (114.27 km/hr), beating Ricardo Caron (Fiat) and Blanco in his trusty Reo.

It is ironic that Karstulovic's first and only win in the *Gran Premio* should have been in a high-speed event like this: he had made his name over far more rugged terrain. Born in Antofagasta in 1895, the lanky and easy-going 'Kartulo' began his motoring exploits at the age of seventeen, when he drove a car up the difficult San Cristobal peak in Chile. Near-impassable roads had an irresistible attraction to him: in 1926 he drove a Renault over the southern Andes using a pass normally reserved for goats. He also liked long distances: in 1927 he drove from Jujuy through Buenos Aires to the Straits of Magellan in only three stages—a distance of about three thousand miles. And in this run he was prophetic.

TURISMO
DE CARRETERA

1935–49

The great romantic age of South American road racing began on 14 March 1935, with the running of the *Gran Premio Internacional*, an event of 2,733.6 miles (4,409 km)—treble the length of any earlier *Gran Premio*—over every possible terrain from Buenos Aires to Santiago de Chile and back (see Map 9). Officially it was a rally, since there were still restrictions on open-road races in Argentina, but all the leading racing drivers competed—and most finished well down the field after losing points for exceeding the set average speeds.

The first stage, Buenos Aires to Mendoza, was won by Hector Suppici Sedes (Ford) from Uruguay; the second, across the Andes to Santiago, was won by Raul Riganti (Plymouth); the third and fourth, south to Temuco, then back across the Andes to Neuquen, were won by Juan Malcolm (De Soto)—and so on. But the final winner, with 203 points lost, was the unknown Arturo Kruuse (Plymouth), a Patagonian, who, like the Scandinavian rally drivers of recent years, had the background that produces natural rally drivers.

The following year, 1936, the rally restrictions were removed from the *Gran Premio*, and its length was increased by another fifty per cent, to 4,256 miles (6,865 km). The route was similar to that of 1935, but, after the return crossing of the Andes, a loop south to Comodoro Rivadavia, Argentina's Patagonian oil town, was added. This race proved the greatest victory of Raul Riganti's career: he averaged 45 mph (76.5 km/hr) for 89 hrs 47 min. 20 sec., bringing his Terraplane home two hours in front of the duelling Fords of Antonio Vazquez and Angel lo Valvo—yet without winning one of the nine individual stages. Fourth was Julio Perez (Chevrolet), cheered on by his 14-year-old nephew, José Froilan Gonzalez.

Third-finisher Angel lo Valvo went on to win the *Gran Premio* the following year, 1937, and won it again in 1939: a remarkable feat, since he seldom competed in any race but the *Gran Premio*. For him money was the sole point in racing, and the big race naturally paid the most. Not that this can be compared with a novice jumping straight into a modern racing car and winning: the cars used in the *turismo de carretera* (highway touring) races of the mid-'thirties were more or less standard American sedans of the period, with 3.5-litre engines and top speeds of about 80 mph (130 km/hr). Speed equipment to increase engine power did not appear until the end of the 'thirties—until then, the cars were simply stripped where

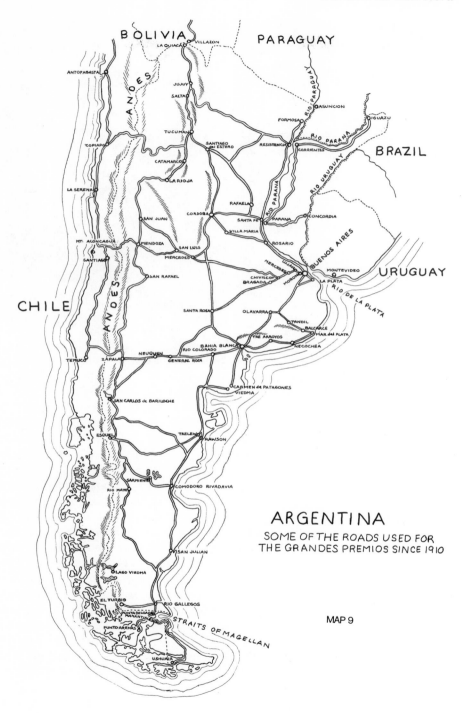

ARGENTINA

SOME OF THE ROADS USED FOR
THE GRANDES PREMIOS SINCE 1910

MAP 9

95. Maintenance during a *Gran Premio*. The changing of major components—engines, gearboxes, rear-axles—was common in the long races, and this work became a highly developed art. Juan Galvez once changed all pistons and con-rods in a Ford engine in forty-five minutes

possible to reduce weight, and strengthened where necessary to stop them being shaken to pieces.

The 1937 event that lo Valvo won was not an *internacional*: the route stayed inside Argentina, although it was just as long as the 1936 race. The enthusiasm generated by the *Gran Premio* was now immense, and in 1938 two such races were held: the regular *Gran Premio* in the north, and a *Gran Premio del Sur Argentino*—a southern Argentine Grand Prix. The southern race, which went all the way south to Rio Gallegos, on the same latitude as the Falkland Islands, was won by Hector Suppici Sedes (Ford)—local boy Arturo Kruuse could only manage third—and the northern race was won by hard-charging Ricardo Risatti, who treated this 4,582 mile (7,390 km) race as though it were a sprint. But he did have a special incentive: his wife was critically ill, and Risatti, a devout Catholic, believed that only a pilgrimage to Lourdes could save her. When he passed his home in southern Cordoba province during the race he had time to rush inside and tell his wife he was leading, and would soon have the prize money to take her to Europe. But it was

96. A *Turismo de Carretera* coupé crashes at Santa Fé

97. Juan Galvez. Photo taken at the Buenos Aires autodrome, 1947

found that she was too sick to move, and she died soon afterwards. Risatti himself was killed racing after the war. Their son, Jesus Risatti, raced successfully in the 'sixties.

Among the also-rans in the 1938 northern *Gran Premio* was 26-year-old Oscar Alfredo Galvez. Before the year was out he would be joined as co-driver by his brother Juan, two years younger. A year after Oscar's début, another young man would make his *Gran Premio* début, a 28-year-old named Juan Manuel Fangio. The day of the titans had dawned.

Los Galvez came from Buenos Aires, where their father owned a small garage. They grew up surrounded by engines, and started working for their father at an early age. Fangio's father in Balcarce was a house painter, but Juan went to work in a garage at the age of ten, doing menial jobs, passing spanners to the adult mechanics. His first experience of driving was on a wooden cart powered by an ancient Evans motorcycle engine. The apprentices at the garage took turns every week to drive the cart, loaded with junk, to the dump outside the town. The Galvez brothers got off to a grander start: they had an old Model T Ford when Oscar was only sixteen. When Fangio was sixteen he ran away to Mar del Plata with two friends, looking for work and adventure. Fangio Senior found them five days later, and Juan returned, without much reluctance, to Balcarce and his beloved engines. With help from his brothers and friends he built a workshop in the courtyard of their house. He was now a proper mechanic, and soon found plenty of work to do, often out on farms under the blazing sun, where he sipped *maté* to quench his thirst as he struggled to coax a tractor or a threshing machine back into life.

Fangio's first experience of racing came early, in 1928, when he was seventeen and rode as riding mechanic for a Señor Ayerza in a minor road race. But soon afterwards he fell seriously ill with pneumonia, and then, after a lengthy recovery, came his military service. It would be six years before he would again take part in a race.

By then he had his own garage business, in partnership with his lifelong friend José Duffard. The business went well, although still not well enough for a working-class boy like Juan to buy his own car. But in 1934 he managed to borrow a Ford and enter it in a minor road race. A connecting rod broke, and Juan had to repair the car for nothing to placate the furious owner. It was not until 1936 that Fangio saved enough money to buy his own Model A. With the help of friends he converted it into a racing two-seater in the style of the 'twenties—every modification being celebrated with accordion music and huge glasses of *maté*, if the English edition of Fangio's autobiography is to be believed—and turned up with it at his first race in December 1936. But he arrived late after staying up all night rebuilding the ignition system, and was black-flagged for starting late.

The Model A was never raced again. Instead, Juan and his younger brother Reuben built another Ford using a Model T chassis and a V8 engine. Fifteen months later, in March 1938, he finished a brilliant third in his heat for the Neco-chea circuit race, and went on to finish seventh in the final. At last he was getting somewhere. In September 1938 he gained his first experience of cross-country road racing, as co-driver to Finochietti in the *Gran Premio de la Republica*: they finished seventh. But the following month he suffered a serious emotional set-back when he competed in the disastrous race over the eight-mile circuit at Tres Arroyos ('Three Creeks'), a race in which five men were killed.

So, just as the Galvez brothers were establishing themselves in racing, after long years of clandestine drag races, it looked as though Fangio's racing career was finished. But Juan's spirits slowly revived, especially when his friends in Balcarce started a subscription to buy him a road-racing coupé. Despite his initial scepticism, the fund began to grow: the wealthy might give 500 pesos; a child one peso; and two benefits were held at the local movie theatre. Meanwhile he had a last race in the V8 Special, finishing eighth at La Plata, and then acquired an old Chevrolet coupé—the fund was not yet large enough to pay for a new Ford—to make his *Gran Premio* début in October 1939. He had missed the southern *Gran Premio* in March, won by lo Valvo, but now at last he was entering the big time. In five years of racing he had started in only six races, as either driver or co-driver. Today a novice racing driver would expect to gain the same experience in six weeks.

98. Juan Manuel Fangio, 1938, in his home-built Ford Special.
Chassis is Model T; the engine a V8

At the end of the first stage, 665 miles (1,074 km) Buenos Aires–Cordoba–Santa Fé, Fangio was eighth, despite a long stop at Pergamino, an hour and a half after the start, to change a broken con-rod. The engine was losing oil, so Fangio and his co-driver, Hector Tieri, fitted a length of rubber hose into the oil filler and led it back into the cockpit, enabling Tieri to pour oil into the engine while on the move, and to blow down the hose to increase oil circulation—at the price of smoke and poisonous oil fumes blowing back into the cockpit.

The competitors were shipped across the Paraná River to the town of Paraná, from where the second stage crossed Entre Rios province to Concordia on the Uruguay border. It proved a triumph for Oscar Galvez, who moved to the front of the field in heavy rain, while the near-asphyxiated Fangio dropped back to seventeenth. And that proved to be the end of the race, for the third stage was completely washed out—in 1939 there was not a single paved road in the whole of the province. Oscar Galvez (Ford) was declared the winner, with Tadeo Taddia (Chevrolet) in second place.

The race was restarted a week later from Cordoba as the *Gran Premio Extraordinario*. Fangio, with little money and no help from General Motors, had trouble preparing his Chevrolet for the race, but he found a friendly garage in Cordoba where he got all the help he needed—an apprentice even went out and stole some racing oil for him. On the first stage, Cordoba–Santiago del Estero, Fangio finished fifth, ahead of all the other Chevrolets. General Motors suddenly became very friendly, and agreed to pay all his bills. Fangio continued to lead the Chevrolets, and on the fourth stage, Catamarca–San Juan, he defeated all the Fords as well to win outright. For the first time in his life he saw his name in headlines. But his fame was short-lived. On the next stage, to San Luis, he went too fast into a corner and rolled the car over. It had to be towed into San Luis—and the newspapers that had hailed him twenty-four hours before were silent. He had almost decided to retire from the race when he ran into two friends from Balcarce. They soon cheered him up, and helped him and Tieri to repair the car.

The final winner of the 2,746 mile (4,430 km) *Gran Premio Extraordinario* was Oscar Galvez (Ford), averaging 61.4 mph (99 km/hr). Second was Daniel Musso (Ford), followed by Rosendo Hernandez (Ford) and Pablo Mesples (Ford). Fangio was fifth, the first Chevrolet to finish, two and a half hours behind the Galvez brothers.

So, in only his second season of serious racing, Oscar Galvez had become the man to beat. It was not only Oscar's driving ability: *Los Galvez* were already setting new standards in the tuning and preparation of their cars, and in the organisation of their team. Their engines were the most powerful—after the war they were the first to see that a long-stroke Mercury crankshaft could be installed in the Ford engine, increasing capacity from 3.6 to 4 litres—and they were the first to fit oversized radiators to make sure they stayed powerful and reliable. Their support crew, who were the first to use an intelligence system to keep their drivers informed on the state of the race, drove Fords identical to the race cars, so that a supply of run-in spares was always available.

They didn't ignore safety precautions: after tumbling over a cliff during a race in 1940—Oscar was seriously injured, and earned the name *Aguilucho* (Little Eagle)—they were the first to install roll-over bars and to use crash helmets. But when they felt it necessary they could ignore safety precautions: to save time they evolved the hair-raising technique of taking in five-gallon petrol cans through the window and emptying them into the tank through a filler inside the car, while the car was moving. After this strenuous exercise they could then cool off by sipping water through a tube from a vacuum flask installed behind the seats. Strangely, one aid that *Los Galvez* never used was pace-notes—they preferred to rely upon experience and initiative.

99. Fangio (Chevrolet) during the *Gran Premio Internacional del Norte*, 1940, his first victory

The third great encounter between Oscar Galvez and Juan Manuel Fangio came in September 1940, in the *Gran Premio Internacional del Norte*, a 5,856-mile (9,445-km) race from Buenos Aires to Lima and back. Now Fangio had his new car: not a Ford, as planned, but a Chevrolet, simply because the Balcarce Ford agent did not have a suitable car available, but the GM agent did. The Chevrolet was a good car, as Fangio proved as he left the pre-dawn start in Buenos Aires, with its floodlighting, cheering crowds, flags and banners, and took an immediate lead. As dawn broke over Cordoba he fought off a fierce challenge from Oscar Galvez, who loomed up in his mirrors, and went on to arrive in Tucuman first and win the stage.

North into the mountains, on to the high plateau of the Bolivian *Altiplano*, through Potosi, from where the Spanish Empire once mined fabulous riches in silver, the Galvez class began to show, and Oscar, brother Juan beside him, took the lead—until they were delayed by engine trouble short of La Paz. Fangio re-took the lead. La Paz, and finally Lima, a beautiful city that was for drivers and crews only dimly-lit garages and oil-stained floors. Soon after Lima the Galvez Ford stopped for good—leaving Fangio with the job of nursing his Chevrolet, now comfortably in the lead, the 2,000 miles or more back to Buenos Aires. He was drawn into a dangerous duel with Domingo Marimon (Ford), the Cordoba province undertaker, whose son Onfre was to race in Europe in the early-'fifties, and beat him to win the La Paz–Potosi stage, but then he wisely eased up, finishing ninth, seventh, and fifth in the final three stages. He won by over an hour.

Those thirteen days of racing proved beyond dispute that Fangio was a driver of the very highest class. Millions of Argentinians adopted him and became *Fangistas*, implacable enemies of the millions of others who were already *Galvistas*. In the years ahead the rivalry between the two groups of fans was even to lead to violence. But Fangio and *Los Galvez* always remained the most friendly of rivals.

After averaging 53.5 mph (86.18 km/hr) for 109 hrs 36 min. 16.8 sec.—over four and a half days of speed—Fangio drove his race car home to Balcarce, where he was greeted by crowds lining the streets, little girls giving him flowers, endless handshakes that made his hand throb, endless slaps on the back that made him feel like a punchbag, and a civic reception from the mayor, who added his name to the Balcarce Roll of Honour.

Fangio was national champion in 1940, and again in 1941, when racing continued, despite the war and the resulting shortages, although there was no *Gran Premio* that year. There would not have been one in 1942, either, if it had not been for a group of citizens in Esquel, a town in the foothills of the Patagonian Andes, in Argentina but barely fifty miles from the Pacific, who organised a southern *Gran Premio* without the sanction of the ACA. The race started at Mercedes, in Buenos Aires province, an industrial town about sixty miles from the capital, went right south to Punta Arenas on the Straits of Magellan, the most southerly city in the world, then returned north to Bahia Blanca—a total distance of 4,459 miles (7,192 km). All the top drivers entered. It was a gruelling race: both Fangio and Oscar Galvez were slowed by engine trouble, finally finishing tenth and fifth respectively. The winner, scoring the only major victory of his career, was Esteban Fernandino (Ford), from wealthy young Ricardo Harriague (Ford) and the ever-reliable Daniel Musso (Ford). Musso had finished second in the two previous *Grandes Premios*, and was to go on showing a remarkable ability to finish consistently among the leaders, although he was never to win a *Gran Premio*. In nine straight races, from 1939 through until 1951, he was in the first five on seven occasions, scoring two seconds, two thirds, and three fifths.

At the end of 1942 Argentine motor racing finally stopped, except for some midget car events in small stadiums, which kept some drivers happy during the bleak

100. Daniel Musso, Mar del Plata, 1942

101. Angel lo Valvo (Ford) in the 1947 *Mil Millas Argentinas*,
Buenos Aires

war years. Others turned to power-boat racing. Fangio stayed at home and concentrated on rebuilding his faithful Chevrolet coupé and building a new Chevrolet-based single-seater for circuit racing. It was not easy, with the American-owned car factories of Buenos Aires shut down and no spares being manufactured, but faithful friends would often bring him any parts they could find. To keep in practice he would drive for hundreds of miles across Argentina. Stopping in small towns he would be recognised by racing enthusiasts, and would spend many happy hours sipping *maté* or coffee and talking about racing. When racing began again early in 1947, with Argentina under the régime of General Perón, Fangio was thirty-five years old.

The big road races began again in November 1947, with the *Gran Premio Inter-nacional*, a trans-Andes race similar to the 1935 and 1936 races. Chevrolet were now more active in racing, and Fangio was no longer alone against the Fords. Before the start he was offered a new camshaft for his car, but, with no time to test it, he gave it to his friend Domingo Marimon, who promptly won the first stage, 897 miles (1,446 km) from Buenos Aires to Santiago de Chile. Fangio won the

102. Fangio in the 1947 *Gran Premio Internacional*

second stage, Santiago to La Serena, north on the Pacific coast, but then the Fords began to move into the picture, Esteban Fernandino winning the third stage, to Copiapó. Then came the most difficult section of all: the return crossing of the Andes by the near-15,000 feet San Francisco Pass. It was the critical stage of the race, and Fangio took an immediate lead on the dark climb up the pass—until, near the top, he slid into a snowdrift. Clouds of steam rose as the snow melted under the engine's heat, but the car was undamaged. Fangio and his mechanic waved down Oscar Galvez, who didn't hesitate to stop and try to help pull the car back on to the road. Other rivals stopped, including Esteban Fernandino and Juan Galvez—now a driver in his own right—but still the Chevrolet stayed stuck. As other drivers came through without stopping, the helpers were forced to leave. Oscar Galvez won the stage, Copiapó to Tucuman, and Fangio finally managed to jack his car back on to the road and finish tenth, an hour behind.

The final overall winner was Oscar Galvez, from Eusebio Marcilla (Chevrolet). Fangio was sixth. One stage, Tucuman–Resistencia, was won by an ex-RAF pilot, George 'Jorge' Daly (Dodge), who alternated his race driving with taking photographs by the roadside. Years later, in 1958, he was to drive a Volkswagen in the race for standard production cars run concurrently with the T C *Gran Premio*, and, on a muddy Catamarca–San Juan stage, beat all the T C cars, led by Oscar Galvez. After retiring he devoted himself to importing whisky. He died in Buenos Aires in 1971.

Circuit racing was becoming increasingly important in Argentina, a trend that has continued to the present day. Fangio had his Chevrolet-based single-seater, then a Maserati supplied by the A C A. *Los Galvez* had Alfa Romeos. Among the most successful locally-built cars was the Cadillac special of Clemar Bucci, the son of the late Domingo Bucci. Clemar Bucci went to Europe in 1948, along with Pascual Puopolo, Oscar Galvez, and Juan Manuel Fangio. Of these, of course, only Fangio persisted in Europe and became an established Grand Prix driver. But the 1948 trip was a disappointment even for him.

The highlight of 1948 came in October and November, with the running of one of the great motor races of all time: the *Gran Premio de la America del Sur*—the Grand Prix of South America—known in Argentina simply as *La Caracas*. It was not the longest race ever held in South America—although many books will tell you that it was—but for sheer grandeur it surpassed all others. It started in Buenos Aires, the capital of Argentina, and then proceeded north through the capitals of Bolivia (La Paz), Peru (Lima), Ecuador (Quito), Colombia (Bogota), to the finish at Caracas, the capital of Venezuela—a distance of 5,937 miles (9,576 km).

Oscar Galvez won the first stage, a massive 1,049 miles (1,693 km) from Buenos Aires to Salta—the first 1,000-mile stage ever in an Argentine road race—with Fangio floundering in seventy-ninth place with a multitude of mechanical problems. This not only meant he had lost a lot of time, but that he had to start the second stage in seventy-ninth position, with the prospect of having to pass seventy-odd cars before he was among the leaders. And this is what he did, arriving at La Quiaca on the Argentine–Bolivia border in fourth position, although still well down the field on general classification.

But Fangio's mechanical problems continued—he would have had to retire had not a complete stranger offered him the back-axle out of his own Chevrolet—while Oscar Galvez won the first three stages, and brother Juan the fourth, making it a solid *Los Galvez* one-two by La Paz. Fangio fought back and took the fifth stage, La Paz–Arequipa, the only Chevrolet driver to win a stage in the entire race, but on the sixth stage, a hundred kilometres before Lima, a back wheel fell off and he limped in many miles behind.

In Lima there was supposed to be a complete day's break, but a revolution caused the organisers to send the drivers on their way without even a complete night's sleep. Fangio left in twenty-fifth position, but quickly forced his way to the front. By his own account he even shook off Oscar Galvez, and was alone on the road near Trujillo when he misjudged a corner and crashed.

The Chevrolet rolled repeatedly and finally stopped with only Fangio in the car. His co-driver and friend, Daniel Urrutia, had been flung out, and lay in a pool of blood. Fellow-Chevrolet driver Eusebio Marcilla stopped immediately and rushed

103. Juan Galvez (Ford) is escorted to the Automovil Club
Argentino after winning the 1951 *Gran Premio*

the dazed Fangio and the unconscious Urrutia to the nearest hospital. Urrutia was dead on arrival, but the truth was kept from Fangio. He only learned of his friend's death the next day, when a garage pump attendant offered his condolences.

The crash causes controversy in Argentina to this day. It is said by some that Fangio was dicing with Oscar Galvez at the time, and that the two cars touched. *Fangistas* were quick to call Galvez a murderer, and the argument dragged on for years, in the way that football fans will go on disputing a referee's decision until the players concerned are fat and middle-aged.

Fangio's crash certainly overshadowed the end of Arturo Kruuse's career: he crashed heavily in the same stage and never raced again.

Meanwhile the Galvez brothers stormed ahead, leading comfortably—until the very last stage, from Valera to Caracas. Juan Galvez, intent on winning the bonus money for fastest time on this stage, lost control of his Ford about 150 miles from the finish and slid into a deep ditch. Brother Oscar arrived and naturally tried to tow Juan's car back on to the road. He not only failed but also immobilised his own car by burning out the clutch. *Los Galvez*, the conquerors, were stuck. Oscar, an excitable man as racing drivers go, began screaming for help, and it came in the form of a kind soul who towed the crippled Ford into Caracas. Oscar was cool enough to coast the last kilometre alone, but he was still disqualified for receiving outside assistance.

One man who knew nothing of this was Domingo Marimon (Chevrolet), who arrived in Caracas pleased with what he thought was third place. He had settled down in the automobile club and lit up a cheroot when a man rushed in to tell him that he had just won the greatest race of all time. His response, in Argentine Spanish, was 'Don't be so bloody stupid'.

But he had, averaging 50 mph (80.73 km/hr) for 118 hrs 37 min. 18 sec. Second was Eusebio Marcilla, only twelve and a half minutes behind—a certain winner had he not stopped to help Fangio. A very deflated Juan Galvez was third, after losing four hours in that ditch.

Domingo Marimon was certainly one of the most colourful characters in motor racing, and surely the only one who ever made money out of smuggling corpses. By profession he was, and is, an undertaker in the tourist town of Cosquín, near Cordoba. Many old people retire there, and when they die they frequently become Domingo's customers. At one time there was a heavy tax on taking bodies across a state line in Argentina, so if anybody had to be buried outside Cordoba province Domingo used the technique of dressing his corpses in street clothes and propping them up in his car as though they were just asleep. He carried dozens of corpses across state lines in this way before the police found out.

A few weeks after *La Caracas* Oscar Galvez had a chance to get his revenge: a race, officially the second stage of the *Gran Premio de la America del Sur*, but arousing little public enthusiasm, was run from Lima south to Santiago de Chile, then across the Andes to Buenos Aires. Oscar led from start to finish, beating Rosendo Hernandez (Chevrolet). Unseasonal snow meant that the cars had to cross the Andes by train, thus removing the most interesting section of the route.

The 1949 *Gran Premio de la Republica* was even longer than *La Caracas* of the year before. At 6,842 miles (11,035 km) it was second only to the 1908 New York–Paris race in length—in effect it was the southern and northern *Grandes Premios* of 1938 and 1939 combined into one race, with Rio Gallegos being reached in the south, and Jujuy in the north. But after the drama of *La Caracas* it was another anti-climax. Juan Galvez led from start to finish, winning five out of twelve stages. Fangio won three stages, and finished a rather dispirited second, two hours behind —and immediately sold his beloved old Chevrolet to an amateur. The death of Daniel Urrutia had soured him to road racing; he had started the 1949 race against the advice of his Italian mechanic, Amedo Bignami, who knew that driving a Chevrolet on dirt was a totally different art from driving a Grand Prix car on a track; so he decided, sadly, to turn his back on the races that had made him famous. He had met *Los Galvez* seventeen times in combat, and had won eight to their five. He was the greatest of the great, and now had new fields to conquer.

104. The Emiliozzi brothers, Dante and Torcuato, in their hand-
built Ford coupé

After Fangio

While Fangio performed his great feats in Europe, the 'fifties in Argentina became
the decade of *Los Galvez*. Between 1947 and 1961—fifteen seasons—they were
beaten only once in the national *turismo de carretera* championship—by Rodolfo
Alzaga, nephew of 'Mococo' Alzaga Unzue of the 'twenties, in 1959—and beaten
only five times in the *Gran Premio* itself.

Juan Galvez's first *Gran Premio*, in 1949, was the start of the first hat-trick in the
history of the race. He won again in 1950 and 1951, and when he was beaten in 1952
it was by exactly 31.2 seconds after more than 33 hours of racing; the winner was
fellow Ford driver Rosendo Hernandez. That year an attempt was made to slow
the TC down by limiting engines to one carburettor only, but it made little
difference, so all engine restrictions were removed again for 1953—a move that
pleased a very clever young man named Dante Emiliozzi, who had his own overhead valve conversion for the faithful old Ford flathead running that year.

The 1953 *Gran Premio* was the shortest since 1934: it shrank to a miserable
1,013.5 miles (1,633 km), run in two stages—Buenos Aires–Cordoba, and Cordoba–Buenos Aires, by slightly different routes. But this lowland route did result
in the fastest *Gran Premio* of them all: Dante Emiliozzi, crewed by his brother

105. *Turismo de Carretera* coupés in typical northern Argentina mountain scenery during the 'fifties

Torcuato, beat Juan Galvez by five minutes to win at 102.76 mph (165.57 km/hr). But *Los Galvez* bounced back to win again in 1954 (Oscar), 1956 (Juan), 1958 (Juan), and 1960 and 1961 (both Oscar). The saga of *Los Galvez*, begun in the 'thirties, finally ended in the 'sixties. Juan was killed in the first race of the 1963 season, at Olavarria, Buenos Aires province, while trying to catch Emiliozzi's faster car. He was forty-nine years old. Oscar, aged fifty-one, went on racing, but retired after a crash in 1964, and went on to manage the Ford team, with works and dealer support.

Things were now tougher for Ford. In 1956 the engines of TC cars were limited to 4 litres, giving 6-cylinder engines a better chance against the Ford V8s. Slowly, very slowly at first, Chevrolet began to break the Ford stranglehold. In 1962 Chevrolet sixes won six out of twenty-one TC races (not all of them road races); in 1963 they won five out of eighteen; and in 1964 they moved ahead, winning twelve to Ford's nine, with Dodge winning three. And all nine Ford wins were scored by Dante Emiliozzi, who was on his winning streak of four national championships: 1962–5. But, strangely, his 1953 win was his only one in the *Gran Premio*.

Marcos Ciani won the *Gran Premio* for Chevrolet as early as 1957, and Felix Peduzzi won it for them in 1962, Carlos Pairetti in 1963, and Juan Manuel Bordeu in 1964. And it was Bordeu who became the first Chevrolet driver to win the TC championship since Fangio in 1941. Appropriately, Bordeu came from Balcarce and received much help and encouragement from Fangio, although the old master could have seen little of himself in Bordeu, for the young man was from a wealthy, land-owning family. He began racing in 1954, and in 1959 and 1960 he raced Formula Junior single-seaters in Europe, and was often photographed with his mentor. There was talk of a new generation of Argentine Grand Prix drivers, to repeat the feats of Fangio, but it didn't work out that way—Bordeu did no racing in Europe after 1963. Instead, at the age of thirty, he beat Emiliozzi by five minutes to win the 1964 *Gran Premio*, and he finally won the championship in 1966.

All this time the rivalry between the Ford fans and the Chevrolet fans remained as intense as it had been in the days of the *Galvistas* and *Fangistas*. Fans at the roadside and trackside still came to blows if they heard an opinion they disagreed with expressed anywhere near them. And when Felix Peduzzi, a successful Chevrolet driver since the late-'forties, decided to switch to Ford in 1965, there was such an uproar—as if Pelé were joining Manchester United—that he gave in and stayed with Chevrolet.

But if the fanaticism remained the same, the cars were changing. In 1964 the former Ferrari Grand Prix driver José Froilan Gonzales—one of the rare Argentine drivers with almost no *turismo de carretera* experience—imported a Chevrolet II from the USA for Jorge Cupiero to drive. It was low and sleek beside the pre-war style coupés that were still dominating Argentine racing after thirty years, and the fans responded by throwing stones at it. But there was no stopping progress, and soon the tracks and roads were full of heavily-modified Falcons, Mustangs, Valiants, and *Chevytus*, with the odd coupé lingering on—Bordeu still raced one in 1968. By now the supply of 'thirties body shells had run out, so they were coachbuilt at vast expense.

This revolution in TC racing led for a time to the building of race cars that bore almost no relationship to the production original, but regulations were tightened in 1971 to make the cars basically stock, although with continuing freedom to modify engines. In the long run a bigger revolution was the appearance of the Torino in 1967.

The story of the Torino began, like so many others on the American continent, with one Henry J. Kaiser, born of poor German parents in Sprout Brook, New York, in 1882. He went to work at thirteen, and later built the highways of Cuba, the levees of the Mississippi, the Hoover Dam, parts of the San Francisco Bay Bridge, and the Liberty ships. After the Second World War he bought the largest aircraft factory in the world, the Ford plant at Willow Run, and set about making cars in it. They were a limited success, despite his purchase of Willys-Overland in 1953, and the production of cars, although not of the evergreen Jeep and its variants, ended after ten years, in 1956. But in the meantime he had started plants

106. Juan Manuel Bordeu, with co-driver Antonio Winter and the works Mercedes-Benz 300SE in which they finished fourth in the 1963 *Gran Premio Standard*, behind Böhringer, Glemser, and Ewy Rosqvist

107. Carlos Pairetti raced this Plymouth Barracuda with Chevrolet
engine. Regulations were later tightened to exclude imported
cars like the Barracuda

in Argentina and Brazil, where labour was cheap and the market less competitive.

In 1966 Kaiser's Argentina plant, I K A, began producing a licence-built development of the American Motors Rambler, which soon had a new body designed
by Pinin Farina and a 3.8-litre, 6-cylinder overhead camshaft engine from Willys.
In 1967 I K A was acquired by Renault, and went racing—and promptly scored a
one-two victory in the *Gran Premio*, Eduardo Copello leading home Mario Tar-
ducci. There was no race in 1968 and 1969, but when it was held again in 1970 Luis
di Palma won it for Torino, and Carlos Marincovich repeated the feat in 1971. The
Torino is the one Argentine car to have raced in Europe: in 1969 it came near
to winning the Nürburgring 84-hour event in Germany, a cross between a rally

108. Eduardo Copello (Torino) at Bragada, 1967

and a race, but sadly it never returned to Europe. Usually it was Europeans who invaded Argentina.

The perfect opportunity came in 1957, with the introduction of the *Gran Premio Standard*, a production car race run concurrently with the TC race. It was run on a class basis, giving small European cars a chance. No European drivers appeared until 1959, when Edgar Barth from Germany and Paul Frère from Belgium drove for NSU in the 750 cc class. Frère retired, and Barth was beaten by Juan Manuel Bordeu.

In 1960 the race was run independently from the TC *Gran Premio*, and as an international event. And it attracted an international rally driver of the very

109. Walter Schock (Mercedes-Benz 220 SE) winning the 1961
Gran Premio Standard

highest class, Gunnar Anderson from Sweden with a Volvo, who won the 2,864-mile (4,618.7-km) race comfortably, beating local driver Gaston Perkins (Alfa Romeo) by well over an hour. The following year, 1961, the locals were in even worse trouble; Mercedes-Benz entered a team of 220 SE cars, and Walter Schock from Germany won for them, with his team-mate Hans Herrmann just three minutes behind. The first local, veteran Oscar Cabelan (Alfa Romeo), was two and a half hours back.

To rub the point in, Mercedes-Benz returned in 1962 with their ace women rally crew, Ewy Rosqvist/Ursula Wirth, who set Latin American *machismo* on its ear by not only winning the race, but also all six stages in doing so—an unprecedented feat that will probably never be repeated. Mercedes-Benz won twice more, in 1963 and 1964, each time scoring a one-two-three with the same drivers in the same order: first, Eugen Bohringer, the tubby little Swabian who did not become a rally star until he was in his late-thirties; second, young Dieter Glemser; and, third, Ewy Rosqvist—or Baroness von Korff, as she became in 1964. Four

110. Eugen Böhringer and Ewy Rosqvist, Argentina, 1964

wins in four years for Mercedes-Benz; five wins in five years for European drivers; and the Argentinians were left in peace.

Peace, that is, until 1967, when Sobieslaw Zasada arrived from Poland with a Porsche 911. He had none of the Mercedes-Benz factory resources behind him, yet he still managed to win, beating the quickest Torino by a quarter of an hour.

For ten years the *Gran Premio Standard* was confined to the familiar road racing country of Buenos Aires, Cordoba, and the country to the north, but in 1969 it became the Grand Prix of Patagonia, sponsored, as it had been from the beginning, by the Argentine national oil company YPF—appropriately, since much of Argentina's oil comes from Patagonia. As in the unsanctioned 1942 *Gran Premio*, cars crossed into Chile to the most southerly city in the world, Punta Arenas. Strangely, only the 2-litre cars did this section: the bigger cars were ferried across the Straits of Magellan, and raced on through Argentine Tierra del Fuego to reach Ushuaia, the most southerly town in the world, overlooking the Beagle Channel. The honour of winning this Rio Gallegos–Ushuaia–Rio Gallegos stage went to Luis di Palma (Torino), but by the time the competitors had returned up the full length of Patagonia—shadowed, as always, by the aircraft of the broadcasting companies—to the finish at Santa Rosa, the winner was 'Larry' Rodriguez Larreta, yet another second-generation Argentine racing driver, from Cesar Malnatti and Carlos Ruesch, all three in Torinos.

But despite these rare races with an epic quality, road racing in general declined in the 'sixties. Starting in the late-'fifties, as traffic density increased, it became harder to close public roads for racing. More autodromes were built; road circuits got smaller and smaller. Not that the road racing enthusiast has much cause for complaint when he compares Argentina with other countries.

Take 1972, for example. The TC championship was decided over fifteen rounds that year: among these races were the thirteenth *Vuelta de Hughes*, run over four 88-mile (142.3-km) laps; the tenth *Vuelta de Salta* (five 74.4-mile/120-km laps); the eleventh *Vuelta de Cordoba* (eleven 29.5-mile/47.6-km laps of the Los Condores circuit); the twenty-third *Vuelta de Santa Fé* (four 88-mile/142.4-km laps); the third *Vuelta Ciudad de Chivilcoy* (four 80-mile/128.7-km laps); the second *Gran Premio de la Montana* (a four-stage Mickey Mouse road race in the rocky hills near Cordoba); and the forty-eighth *Gran Premio de Turismo de Carretera*, also rather Mickey Mouse compared with the days when it went to Lima or Caracas, but still a healthy 2,353.4 miles (3,792.4 km) over five stages—Rafaela–Santiago del Estero–Formosa–Salta–La Rioja–San Francisco.

The winner of the 1972 *Gran Premio* was the late Hector Luis Gradassi from Cordoba, a city still equally famous for *automovilismo* and radical politics. Driving his Ford Falcon, Gradassi won the championship as well, and other Ford drivers were second, third, and fifth. Juan Manuel Bordeu was fourth in a Dodge; Jorge Martinez Boero sixth in the first Chevrolet; and Juan Traverso eighth in the first Torino—once again Ford were on top.

These four makes—Ford, Chevrolet, Dodge, Torino—are the only ones to

111. Dieter Glemser (Mercedes-Benz 300SE) in the sub-Andean highlands on his way to second place in the 1963 *Gran Premio Standard*

112. Ewy Rosqvist/Ursula Wirth (Mercedes-Benz 220SE) winning the 1962 *Gran Premio Standard*

113. *Turismo de Carretera*, Oncativo, Cordoba, 1967

114. Hector Gradassi (Ford) at Capilla del Monte, Cordoba

contest TC racing, but almost equally popular now are the smaller, near-standard *turismo nacional* class cars. Carlos Reutemann, the best Argentine Grand Prix driver since Fangio, made his name in small Fiats (although in *turismo mejorada*— improved touring—rather than *turismo nacional*), and the T N class is also contested by Renault and Peugeot, who, like Fiat, have local factories. A leading T N

115. Juan Manuel Fangio in retirement

driver is Oscar 'Cacho' Fangio, the son of the great Juan Manuel. And many of the stars of T C racing compete in T N on special occasions, such as the annual T N *Gran Premio*, successor to the international race that Mercedes-Benz used to dominate, which is generally as long and tough as the T C *Gran Premio*.

INCAS AND OTHERS

Argentina, for all its problems, remains the dominant motor racing country of South America. So much so, in fact, that there is little incentive for the successful Argentinian driver to race in Europe or North America, for there are so many local races. Like the Galvez brothers, the majority of leading Argentinian drivers in recent years have stayed at home.

But what of racing—particularly road racing—in the rest of Latin America?

Brazil, of course, has produced Emerson Fittipaldi, and Fittipaldi competed in the last road race ever held in Brazil, in 1968, a flat-out blind along a stretch of motorway between Curitiba and São Mateus do Sul. He led easily in his Fitti-Porsche prototype until the engine failed. The rest of the field was a muddled collection of production cars and *carretera* specials. An Alfa Romeo GTA won.

Oil-rich Venezuela looks a likely candidate for healthy motor sport, but, apart from a brief period of international interest in the late-'fifties, little has been done. In 1958 Jean Behra from France won a *carretera* Grand Prix of Venezuela in a Ferrari 250 GT. Jo Bonnier, who kept a house in Caracas at the time, competed for the fun of it in a Volvo. But the course, in three stages, Caracas–Agaviva–Valencia–Caracas, was of only 469 miles (755 km), although mountainous.

A country with a surprisingly long motor racing history is Peru, which ran a *Gran Premio Nacional de la Carretera* as early as 1924. Argentine-organised races such as the Buenos Aires–Lima–Buenos Aires and *La Caracas* attracted interest and entries from Peru, but the only success went to the experienced Arnaldo Alvarado, who was fifth in the 1948 Lima–Santiago de Chile–Buenos Aires race driving a Ford. Alvarado is not only a racing driver, but a political figure as well, and at times emulates the late Errol Flynn in being followed around by a group of troubadours singing ballads in praise of his driving, wisdom, and *machismo*.

He probably holds the world longevity record for racing drivers: in 1936 he won a race from Pisco, on the Pacific coast, to Ayacucho, Pizzaro's colonial city, which lies in a valley at 9,500 feet (2,900 m), by what is alleged to have been a margin of six days; and he won the Peruvian *Gran Premio*—better known as the *Caminos del Incas*—as late as 1967, and was still going strong in the 'seventies, finishing fourth in 1971—with his grandson as co-driver—and fifth in 1972. His sons also race, but none has yet gained the fame of old Arnaldo, the *Rey de las Curvas*—the King of the Curves.

116. Recende Dos Santos (Mercedes-Benz 300 S L) winning the 1957
Caracas–Cumana–Caracas road race in Venezuela

To win the *Caminos del Incas* a driver does need a mastery of curves. There are tens of thousands of them on the 1,500-mile (2,500-km) course, many of them clinging to rocky crags at altitudes of up to 16,000 feet (4,000 m). Once when a car went over the edge it took three weeks to find the co-driver's body. An Indian had seen the crash, but, with the lethargy for which the descendants of the Incas are famous, had just shrugged and gone home, telling nobody. This lack of involvement does not extend to the towns: the local radio stations broadcast commentaries on every minute of the race—almost thirty hours in all.

The *Caminos del Incas* gained much publicity in the late-'sixties when the desperate Cuzco–Ayucucho–Huancayo section of the course was chosen to form

117. Teodoro Yangali, 'El Zorro' (Ford Mustang), in the 1970
Caminos del Incas

118. Venezuela, 1958. Jo Bonnier, who had a home in Caracas at
the time, with Jean Behra, who drove a Ferrari to victory in
the 1958 Venezuelan road race Grand Prix. Bonnier competed
in a Volvo

119. Dr Jorge Burgoa (Jaguar E-type) averaging over 60 mph to win the 1966 Bolivian *Gran Premio Nacional*, beating Willy Zalles's Ford Mustang by over an hour. The race had only twenty-one starters, and nine finishers. Dr Burgoa, sharing a BMW with two other Bolivians, finished thirteenth in the 1970 World Cup Rally

part of the 1970 World Cup Rally. Nominally the Peruvian event was now a rally, too, but nobody was fooled. Tony Fall was sent out from Britain with a works Ford Escort in 1969 to sample the high-altitude Inca roads under competition conditions, and he won the *Caminos del Incas* easily. Hannu Mikkola, the Finnish winner of the 1970 World Cup Rally, returned to Peru in 1970 to race in the Peruvian classic himself, but he retired a few miles after the start, leaving local driver Henry Bradley—another veteran of *La Caracas*—to win in an Escort entered by a local dealer. After 1970 Peruvian motor sport reverted to its closed world.

Almost every country in Latin America—except perhaps some of the smaller republics of Central America—has held some sort of road race at some time.

Mexico has held many events, apart from the *Panamericana*, but the only race that has attracted interest outside its borders is the Baja 1,000 off-the-road race, a car and motorcycle scramble down the peninsula of Baja (Lower) California. It is hardly an indigenous Mexican event: more of a tribal cult for the motorcycle and dune-buggy freaks of Los Angeles.

In the majority of Latin American countries anyone who wants to race seriously has got to emigrate: Emilio Karstulovic left Chile for Argentina; Hector Suppici Sedes crossed from Uruguay to race in Argentina. Argentina, in turn, exported some of its races: its *Gran Premio*, at various times, ran into Chile, Bolivia, Peru Ecuador, Colombia, and Venezuela. This has stopped now, although as recently as 1970 the *Gran Premio Standard* ran into some thinly populated parts of Bolivia and Paraguay. Sobieslaw Zasada competed, making his second attempt to win this race, this time in a BMW, but had to be content with second.

A curiosity in South America has been the state-sponsored racing drivers of Bolivia. When one of the minute *élite* of Bolivian racing drivers goes abroad to race—in the *Caminos del Incas* or the World Cup Rally—his car is painted to advertise one product: Bolivia. Who wants to buy Bolivia? One of these drivers, a Dutch-born refugee from the Second World War named Dieter Hubner, who imports tyres into Bolivia, gave up racing in 1970, very disenchanted, after a decade as a local idol. What was the point in driving a 500 bhp Ford Mustang around first-gear hairpin bends on mountain mule-tracks at altitudes higher than the peak of the Matterhorn? He may have asked, too, what was the point, in a country where the population is seventy per cent Indian and has little to do with any market economy, of racing against a few friends—twenty cars is a huge field in Bolivia—in a car the value of which would pay a peasant's wage for a hundred years?

A French mountaineer, the late Lionel Terray, had a simple phrase to describe his own kind: conquistadors of the useless. It is a phrase that perhaps cannot be applied to all racing drivers—some gain wealth and fame, and entertain millions—but among the few enthusiasts of Bolivia, driving along the dusty, desolate roads of the *Altiplano* in cars so priceless that they might as well have been beaten from solid silver, the phrase must seem very apt.

THE RALLY—
AND THE FUTURE

Has the road race any future? At first glance it would appear to have very little. The *Mille Miglia* and the *Targa Florio* have gone; the road races of Latin America are fading; only one world championship Grand Prix, that of Monaco, is held every year on a road circuit. It's too early to judge whether Long Beach will survive for long. The Montjuich circuit in Barcelona seems, after the crash in 1975 which killed four bystanders, to be finished. The fifty-year-old Spa-Francorchamps circuit in Belgium has not been used for Formula One since 1970: its survival is equally doubtful. Le Mans survives, but continues to be unpopular with many of the best drivers. Disenchantment with the old road circuits has gone just as far among motorcyclists: the Isle of Man Tourist Trophy circuit seems to have no future for world championship racing.

With perhaps a brighter future is the 5-mile (8-km) Charade circuit overlooking Clermont-Ferrand in central France: it was opened in 1958, completely against the spirit of the times, and is still used today.

But the truth is that there are still a number of very hairy road races in Europe— races that many enthusiasts are scarcely aware of. You won't find them listed in any calendar of races, because officially they're not races at all, but superior specimens of that most mystifying hybrid, the rally.

A race is a race is a race, but a rally can be almost anything. The word 'rally' most accurately suggests a regular gathering of enthusiasts, and many rallies have been just that—rallying has always been a more social sport than racing. Even international rallies have at times been very friendly, even uncompetitive, affairs. There was a Dutch driver who drove the same Ford V8 in the 1934 and 1947 *Coupe des Alpes*. Even into the early-'fifties one might see competitors using a stop to take photos of the mountain scenery, although rallying was by then starting to get tougher. As late as 1947 a British *Coupe des Alpes* competitor, who had finished sixth in the 2-litre class, complained in *Autocar* that he had worn out a set of tyres in only 2,000 miles. Today, in rallying as in racing, tyres are almost as expendable as petrol.

The development of the modern rally is long and complex. The first-ever

120. Rally or Race? Erik Carlsson (Saab) in the 1963 Monte Carlo Rally

motor competition, the 1894 Paris–Rouen trial, was a test of reliability, not speed, but has no obvious connection with the sport we know today as rallying—rather it is the father of all motor sport. The early inter-city races of Europe were closer to rallying: they had control points, and neutralised, non-racing sections through towns—the opposite of a rally such as the *Tour de France*, which has long sections covered at a low average speed broken up by short speed sections. The 1902 Paris–Vienna race had a neutral section right through Switzerland, where racing was forbidden; it also introduced motor sport to the mountains, by crossing the Arlberg Pass. That year also saw the start of the longest-surviving speed event of all, the Mont-Ventoux hillclimb in the South of France, an area that has always been important for road racing, both for the classic round-the-houses Grands Prix of Monaco and Pau, and for high-speed mountain rallies.

The sport of rallying is one year older than the *Targa Florio*: it began in 1905 with the Herkomer Trial in Germany, an event sponsored by a Bavarian-born professor, Hubert von Herkomer, who became a British subject. Reacting against the overwhelming professionalism of early motor sport, Professor Herkomer restricted his competition to amateur drivers only. The route was a 1,000-km tour of southern Germany, starting and finishing in Munich. There were two speed sections, a hillclimb on the Kesselberg and a race in Munich's Forstenrieder Park, and there was a beauty contest for the cars—a *concours d'élégance* of the sort that was very popular in rallying until well into the 'fifties, although there are no records from 1905 of anyone trimming his car seats with mink or chroming the undersides of his mudguards. A set time was allowed for repairs after each section, and anyone who overran these limits was awarded penalty points.

Of eighty-nine starters, twenty-six finished without loss of points, so in 1906 the Herkomer Trial was made tougher, with a longer route running from Munich through Linz to Vienna (where a hillclimb was held on the Semmering), then back to Munich via Innsbruck. Entries came from as far away as the USA.

With the 1906 Herkomer Trial the pattern for most future rallies was laid down: long distances, mountains, hillclimbs, races, *concours d'élégance*, discreet cheating (standard cars that weren't quite standard), and numerous and complicated regulations, many of them petty.

Which brings us back to where we started: a rally can be almost anything—and some of them try to be everything at once.

The most famous of all is the Monte Carlo, which started in 1911. At first it was simply a drive to Monte Carlo from various starting points around Europe. From 1925 a 50-mile (80-km) mountain trial was added to the end of the run as a final elimination test. A decade later this had become too simple, so a driving test was added to the end of the mountain trial. Later they introduced a race around the Monaco Grand Prix circuit. Hillclimbs were thrown in. Elaborate handicapping systems were tried. Elaborate handicapping systems were dropped.

The Monte Carlo, along with many other rallies, has suffered a constant crisis of identity. To the challenges of man against the road, man against machine, man against man, is added a new challenge—man against bureaucracy. Rallying is a uniquely twentieth-century sport, dependent for its very existence on time-clocks and paperwork and regulations. A Grand Prix could be run successfully without even a stopwatch present—anyone with eyes could see who won—but in rallying there can be no such escape.

But in the best rallies this complexity is largely a defence, a smokescreen—a way of hiding from the outside world the fact that these rallies are nothing less than legalised road races. The French and the Belgians are particular masters of this subterfuge—in Britain and Scandinavia, where laws are stricter, rallies are held far more on private roads.

Belgium has a long tradition of rallying, and of the *élite* group of rallies that are, or were, really thinly disguised road races, the best of all is generally considered to have been the pre-1965 *Marathon de la Route*, organised by the Royal Motor Union of Liège. It began in 1931 over a route Liège–Rome–Liège, and retained this basic route until 1960, after which it became known as the Liège–Sofia–Liège—the roads of western Europe were becoming too crowded for such a high-speed event. The formula for the *Marathon* was simple: to send the competitors across Europe and back for four days and four nights over the worst possible roads at the highest possible average speed. There was an absolute minimum of regulations (no petty restrictions on modifications to cars, therefore no reason for any competitor to lodge a protest against another—the winner was decided on the road and never in a committee room), and there was a positive attitude towards the threat of the outside world (in the drivers' briefing there was inevitably a warning to 'Watch out for the police in Germany'). The declared ambition of the organisers was to hold a rally in which only one car would succeed in staggering back to Liège.

It was road racing at its best—the nearest that Europe has had to the Argentine *Gran Premio de Turismo de Carretera* since the great inter-city road races came to an end in 1903—and it is no accident that two of the best *Targa Florio* drivers of the last twenty years, Olivier Gendebien (who scored three wins) and Willy Mairesse (two wins), were both Belgians and both former winners of the *Marathon de la Route*. Gendebien won in 1955, Mairesse in 1956, both driving Mercedes-Benz 300 S Ls.

Gendebien, who gained his place in the Ferrari works team in 1955 by winning the most rally-like of races, the *Coppa Dolomiti* (for many years the circuit was used as a stage in the *Coupe des Alpes*, with the race being run on the same day), also won the *Tour de France* for three consecutive years, 1957–9, with another Belgian, Lucien Bianchi, as co-driver. Bianchi was also a driver in his own right, who won the *Marathon de la Route* in 1961, the *Tour de France* in 1964, and came within hours of winning the London–Sydney Marathon in 1968.

Willy Mairesse won the *Tour de France* twice, in 1960 and 1961, and was favoured instead of Gendebien with Ferrari Formula One drives. To some he was a figure of fun: his background was as poor and provincial as Gendebien's was rich and cosmopolitan, and he was a frequent crasher—five wrecks in 1957 was probably his record—but he was a driver of indomitable courage and potential greatness, and his death by suicide on his sickbed in Ostend in 1969 must be the saddest end that any racing driver has had to endure.

The list of rally drivers who became outstanding racing drivers, or racing drivers who found they could also excel in rallies, is long and varied. Vic Elford is the most obvious recent example. Jo Bonnier rallied for five seasons before turning to racing. Another Scandinavian, Leo Kinnunen, was Finnish rally champion in 1967, although he had started out as a racing driver and returned to racing with exceptional success. Peter Collins was a member of the very successful Rootes rally team in the early-'fifties. Karl Kling drove for Mercedes-Benz in trials—similar to the modern forest rally, but with mountains thrown in—in the late-'thirties, became a Grand Prix and sports car driver after the war, won the *Panamericana* in 1952, and, when nearly fifty, won the 1959 Algiers–Cape Town Rally. Second in this 8,700-mile (14,000-km) event were Olivier Gendebien and his wife in a Citroën.

Two old-timers who turned to rallying in later years were Louis Chiron (who won the 1954 Monte) and Gigi Villoresi (who won the 1958 Acropolis Rally in Greece). And there is Stirling Moss, not only one of the greatest Grand Prix and sports car drivers of all time, but a winner of a *Coupe des Alpes en Or*—an Alpine Gold Cup—awarded to those who finish unpenalised in three successive Alpine Rallies.

Gérard Larrousse is a more recent convert from rallying to racing: in 1969 he won the Tour of Corsica, a rally that is short—lasting about twenty-four hours—but very fast and tough. A similar event on the French mainland is the *Ronde Cévenole*, run over four laps of a *Targa Florio*-like circuit in the hills north of Montpellier in the South of France. In 1969 it was won by a future Ferrari Grand Prix driver, Ignazio Giunti, who drove an out-and-out competition car, an Alfa Romeo Tipo 33 V8.

There is nothing very unusual about competition cars being successful in rallying. Before the Second World War Bugatti had repeated success in the *Marathon de la Route*. In Italian rallies there was little to touch Alfa Romeo. But, in general, rallies have tended to attract heavier, more solid cars. Before the war the big 6-cylinder Hotchkiss and Delahaye saloons from France were very successful. They went on winning until the early-'fifties, by which time the best car of this type in the world was the Jaguar, which won numerous rally and race victories in both saloon and sports versions.

By the mid-'fifties the Jaguar XK120 had to give best to the Mercedes-Benz 300SL, which, in turn, was ousted by the Ferrari 250GT in speed events, and, surprisingly, by the relatively cheap and crude Austin Healey in events that were too tough for the thoroughbred Ferrari. Mercedes-Benz hit back briefly with their 250SL, and they had many successes with their increasingly powerful saloons.

It was in the later Mercedes-Benz models that Eugen Bohringer had his remarkable successes. He had started competing in hillclimbs and circuit races in 1958, when already in his mid-thirties, and after only two seasons had been

121. Rally or Race? Gérard Larrousse and his navigator, journalist Johnny Rives, during the 1971 *Tour de France*. Their car is a 3-litre V12 Matra of the type that won Le Mans in 1972 and 1973, and also took the World Manufacturers' Championship in 1973

offered a place in the Mercedes-Benz rally team. In the next four years, before his retirement, he became a legend. He won the *Marathon de la Route* twice (1962 and 1963), the Acropolis twice (1962 and 1963), and the Argentine *Gran Premio Standard* twice (1963 and 1964). All these are events so tough that only one other driver, Mercedes-Benz's Walter Schock, has ever won any two of them—he won the *Gran Premio Standard* in 1961, and the Acropolis twice, in 1956 and 1960.

After *Marathon de la Route* moved to the Nürburgring in 1965, the Acropolis took over as Europe's toughest road event. It is shorter, but with two and a half days of non-stop driving it is a very formidable challenge. And official support from the Greek government, through the Greek tourist board, has given it protection against the dark forces of civilisation and reason.

Similar protection is given to Kenya's East African Safari Rally, which is easily the world's premier rally outside Europe. It has its origins in the Nairobi–Johannesburg road race of 1936, a 2,700-mile (3,350-km) event which ran through six countries: Kenya, Tanganyika (now Tanzania), Northern Rhodesia (now Zambia), Nyasaland (now Malawi), Mozambique, and South Africa. Forty cars left Nairobi, and over thirty survived to be cheered into Johannesburg by a crowd of 40,000. The winners were F. R. H. Hopley/C. L. Englebrecht (Terraplane), who averaged 46.2 mph (74.4 km/hr) for 59 hrs 10 min.

Unlike the Argentine *Grandes Premios* of the same period, the Nairobi–Johannesburg did not lead to greater things, and Africa produced no Fangio or Galvez. But, ironically, when European works teams began to contest the East African Safari Rally in the 'sixties—the event had started, as the Coronation Rally, in 1953—they found it a much harder nut to crack than the Argentine races. The *Gran Premio Standard* fell with comparative ease to Volvo, Mercedes-Benz, and lonewolf Zasada in his Porsche, but it was not until 1972 that a European driver, Finland's Hannu Mikkola in a works Ford, managed to beat the locals in the Safari. Among those who tried and failed are Eugen Bohringer, Erik Carlsson, Pat Moss, Rauno Aaltonen (a former co-driver for Bohringer—as a driver he won the final *Marathon de la Route* of 1964 in an Austin Healey), Lucien Bianchi, Olivier Gendebien, Gunnar Anderson (1960 *Gran Premio Standard* winner), Sandro Munari, Timo Makinen, and Sobieslaw Zasada.

The Safari is the most extreme case of a long road event favouring the driver with an intimate knowledge of local conditions—more extreme even than the *Mille Miglia*. Drivers who excel in such events can be quite mediocre elsewhere, and often appear to be uncompetitive persons who have little interest in driving elsewhere. They are very different types from the successful Grand Prix driver, who must be emotionally and physically sharper and tougher if he is to survive the sheer intensity of the modern Grand Prix—or the modern 1,000-km sports car race, which is no more than an extended Grand Prix.

Opinions vary as to what was the toughest road race of all time. Piero Taruffi found the *Targa Florio* the toughest of his 34-year career. Stirling Moss found the Nürburgring 1,000-km sports car race tougher. Vic Elford agrees with Moss, because of the higher G-forces at the Nürburgring, compared with the slow Madonie circuit: 'In the *Targa* the strain comes in your wrists and arms, but at the end of the Thousand Kilometres you're beginning to feel a bit sore around the kidneys.'

Rallies tend to put less stress on a crew than a race, because in a rally periods of intense concentration—speed sections—are followed by relatively relaxing

122. Rally or Race? Bernard Fiorentino (2.2-litre Simca C G)
winning the 1971 *Ronde Cevenole* in southern France

stretches. And even if speed sections are long and schedules tight—as in the
Marathon de la Route—the crew are obliged to relax if they want to survive through
to the finish. In this respect the *Mille Miglia* was close to a rally: drivers were forced
to pace themselves carefully and finish with energy in hand if they were going to
finish at all. The British photographer Louis Klemantaski, who crewed in the
Mille Miglia half a dozen times, and who was with Peter Collins's winning Ferrari
in the 1956 *Giro di Sicilia*, has said: 'Reading the pace-notes I knew more about the
road ahead than the driver did, and I could never understand why he wasn't going

faster.' That safety margin always had to be there. Seldom is a long-distance driver subjected to that almost unendurable fatigue that may strike even the fittest young driver only forty minutes into his first Grand Prix.

With the increasing competitiveness of rallies, and with the decline of the long-distance road event, there has been a tendency for rallying to move closer to racing —not least in types of cars that are needed to win. The big, heavy saloons have gone; even the Grand Touring type of car—the Lancia Aurelia, the Porsche 356 and 911—is less favoured. Today's rally cars—the Alpine-Renault, the Simca C G, the Lancia Stratos—are built for competition and little else. Cars of a similar nature have been rallied in the past: the big Austin Healey had heavy steering, a

123. *Targa Florio*, 1973

hot and poorly ventilated cockpit, and the uncomfortable habit of taking road shocks through its undertray and the crew's backsides rather than through its suspension—all one can say in its favour is that it was successful. But the Healey was an old car even when new—it owed little to racing car design of the 'fifties—whereas the modern rally car is a very close cousin to the rear-engined racing and sports-racing car of today.

The Alpine, in fact, was a pioneer of the rear-engined competition car, the first prototype being built in 1952, using Renault 750 components. After three years of rallying and racing it went into production in 1955. It was not until the late-'sixties that it became a major force in international rallying, but when it did it proved that a lightweight, wiry, competition-bred machine can survive the toughest rallies just as well as a much heavier production car. Rallying had sired its first thoroughbred.

The pure road race is dead in Europe—will the rally-as-road-race go the same way? The answer, sadly, is probably, eventually, yes. All the arguments used to stop road racing—the danger, the inconvenience—apply almost equally to rallying. 'Almost', but not quite, because rallies are invariably held on roads—in the mountains, through forests, often loose-surfaced or snow-covered—where really high speeds are impossible. In racing, as on the road, Speed Kills, as the appalling safety record of such high-speed circuits as Indianapolis, Monza, Le Mans, Spa, and the *Mille Miglia* shows. Safety lies in corners, and lots of them. Perhaps, with care and diplomacy, rallying—and road racing—may have a future.

APPENDIX: THE CARS

In writing a history of Grand Prix racing it is possible to trace the technical development of the competing cars as a smooth line on a graph: continuing improvement, with rare lapses, has gone on year after year since the beginning.

Road racing, as defined by this book, has shared in this development to a large extent; but many other factors complicate the story. For instance, the 180 mph German Grand Prix cars of the mid-'thirties—considered by many to be the most exciting cars that motor racing has ever produced—had no part in road racing. If anything, these colourful monsters drew money and interest away from European road racing. During that period, arguably, the most exciting road racing in the world was taking place in Argentina, with near-standard American sedans and coupés with a top speed of barely 80 mph. The *Mille Miglia* of that period was contested by sports versions of obsolete Alfa Romeo Grand Prix cars, their engines detuned for 1,000-mile reliability.

Any look at the technical history of road racing reveals a muddle of surprises and contradictions. The car that won the 1952 *Targa Florio* was no more powerful than the car that won the 1919 race. The speed increase, however, was sixty-nine per cent. The 1919 winner was a Grand Prix car; the 1952 winner was a hard-top tourer—which tells us more, perhaps, about the development of the motor car in the twentieth century than any dry technical analysis ever could. And it tells us a lot about road racing: about its central position between Grand Prix racing and everyday motoring; about its constantly shifting relationship with both.

If one looks at the 67-year history of the longest-surviving of all road races, the *Targa Florio* (although the Argentine *Gran Premio* will, I hope, take this title away from the *Targa* in 1976), we see that it has been won by almost every conceivable type of car: racing cars, sports cars, sports-racing cars, touring cars. The first race, in 1906, fell to one of the greatest all-rounders of the Edwardian era, the Itala, winner of the Peking–Paris Trial in 1907; the last, in 1973, fell to another great all-rounder, the Porsche 911, winner of dozens of the world's toughest rallies, and also of an Argentine *Gran Premio*. Two cars, separated by sixty years; yet close together in representing the very finest in motoring. One feels that is the way Vincenzo Florio, who died in 1958, in the same year as the *Mille Miglia*, would have wanted it.

The following table lists a selection of the most successful road racing cars in the years encompassed by the *Targa Florio*. It should be taken as a rough guide only: much of the information has inevitably come from manufacturers, and manufacturers are doting parents who tend to exaggerate the virtues of their offspring. Apparently authoritative journals and books, for example, will tell you that the Ferrari in which Taruffi won the 1957 *Mille Miglia* had a power output of 430 bhp—a figure that is highly improbable in the light of the car's observed performance. Independent Italian sources give the output of the car as 350 bhp, and that is the figure quoted here. The maximum speeds quoted are in most cases the optimum obtainable: these, too, should be taken as approximate only.

The abbreviations and contractions used should be self-explanatory. In the case of some Alfa Romeo models, such as the 6C-1750SS, the number of cylinders (6) and the cubic capacity (1.75 litres) is indicated, so I have not repeated this information. For further reading, see the Bibliography.

RACE	WINNING CAR	POWER	WEIGHT	MAXIMUM SPEED
1906 *Targa Florio* 1907 Peking–Paris	Itala 6.7 litre 4-cyl.	40 bhp at 1,250 rpm	2,200 lb. 1,000 kg	70 mph 110 km/hr
1911 *Targa Florio* 1912 *Giro di Sicilia* 1914 *Giro di Sicilia*	Scat 4.5-litre 4-cyl.	45 bhp	—	70 mph 110 km/hr
1919 *Targa Florio*	Peugeot 2.5-litre 4-cyl.	80 bhp at 3,000 rpm	2,350 lb. 1,070 kg (laden)	92 mph 150 km/hr
1920 Mugello 1921 Mugello	Alfa Romeo 6.1-litre 4-cyl.	82 bhp at 2,400 rpm	—	92 mph 150 km/hr
1922 *Targa Florio*	Mercedes 4.5-litre 4-cyl.	115 bhp at 3,000 rpm	2,970 lb. 1,350 kg (laden)	116 mph 187 km/hr
1923 *Targa Florio*	Alfa Romeo R L 3.1-litre 6-cyl.	95 bhp at 3,800 rpm	—	97 mph 157 km/hr
1924 *Targa Florio*	Mercedes 2-litre 4-cyl. blown	120 bhp at 4,500 rpm	2,580 lb. 1,170 kg (laden)	115 mph 185 km/hr
1925 *Targa Florio*	Bugatti 35 2-litre 8-cyl.	100 bhp at 5,000 rpm	1,960 lb. 890 kg (laden)	112 mph 180 km/hr
1927 *Mille Miglia*	OM 2-litre 6-cyl.	+ 65 bhp at 4,000 rpm	1,800 lb. 820 kg	+ 85 mph + 140 km/hr
1928 Mugello 1929 Mugello	Talbot 1.5-litre 8-cyl. blown	145 bhp at 6,000 rpm	2,000 lb. 910 kg (laden)	130 mph 210 km/hr
1929 *Mille Miglia* 1930 *Mille Miglia*	Alfa Romeo 6C–1750SS blown	85 bhp at 4,500 rpm	1,875 lb. 850 kg	100 mph 162 km/hr
1930 *Targa Florio*	Alfa Romeo P2 2-litre 6-cyl. blown	156 bhp at 5,500 rpm	2,240 lb. 1,020 kg (laden)	140 mph 225 km/hr

RACE	WINNING CAR	POWER	WEIGHT	MAXIMUM SPEED
1931 *Mille Miglia*	Mercedes-Benz 7.1-litre 6-cyl.	280 bhp at 3,500 rpm	2,500 lb. 1,140 kg	150 mph 240 km/hr
1934 *Giro d'Italia*	Lancia Astura 3-litre V 8	82 bhp at 4,000 rpm	2,400 lb. 1,090 kg	92 mph 150 km/hr
1936 *Gran Premio Internacional* Argentina 1936 Nairobi–Cape Town	Terraplane 3.5-litre 6-cyl.	88 bhp at 4,200 rpm	2,800 lb. 1,270 kg	80 mph 130 km/hr
1936 *Mille Miglia*	Alfa Romeo 2900 A 8-cyl. blown	210 bhp at 5,400 rpm	2,240 lb. 1,020 kg	140 mph 225 km/hr
1940 *Coppa Brescia*	B M W 328 2-litre 6-cyl.	120 bhp at 5,000 rpm	—	125 mph 200 km/hr
1948 *Mille Miglia* *Giro di Sicilia* 1949 *Mille Miglia* *Giro di Sicilia*	Ferrari 2-litre V 12	130 bhp at 6,600 rpm	1,430 lb. 650 kg	130 mph 210 km/hr
1951 *Mille Miglia*	Ferrari 340 4.1-litre V 12	250 bhp at 6,600 rpm	2,000 lb. 900 kg	170 mph 280 km/hr
1952 *Targa Florio*	Lancia Aurelia GT B 20 2-litre V 6	80 bhp at 5,000 rpm	2,550 lb. 1,140 kg	100 mph 162 km/hr
1952 *Panamericana*	Mercedes-Benz 300 S L 3-litre 6-cyl.	215 bhp at 5,200 rpm	1,920 lb. 900 kg	150 mph 240 km/hr
1954 *Mille Miglia* *Targa Florio* *Giro di Sicilia*	Lancia D 24 3.3-litre V 6	240 bhp at 6,500 rpm	1,650 lb. 750 kg	170 mph 280 km/hr
1954 *Gran Premio* 1956 *de Carretera,* Argentina	Ford 3.6-litre V 8	200 bhp at 4,500 rpm	3,000 lb. 1,370 kg	120 mph 190 km/hr
1955 *Mille Miglia* *Targa Florio*	Mercedes-Benz W 196 R 3-litre 8-cyl.	300 bhp at 7,450 rpm	1,830 lb. 830 kg	180 mph 290 km/hr
1956 *Targa Florio*	Porsche R S 1.5-litre 4-cyl.	135 bhp at 7,200 rpm	1,300 lb. 590 kg	150 mph 240 km/hr
1957 *Mille Miglia*	Ferrari 412 M I 4.1-litre V 12	350 bhp at 7,700 rpm	1,940 lb. 880 kg	170 mph 285 km/hr

RACE	WINNING CAR	POWER	WEIGHT	MAXIMUM SPEED
1957 *Giro di Sicilia* 1958 Venezuelan GP	Ferrari 250 GT 3-litre V 12	220 bhp at 7,000 rpm	1,980 lb. 900 kg	160 mph 260 km/hr
1958 *Targa Florio*	Ferrari 250 Testa Rossa 3-litre V 12	280 bhp at 7,200 rpm	1,760 lb. 800 kg	170 mph 280 km/hr
1960 *Gran Premio* *Standard,* Argentina	Volvo P V 544 1.6-litre 4-cyl.	+ 85 bhp at 5,500 rpm	2,500 lb. 1,140 kg	+ 90 mph + 145 km/hr
1963 *Gran Premio* 1964 *Standard,* Argentina	Mercedes-Benz 300 S E 3-litre 6-cyl.	+ 160 bhp (net) at 5,000 rpm	3,570 lb. 1,620 kg	+ 108 mph + 174 km/hr
1964 *Targa Florio*	Porsche 904 2-litre 4-cyl.	180 bhp at 7,000 rpm	1,630 lb. 740 kg	160 mph 260 km/hr
1965 *Targa Florio*	Ferrari 275 P 3.3-litre V 12	320 bhp at 7,700 rpm	2,050 lb. 920 kg	180 mph 290 km/hr
1968 *Targa Florio*	Porsche 907 2.2-litre 8-cyl.	270 bhp at 8,600 rpm	1,320 lb. 600 kg	170 mph 280 km/hr
1970 *Targa Florio*	Porsche 908/3 3-litre 8-cyl.	350 bhp at 8,400 rpm	1,180 lb. 530 kg	180 mph 290 km/hr
1972 *Targa Florio*	Ferrari 312 P 3-litre 12-cyl.	440 bhp at 10,800 rpm	1,440 lb. 655 kg	190 mph 305 km/hr
1972 *Vuelta de* *Chivilcoy,* Argentina	I K A Torino 4-litre 6-cyl.	360 bhp at 6,000 rpm	3,000 lb. 1,370 kg	160 mph 260 km/hr
1973 *Targa Florio*	Porsche 911 Carrera 3-litre 6-cyl.	325 bhp at 7,500 rpm	2,000 lb. 900 kg	170 mph 280 km/hr

SELECT BIBLIOGRAPHY

BERNADO, Ferruccio, *History of Lancia from 1906* (Lancia Revue, Turin, 1969).

BORGESON, *see* THOMPSON.

BOROCOTO, *see* LORENZO.

BRADLEY, W. F., *Ettore Bugatti* (Foulis, London, 1959).
  Motor racing memories, 1903–1921 (Motor Racing Publications, London, 1961).
  Targa Florio (Foulis, London, 1955).

BUHNAU, Ludwig, *Eiskalt auf heisssen Strassen* (Arena, Wurzburg, 1971).

CANESTRINI, Giovanni, *La favolsa Targa Florio* (L'Editrice dell'Automobile, Rome, 1966).
  Mille Miglia (L'Editrice dell'Automobile, Rome, 1967).

CARACCIOLA, Rudolf, *Mercedes Grand Prix ace: an autobiography*, translated from the German (Foulis, London, 1955). New translation, *A racing car driver's world* (Farrar, Straus, New York, 1961). Also published as *A racing driver's world* (Cassell, London, 1962; Ambassador, Toronto, 1962).

CARLI, Emanuele Alberto, *Settant'anni di gire automobilistiche in Italia* (L'Editrice dell'Automobile, Rome, 1967).

COURT, William, *Power and glory: a history of Grand Prix racing, 1906–1951* (Macdonald, London, 1966).

DAVEY, *see* PRITCHARD.

DOODSON, Mike, *Carlos Reutemann: following in Fangio's footsteps?* (*Motoring News* 768, London, 25 November 1971).
  Looking at the scene in Brazil and Argentina (*Motoring News* 771, London, 16 December 1971).
  Oreste Berta: a young man with a vision (*Motoring News* 770, London, 9 December 1971).

FANGIO, Juan Manuel, *with* GIAMBERTONE, Marcello, *My twenty years in racing*, translated from the French (Temple Press, London, 1961; Ambassador, Toronto, 1961).

FERRARI, Enzo, *My terrible joys: the Enzo Ferrari memoirs*, translated from the Italian (Hamish Hamilton, London, 1963).

FERSEN, *see* SLONIGER.

GEORGANO, G. N. (ed.), *The complete encyclopaedia of motor cars* (Ebury Press, London, 1968; Dutton, New York, 1968; Clarke, Irwin, Toronto, 1968).
  The encyclopaedia of motor sport (Ebury Press & Michael Joseph, London, 1971; Viking, New York, 1971).

GIAMBERTONE, *see* FANGIO.

HANSEN, Ronald, *Racing in the Argentine* (*Autocar*, London, Vol. 106, No. 3186, 11 January 1957).

HERRMANN, *see* SOHRE.

HULL, Peter, and SLATER, H. Roy, *Alfa Romeo, a history* (Cassell, London, 2nd ed. 1969).

KLING, Karl, *with* MOLTER, Gunther, *Pursuit of victory: the story of a racing driver*, translated from the German (Foulis, London, 1956).

LEVINE, Leo, *Ford, the dust and the glory: a racing history* (Collier-Macmillan, New York & London, 1968).

LORENZO, Ricardo 'Borocoto', *Medio siglio de automovilismo Argentino* (Atlantida, Buenos Aires, 1953).

LURANI, Giovanni, *with* MARINATTO, Luigi, *Nuvolari*, translated from the Italian (Cassell, London, 1959).
Racing round the world, translated from the Italian (Foulis, London, 1954).

MARINATTO, *see* LURANI.

MERLIN, Olivier, *Fangio, racing driver*, translated from the French (Batsford, London, 1961).

MILLER, Peter, *Men at the wheel* (Batsford, London, 1963).

MOLTER, Gunther, *Juan Manuel Fangio*, translated from the German (Foulis, London, 1956).
see also KLING.

MORSE, Ralph (photographer), and others, *Racers challenge death in Mexico* (*Life*, Vol. 35, No. 23, 7 December 1953).

MOSS, *see* PURDY.

NEUBAUER, Alfred, *Speed was my life*, translated from the German (Barrie & Rockliff, London, 1960).

NICHOLSON, T. R., *Adventurer's road: the story of the Pekin–Paris, 1907, and the New York–Paris, 1908* (Cassell, London, 1957; Rinehart, New York, 1958).

NIELSSON, Erik, *Argentina's amazing 'TC' racers* (*Motor*, London, Vol. 130, No. 3816, 3 April 1969).

PALM, Gunnar, and VÖLKER, Herbert, *Tricks of the rally game*, translated from the German (Ian Allan, London, 1971).

PRITCHARD, Anthony, and DAVEY, Keith, *The encyclopaedia of motor racing* (Robert Hale, London, 3rd ed. 1973; McKay, New York, 1969).
Italian high-performance cars (Allen & Unwin, London, 1967; Bentley, Cambridge, Mass., 1967).

PURDY, Ken W., *All but my life: Stirling Moss face to face with Ken Purdy* (Kimber, London, 1963; Dutton, New York, 1963).
The kings of the road (Little, Brown, New York, 1952; Hutchinson, London, 1955).

RUETER, John C., *American road racing: the Automobile Racing Club of America in the 1930s* (Barnes, New York, and Yoseloff, London, 1963).

SLATER, *see* HULL.

SLONIGER, Jerrold, and FERSEN, Hans-Heinrich von, *German high-performance cars, 1894–1965* (Batsford, London, 1965). US edition, *Performance cars from Germany* (Bentley, Cambridge, Mass., 1966).

SOHRE, Helmut, and HERRMANN, Hans, *Hans Herrmann—Ich habe uberlebt* (Motorbuch-Verlag, Stuttgart, 1971).

TANNER, Hans, *The Ferrari* (Foulis, London, 3rd ed. 1968).

TARUFFI, Piero, *Works driver*, translated from the Italian (Temple Press, London, 1964).

THOMPSON, Mickey, *with* BORGESON, Griffith, *Challenger: Mickey Thompson's own story of his life of speed* (Prentice-Hall, New Jersey, 1964).

TRAGATSCH, Erwin, *Das grosse Rennfahrebuch* (Hallwag, Berne and Stuttgart, 1971).

VÖLKER, *see* PALM.

INDEX